ROME
AND THE
UNIFICATION OF
ITALY

Arthur Keaveney

CROOM HELM
London & Sydney

© 1987 Arthur Keaveney
Croom Helm Ltd, Provident House, Burrell Row,
Beckenham, Kent BR3 1AT

Croom Helm Australia, 44-50 Waterloo Road,
North Ryde, 2113, New South Wales, Australia

British Library Cataloguing in Publication Data

Keaveney, Arthur
    Rome and the unification of Italy.
    1. Rome—Politics and governments—
    265-30 B.C.   2. Rome—History—Social
    War, 90-88 B.C.
    I. Title
    937′.05   DG257.3

ISBN 0-7099-3121-2

Printed and bound in Great Britain by Mackays of Chatham Ltd, Kent

Contents

Preface

For some years past the peoples of ancient Italy have been the subject of considerable scholarly interest and a number of individual monographs have been devoted to them. In this book, however, I have not concentrated on any one people or area. Rather, what I have tried to do is examine a wider issue, an issue which exercised and affected a number of Italian nations. I have also attempted to show that it had a profound effect on the dominant people of Italy, the Romans. What I speak of may not unfairly be described as the Italian question in Roman history. By this I mean the desire of the Italian nations for the Roman citizenship and the consequence which flowed from it: the unification of ancient Italy. In other words I have attempted, in however imperfect a fashion, to narrate an episode which is significant both in the history of Rome and of Italy as a whole.

The work was greatly facilitated by the grant of a term's study leave by my university in Michaelmas 1983. A version was read by Professor A.F. Norman and by Mr Robin Seager who made a number of valuable suggestions and comments. I hasten to add, however, that they must not be held responsible for anything in the finished product. The map is taken from *Samnium and the Samnites* p. 342 and is here reproduced by kind permission of the author, Professor E.T. Salmon, and the publishers, Cambridge University Press. A special word of thanks must go to the members of Darwin College Secretariat, who turned my hand-writing into typescript. Finally, I should like to acknowledge the help of my wife, Jennifer, and my colleague, Graham Anderson, in reading the proofs.

Arthur Keaveney
Darwin College
University of Kent
at Canterbury

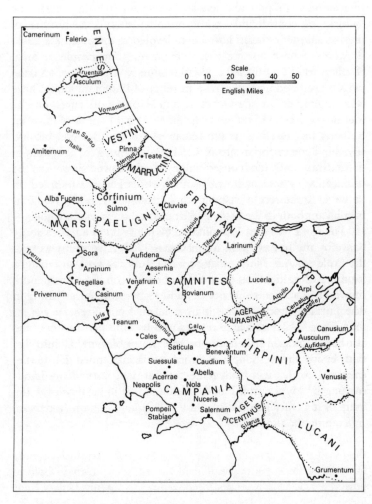

The Social War insurgents.

Introduction

In essence, this is an unashamedly old-fashioned book. It treats of the causes, course and results of the Social War. But these matters comprise what may be called Rome's Italian question and the book can then be seen as an attempt to write the history of that question. Starting from the indisputable fact that a number of Italian peoples rose in revolt in 91 when refused the Roman citizenship, it sets out to discover why that citizenship was wanted in the first place, then why it was refused by the Romans and finally why that refusal provoked a war which had far-reaching consequences for Rome and her empire.

The birth of the Italian desire for citizenship and equality is to be located in the second century and our first task must therefore be the identification of those factors at home and abroad which brought it about. We discover that we are not just dealing with specific grievances but with a complete change of outlook on the part of the Italian peoples. From being subjects they aspire to be the equals of their masters. Once we have established the reasons for this profound alteration in perception we go on to consider its primary political manifestation in the Gracchan age when the demand for citizenship was first heard. We encounter it again in the 90s and here we have to explain not only its strengthening but also the reasons for its failure now as in the past. We shall also see that the Italian question, a major issue in itself, tended to become entangled with other vital issues of the day. It influenced the course of Roman political life and helped to determine the outcome of a number of disputes.

Eventually, the failure of Rome to provide a satisfactory solution to the problem exhausted the patience of the Italians and they broke with her. The story of the Social War is the story of how this bid for independence was crushed. The war did, however, force the Romans to concede the citizenship they had for so long refused. However, it was granted in so imperfect a form that the Italians, once more part of the Roman state, were obliged to resume their previous political agitations. The remainder of our work is, therefore, taken up with an account of how they were able to exert sufficient pressure in order to gain all that they asked and put an end to the Italian question.[1]

Notes

1. In this book 'Italy' is to be taken as referring to peninsular Italy. Cis-alpine Gaul shared in the process of Romanisation which we shall be describing (1.2) but without any of the political consequences which such a process had for the peoples of the peninsula, cf. Salmon (1982) p. 130, 134, 195, n. 261. 'Italians' will be used to refer to Latins and allies together. It should also be noted that some, at least, of the Greek cities of the south remained untouched by the developments we are about to sketch. See Gabba (1976) p. 71 and Sherwin-White (1973) p. 138.

Part One
Rome and Italy in the Second Century

1.1

Romans and Italians Abroad

In 211 during the Hannibalic War, the senate offered Roman citizenship to some Praenestians as a reward for their valour. They, however, refused to accept. More than a century later, in 91, a number of Italian peoples rose in rebellion against Rome when she refused their request for the very citizenship the Praenestians had once spurned. In the subsequent conflict, usually known as the Social War, the consul L. Julius Caesar promised the citizenship to a Cretan in return for an act of treachery. The latter merely laughed and, saying such a thing was of no use to him, asked for money instead.[1]

Here we have represented in miniature what will form the subject of enquiry in this and the subsequent chapter.

Rome, by virtue of conquest, had made herself mistress of the peoples of Italy. Those she dominated were divided into two groups; Latins and allies. The bond which united the Latins to Rome has been described as being of a somewhat 'intangible character'. In contrast, the allies or *socii* had their relations regulated by formal treaties and hence are sometimes referred to as *foederati*. Nominally independent and internally self-governing all these communities were obliged to acquiesce in Roman foreign policy and to supply her with troops. Again, all of them had the privilege of *commercium* which meant they might make valid contracts with Romans. *Conubium* or the right to contract valid marriages with Romans was enjoyed by the Latins and some of the allies. Of the two groups the Latins certainly enjoyed the more favoured position — a circumstance which undoubtedly arose because, culturally speaking, they were close to the Romans. By virtue of the *jus migrationis* they might acquire Roman citizenship if they took up residence in Roman territory and, if in Rome, they might cast a vote in one tribe. As has been

3

well said by A.N. Sherwin-White, 'the Latins apparently felt themselves to be, if not Romans, at least the next best thing'.

Now, it would be pointless to deny that Rome very often in
fact deferred to these people as being her allies and treated them
with courtesy and consideration. But, in the final analysis we
should be constantly aware that they were her subjects. The
arrangements I have described were devised by a superior power
and enforced by her. It was not open to the junior partner to alter
them or seek to withdraw from them. Hence we may speak of the
peoples of Italy as being subordinate to the Romans.[2]

Assuming that the Praenestians were typical of the Italy of
their day,[3] then it is fairly obvious that Rome's Italian subjects
were then content with the state of affairs we have just sketched.
It is also fairly obvious that a great change had been wrought
between that time and 91. Those who had once been happy to be
subordinate, now aspired to be equals. What was once rejected
was now coveted. These ambitions were, however, confined to
the Italians for there is no evidence to suggest that they were
shared by the provincials. Some, like the Cretan, evidently
regarded the citizenship as worthless and it is safe to say all saw
enfranchisement as beyond their wildest dreams. Thus, it seems
logical to suppose that, in the course of the second century, there
had been developments in the Roman world which were of
peculiar significance to the Italians alone. The result of these
developments was a fundamental change in outlook which led
them to desire the citizenship. We must now seek to discover
what those developments were.

Arguably the most striking of these developments was the
physical restlessness of the Italians. Both within and without Italy
we encounter large numbers of her inhabitants who are prepared
to leave their native place in order to seek their fortunes elsewhere. Migration within Italy will concern us in another place.
Here we shall concentrate on movement overseas. Rome's
mastery of the Mediterranean had opened the doors of opportunity to the Italians and they were not slow to stream through
them. All over the Roman world we find men of Italian origin
engaged in banking and diverse commercial activities. Campanians are particularly prominent in these pursuits but we also
hear, to a lesser extent, of Apulians, Lucanians and some few
Picentes. Business contacts with Africa are well attested and we
discover *negotiatores* from southern Italy active in Sicily. Roman
emigration to Spain, which inevitably brought the businessman

with it, seems to have largely come from the Osco-Umbrian districts of central and southern Italy as well as Etruria. Trade between southern Italy and the East was nothing new but now it was wrested from the hands of the Italiotes of the Greek cities. In the East we find men from Campania, Apulia and Samnium together with a few Latins, Etruscans and others from central Italy. The trade was, indeed, worth wresting for it had grown in volume and value as a result of the increasing demand for commodities by the Romans who had been enriched by their conquests.[4]

Obviously some Italians had engaged in business before the second century but their operations had not been on anything like this scale. What, in part, we are witnessing is the growth of an Italian commercial class who were prepared to seize the opportunity offered by Rome's new position of dominance in order to enrich themselves. According to E. Gabba, three consequences flowed from this phenomenon.[5]

In the first place, Roman foreign policy became of vital importance to this new breed of Italians. In Rome itself, just as in Italy, there was now a commercial class. It had taken its rise in the second half of the third century but had only begun to wield power in the second. Since the economic interests of these people dictated that Roman foreign policy should be militaristic and expansionist they were naturally brought into conflict with the rulers of Rome who were basically conservative and aimed at preserving the traditional structure of the state. This fundamental clash of interests becomes more marked and more important in the period after C. Gracchus. It is plainly observable in the struggle between the senate and the *equites* and is further reflected in the oscillations of Roman foreign policy which now favours, now hinders the commercial class. Inevitably the Italian *negotiatores* would support the Roman commercial class in these matters since it was working for ends which they too desired. Such support, however, could only be passive since the Italians lacked the means to influence Roman politics directly. And, seeing how firmly entrenched the oligarchy was at Rome and how difficult it was for their friends to get a coherent foreign policy, the Italians came to the conclusion that they needs must take a hand in the business for themselves. They gradually realised that they would have to acquire the citizenship in order to have a say in affairs and arrange them so as to benefit themselves.

Further, as a direct result of their sojourn in the provinces and their experiences there, the Italian commercial classes became acutely aware of their own merits and, in consequence, profoundly discontented with their relatively low actual status in the Roman scheme of things. Abroad they were treated as were the Romans with all the respect due to members of a conquering race but at home they still continued to be the subjects of a ruling power. This state of affairs at length came to be regarded as intolerable and as one which would have to be rectified. Finally, the *negotiatores* became men of note in their home towns. Investing the profits of their labours in land they became part of the ruling cliques in those towns and some of them are to be found holding public office there.

These, then, for Gabba were among the most important developments which eventually led to the Social War. Both because they felt their intrinsic merits entitled them to it and because their material interests required it, the Italian commercial classes coveted the citizenship, and, when their request was refused, they were, because of the influence they had acquired in their native areas, in a position to bring about the great rebellion.

Gabba's first point raises some very broad issues. Just how aggressive, in fact, were the rulers of Rome? How far may they be said to have consciously followed an expansionist policy of conquest and annexation? These questions are (and will no doubt continue to be) a subject for scholarly debate. Equally, while the acquisition of fresh territories would benefit the businessmen among the *equites*, it is a moot point whether they (or their class as a whole) felt a great need for such expansion. We may also wonder how far they wanted to or, indeed, could shape Roman foreign policy for their own ends.[6] Obviously it would be impertinent (in every sense of the word) for us to pronounce on these matters here but we may be permitted to make one or two observations relevant to the point Gabba wishes to establish. On any view, Roman imperialism can never be described as wholly inimical to business interests whether Italian or Roman. After all, it is that very imperialism which, consciously or not, contributed in a large measure to the growth of this business class in the first place. It was that which furnished its members with their opportunities both within the Roman territories and the neighbouring client kingdoms and, moreover, provided them with protection. In view of the expanse of territory thus opened up to the businessman, it is not impossible to envisage, as some have done, a situation where he, whether Roman or Italian, would be so busy exploiting what he had got that he had no need of or wish for further expansion. His interest in Roman politics would then be directed, not towards fresh aggrandisement but towards making the best possible use of what already lay within his grasp. In this respect, the businessmen among the *equites* had little to complain of since they had been well served by C. Gracchus. When the tribune gave their *ordo* control of the *repetundae* court, he put into their hands a weapon with which to defend their provincial interests and they did not hesitate to use it.

Thus, while it is clearly not impossible that a situation such as that depicted by Gabba could have existed, there are obstacles in the way of a whole-hearted acceptance of his view. We cannot be fully certain that the Roman businessman would necessarily have desired an aggressive foreign policy or that he possessed, for that matter, the means to obtain it. It would therefore follow that his Italian counterpart likewise would have no desire for such a policy, or any wish to help form it by becoming a citizen.[7]

So, in view of this uncertainty, we should, perhaps, if we wished to find an economic motive which might impel the Italian commercial class to seek the citizenship, look elsewhere for it. Gabba has quite rightly stressed that, broadly speaking, both Italian and Roman businessmen had a community of interests. Laying emphasis on this, however, should not blind us to the fact that such an interest would only find expression in the face of a common foe. Where something exceptional occurred which appeared to threaten business enterprise as a whole then we would expect the Italians to be of one mind with the Romans in the matter. In the normal course of events, however, the position of the two groups will more likely have been that of rivals to each other; both parties will have sought the maximum advantage for themselves. The *societates* of the *publicani* may have been largely concerned with tax-farming but their peripheral banking interests will have made them competitors to the Italians who were also active in this field. Likewise, trade, which was one of the special concerns of the Italians, also seems to have interested the *publicani*. Clashes must have occurred in these areas and one suspects that often the non-citizen came off worst. Nor should we forget that the Italians appear to have been shut out of one particularly lucrative area. The *publicani* would seem to have had a near monopoly of the valuable state-contracts, especially those for tax-farming. The speed with which Italians bid for these contracts, once the citizenship had been granted is testimony to how greatly they coveted them and makes it legitimate for us to infer that they must have been aggrieved at not being able to share in them hitherto.[8]

So, if we wish to assign an economic motive to the desire for the citizenship manifested by the Italian business class, we have seen that there is some case to be made for the view that they wished to influence Roman foreign policy in order to broaden their sphere of activity. It seems more likely however that their real reason for wanting enfranchisement was that it would aid them in protecting the enterprises they already had afoot in the Roman world and would also provide them with fresh opportunities there.

But, as Gabba has pointed out, it was not material considerations alone which made the Italian business class look for the citizenship. Leaving their small and relatively isolated communities to seek their fortunes in the wide world must have wrought a profound psychological change in many.[9] To put it in its simplest terms: the Italians began to regard themselves as the equals of the Romans who had once conquered them and this state of affairs is directly attributable to the new circumstances in which they now found themselves. The provincials did not differentiate between them and the Romans. For the native, all men from Italy were Ῥωμαῖοι or Italici and as such were to be treated with due reverence. Gabba has well remarked of the Italians at this time, 'in their commercial activities they could be considered men of high repute and be generally identified with the great political power which in truth they represented.'[10] It is not difficult to see why this should be so. Coming on the heels of the conquerors, many of whom were men of their own race, they were protected by the power and majesty of Rome. They bore a close physical resemblance to the Romans, they spoke (in many cases) the same language and shared some of their privileges. In these circumstances it is not surprising that the provincial should have difficulty telling Roman and Italian apart and that the latter should appear as an overlord in provincial eyes even though he, too, was, in reality, as much a Roman subject as the native.

Initial impressions were reinforced by the behaviour of the Italians themselves who, in the provinces, tended to act in a manner which was akin to that of the Romans. Abroad they and their Roman counterparts were wont to cling together and bond themselves into corporate units, the better to deal with the natives. It is a matter for debate as to whether *conventus* were widespread at this time but it is certain that other more or less formal bodies existed in abundance. The Italici at Cirta, for instance, may be found acting as a group and *collegia* are well attested, most notably at Delos. The consequences of this phenomenon would appear to be chiefly two. Although Roman businessmen and their Italian counterparts could, as we have remarked, have their differences, that essential community of feeling between the two, which we also noted, would appear to be dominant here. In these bodies Roman and Italian met on an equal footing. This sense of common identity, which is most clearly detectable at Delos, will then have played its part in giving birth to the notion that the average Italian was every bit as good as the average Roman. Such an idea will have been further strengthened by the necessity for the mixed body of Italians and Romans to act in concert in a number of their dealings with the natives. These actions will not only have reinforced for the Italians the impression they had that their interests and sympathies, nay their natural place in the world, lay with the Romans but, perhaps just as important, will have taught them to believe that, although both were ruled by Rome, their position should be altogether different from, and more privileged than, that of the provincials.[11]

Nowhere is this state of affairs better illustrated than during Mithridates' invasion of Asia in 88. In the events of that time we see most clearly and dramatically illustrated the close identification of Italian with Roman both in the eyes of the Italians themselves and in the eyes of the provincials. We also witness the kind of gulf which separated the Italian subject of Rome from the provincial. When Mithridates gave the order to massacre everybody of Italian origin the Asiatics obeyed with alacrity and made no distinction whatsoever between Roman and Italian. So far as they were concerned they were all alike members of the hated race which ruled over them. The behaviour of Italians and Romans was all of a piece and now they could expect to pay for it. Indeed the Italians themselves had but lately furnished the most unmistakable proof of their desire to be identified with Rome the oppressing power. The citizenship had just been granted and they immediately donned the characteristic badge of the toga. For long they had comported themselves as the equals of the Romans and the superiors of the other conquered peoples. Now, at last, they had set the seal on their elevated status, blissfully unaware that they would not live long to enjoy it.[12]

Thus far, despite some disagreements on detail, we are in broad accord with Gabba. Psychological and economic factors caused the Italian business classes to covet the citizenship. Material interest and a growing sense of their own worth taught them to aspire to be Romans. After their sojourn abroad they could ill-brook their relatively lowly status and all that went with it, on their return to their native place.[13] We may be fairly certain then that they shared fully in that Italian desire for enfranchisement which by 91 had become universal. However, we must dissent from Gabba when he goes on to claim that these men had the means to realise their ambitions. In other words, the notion that the businessmen first led their communities in the demand for citizenship and then, when it was refused, sent them into war cannot be sustained.

We cannot say what influence the commercial classes enjoyed among the Latins but, if it were in favour of war, it was singularly ineffective since, with the exception of Venusia, they remained quiescent.[14] As regards Etruria and Umbria, it has been postulated that the inhabitants enjoyed but a minor share in Eastern trade. Whatever the truth of this and whatever the extent of their trade with Spain, it is clear that if the businessmen did possess influence in the councils of their area — something which is by no means certain — it did not amount to very much. In 91 the landowners who feared Drusus' agrarian schemes were able to orchestrate substantial resistance to his citizenship proposals. Furthermore, Etruria and Umbria only entered the war in a tardy and half-hearted fashion long after others had irrevocably committed themselves.[15] Indeed, in many parts of Italy, the phenomenon of the *urbs*, so essential for the development of a trader class, was absent, since the population was concentrated in the *pagus*. Thus, in Lucania we find little evidence of trade or industry because the physical characteristics of the country are not favourable to these pursuits. The population there seems to have been composed largely of hunters, pastoralists and farmers. Some traders are of course, to be found but they are of small account when measured against the warlike nobility which dominated the area. Likewise with Samnium. We know of some businessmen but they are in a very distinct minority in a place where there was little trade or industry and where an aristocracy, which had ruled for centuries, continued to hold sway. Even in comparatively Romanised areas such as Picenum or the Marsic country we hear little of the commercial class.[16]

This, in effect, leaves but two areas, Campania and Apulia, for which Gabba's thesis might possibly be valid. But, we must reckon with the fact that neither of these places took the lead in the revolt. They may be fairly described as 'secondary areas' which rose only upon the arrival of rebel armies which had begun the revolt elsewhere. Therefore, the notion that the business class there took the lead in instigating the uprising seems to be untenable. However might it not be true to say, at least, that this class was in the forefront in urging their cities to join the rebels once they had actually appeared on the scene? It could after all be that they were merely awaiting the right moment to translate their desires into action. Unfortunately such a hypothesis does not accord well with the evidence. Members of the trading class are attested as holding magistracies in both Pompeii and Capua. Yet Pompeii joined the revolt only reluctantly while Capua remained conspicuously loyal. Probing the matter a little further we find even more evidence of division. Scholars have stressed that very many of the trader class, active in the East, came from southern Campania. It therefore seems reasonable to postulate that some, at least, of them came from those towns (particularly the coastal ones) directly involved in the Social War. We cannot, however, deduce from this that the businessmen brought these communities into the war. For, even if, in an attempt to accommodate Gabba's thesis in so far as is possible, we made the unprovable assumption that this trader element actually was dominant in the councils of these towns, we still find markedly different attitudes in different places. We know nothing about feelings in Stabiae, Surrentum or Salernum. On the other hand, Herculaneum like Pompeii was an unwilling rebel while Nola and Nuceria embraced the insurgent cause gladly. Thus, even on the broadest possible interpretation of the evidence, we can hardly claim to have discovered in Campania a united business class ready to bring their communities over to the rebel side.

Much the same may be said of Apulia where there is also evidence for the existence of commercial interests in certain places. Again here we learn of towns which had to be coerced into joining the rebellion. Only two voluntary defectors are known: Venusia and Canusium. In the case of the former its Oscanised nature is at least as likely a stimulus to revolt as is the possible presence of traders. With regard to the latter, the business class might have been instrumental in shaping attitudes but we must emphasise that there is no evidence that men of this type held magistracies there.[17]

It would appear, therefore, that while we have no reason to suppose the commercial classes did not desire the citizenship, it is difficult to believe they took the lead in demanding it of the Romans or in making war when it was refused. The most that can be said is that there is a faint possibility that, in one or two instances, they may have persuaded their communities to follow the example already set by others.

In fact, both the agitation for the citizenship and the subsequent rebellion were set afoot by the landed nobility who ruled the various Italian peoples. This is acknowledged by Gabba who does not, in my view, adequately explain it away. Now, it is also well known that some of these rebel leaders had seen military service abroad and this need hardly occasion surprise.[18] There is no need to catalogue the military operations engaged in by the Romans throughout the second century beyond noting they were extensive indeed, and the Italians, whether they liked it or not, were obliged to play their part in them. They were required to supply their share of troops either for active warfare or to act as garrisons.[19] In all cases their contingents would be commanded by their natural leaders, the nobility of whom we have just spoken. Thus, I would argue that it is legitimate to infer that these leaders would, as a result of their provincial sojourn, have undergone a psychological change and a heightening of consciousness akin to that experienced by the commercial classes but that it was one which, in view of the outcome, was of greater historical significance. Abroad the nobility learned to aspire to higher things and they possessed the means to get them.

For the provincials these men, like the traders, must have been Ῥωμαῖοι. If the natives respected (and in places hated) the Italian business class as members of the conquering power and did not differentiate between them and the Romans how much less likely are they to have told apart Roman and Italian soldiers when both, in their very persons, represented the military might of the conqueror? It is not, I think, too difficult to imagine the native deferring with equal respect to Italian and Roman since both alike were his overlords.

We thus see here, as in the case of the commercial men, a gap opening between the Italian soldier and the provincial both of whom, it will be remembered, actually served the same master. A subordinate in his own land the Italian, nevertheless, became a master abroad. This could be illustrated by many concrete examples but is best illuminated perhaps, by drawing attention to the way in which soldiers lived off those they had conquered. Regardless of whether they were Italian or Roman the provincial was obliged, much to his resentment, to supply food, clothing and other necessaries for the soldiers. The most spectacular case is that involving Sulla's troops in Asia in 84. Then the reluctant host had to supply every solder billeted on him with four tetradrachmas a day and an evening meal to which he might bring as many guests as he liked. An officer received fifty drachmas a day and a present of two suits of clothes. It is unlikely that all Roman commanders were as oppressive as Sulla who was partly motivated by a desire for vengeance but this case nicely illustrates and encapsulates the point we wish to make: neither of the parties to the transaction could be in any doubt as to who was the master and who was the servant.[20]

And the very processes which made the Italians aware of their superiority to the provincial also made them feel closer to their Roman fellow soldiers. Both were conscious of having sprung from the same land: Italy.[21] Both spoke the same language for Latin was the language of the camp. Thus, being cousins and comrades in arms in a strange land fighting a common foe it was natural that an *esprit de corps* should develop. Those who shared common dangers would then enjoy the camaraderie of the camp and these circumstances cannot but have contributed to the levelling of barriers between the two groups.[22]

Thus, the Italian upper classes became more aware of their own worth. Their experience of military life in the provinces had taught them to think of themselves as superior to other conquered peoples and as the equals of the Romans. But what of the men they led? What of the great mass of Italian peasantry who served in Rome's armies throughout the period and then made up the bulk of the rebel forces in the Social War? Were they left untouched by their experience of military life abroad? Usually it is held that their feelings are of little account. They simply followed where their betters led.[23] There is obviously a good deal of truth in this view. In general, our sources do not furnish us with much evidence for any kind of sophisticated political thinking among the Italian peasantry. Their role is almost always subordinate and supportive of those who were their lords. Nevertheless it would be wrong to totally deny them any independence of spirit for we receive hints that such indeed existed. As we shall see, there were those who, in the time of Tiberius Gracchus, were prepared to defy their masters when the latters' interests clashed with their own. It is worth remembering also that when the armies of Marius and Poppaedius Silo fraternised the initiative came from the rank and file of both sides. Certainly those who led the rebellion were perfectly well aware they could not always count on blind obedience but must take steps to ensure their followers' morale was maintained. So special care was taken over the distribution of booty and provision was made to dispose of the war dead in such a way as not to depress the spirits of the living.

Furthermore it is I think wrong to suggest that, in fulfilling his traditional role of allegiance to the local baron (something he undoubtedly did), the peasant did not in some measure, share his ideals and have some conception, however limited, of their worth. For instance, rebel coins depicting Italia or showing an Italian bull goring a Roman wolf were doubtless intended as a challenge to the enemy but we should not forget that they were also intended for circulation among the confederates and they must have meant something to those who saw them. The savage outburst of popular fervour at Asculum also serves to illustrate how high and low alike could come to share a common hatred of Rome. Thus, I would argue that up to a point the Italian peasant was aware of what it was he was fighting for. I would further suggest that he had acquired this awareness, in part, in the provinces. Like his betters he had, albeit in a far more limited fashion, become more keenly aware of his separate Italian identity and of his superiority to those whom he helped conquer or police. In consequence he found it easy to respond when his traditional loyalties were invoked.[24]

I would certainly argue that the common man would share his lord's belief that he laboured under a burden of disabilities. The plain fact is that, however much the Italians liked to think of themselves as the equals of the Romans, they were in reality still subordinates and this was made clear to them by the terms under which they performed their military service.

It was, for instance, not uncommon for the Italians to be retained with the colours — often to perform unpleasant fatigue duties — after their Roman counterparts had received their discharge. Again, it was not unknown for them to be recalled to service in an emergency while the Romans got off. It has also been suggested that Roman commanders, regarding the Italians as expendable, used them for particularly hazardous and nasty missions.[25] And, if Italians breached military discipline, they could expect harsher chastisement than their Roman counterparts. With the passing of the Leges Porciae in the second century the *libertas* of the citizen had been secured and *verberatio* became unknown at Rome. The notion then took hold that no citizen should undergo this punishment anywhere in the world since it was repugnant to his status. So *verberatio* disappeared as a punishment in the army as did execution by means of *verberatio* and the axe. But Scipio's treatment of his troops at Numantia and the execution of Turpilius clearly show how an Italian could still undergo these punishments.[26]

Harsh conditions of service were not, however, the only thing which the Italians had to complain of. They were forced to pay for the upkeep of their contingents and this imposition continued after 167 when the Romans were freed from the *tributum*.[27] And this was not all. At the outbreak of the Social War the rebels claimed they furnished yearly double the number of infantry and cavalry which the Romans did. Modern research has vindicated their claim. Although the proportion of Italian to Roman troops obviously varied, throughout the period the Italian contribution was consistently higher.[28]

And if the burdens of empire were greater so the rewards were less. About the viritane distribution of booty there was, in truth, little to complain of since the Italians normally received an equal share with the Romans.[29] Allies might also be admitted to Latin colonies. However, the Italians do not appear to have had any legal claims on the *ager publicus Romanus*. Such land as was given them was given at the discretion of the Romans and, on the one occasion on which we hear of a viritane settlement in the second century, citizens got ten *jugera* while Italians got three. Again, at the time of the Social War, the rebels claimed, with justice, that their efforts had been expended to win an empire for someone else. The conquered territory belonged to Rome alone. It was ruled over by Romans and its tribute was theirs exclusively. The city itself was embellished from the spoils of war but there is little evidence that the money for the adornment of Italian towns came from such a source. At most, a Roman commander like Scipio Aemilianus, Flaccus or Mummius might condescend to dispense some largess.[30]

In the picture we have just painted it is easy to point to elements which would irritate Italians of all classes. Prince and pauper alike can hardly have been best pleased at harsh conditions with the ever present possibility of brutal punishments. However, our main concern must naturally be with the reaction of the upper classes who, of course, had the greater political awareness. In view of their subsequent role in our history, it is important that we divine their response to this situation. It would appear to me that, in the first instance, uncertainty and, sometimes fear, will have been the result.

A characteristic of the history of the second century is the manner in which the position of the Italians vis-à-vis the Romans showed distinct signs of deterioration. We shall have more to say about this anon[31] but, at the moment, we may simply observe that whereas once the Romans had given due weight to the fact that the Italians were, legally speaking, their allies, they now showed a distinct tendency to bring home to them the reality of their status as subjects. Very often Roman actions might simply be neutral or even benevolent but sometimes they could be arbitrary and cruel. But, in all cases, the Italians were made aware of their subordinate position. It was becoming increasingly clear to them that they were almost completely at the mercy of the prevailing temper of their overlords. A commander could do with his Italian troops as he wished. One might be lucky in having a decent general but it was equally possible to find oneself serving under someone who would impose tasks he would not set a Roman or punishments he could not inflict on his fellow countrymen.[32] Again, the generosity of a Mummius serves only to highlight the meanness of others. An Italian could never be sure of such largess; it depended on the whim of the commander as did the distribution of land. A revealing incident occurred in 177. When the consul Claudius distributed the booty he gave citizens twice as much as Italians. This was, of course, unusual but its very singularity serves to underline the point I am here trying to establish: whether or not an Italian got fair treatment depended entirely on the will of the man under whom he served. It could be argued that since booty was a general's to do with as he pleased he was as likely to be stingy with Roman soldiers as Italians. But to deprive a Roman of his due could be dangerous because he was in a position to retaliate. Those Italians who were cheated in 177 could only show their anger by following the triumphal car in silence. Ten years later when Paulus was less lavish than he might have been his Roman soldiers were prepared to vote against his proposed triumph.[33]

So, the Italians became aware of the extent to which their present position left them at the mercy of the power of Rome. How that power might be exercised at any given moment could not be predicted since it depended on individual whim. Hence the growth of feelings of uncertainty and of fear. In these circumstances it is hardly surprising that the subject should begin to think of amelioration and that he should see the citizenship as the obvious solution. If he were to fight alongside Romans then he should be accorded exactly the same treatment as they.

The growing realisation of their own worth insured, however, that the citizenship was not something the Italian aristocrats would beg as a boon from their masters but rather demand as a right. That is to say, anger, as well as fear, was aroused by their present plight. It will be recalled that, at the outbreak of the Social War, the rebels made two great complaints. They were furnishing more troops than the Romans and yet they were banned from that very state for which they had won an empire. The nature of the ties with which Rome bound the Italians to herself made it as legitimate for her to call on them for warfare abroad as in Italy. But although the letter of the law, so to speak, had not changed its spirit had. There could now be no pretence that Rome and her allies were making war to defend their mutual interests. Rather, they were fighting campaigns to further Rome's interests alone and it was Rome's failure to make her interests the Italians' interests also which brought about discontent. Thus, in the pronouncement of the rebels we hear the authentic voice of people who recognise their own worth, are aware of their own importance and are enraged because their present position is not commensurate with the view they have now formed of themselves.[34]

We may now sum up our arguments as follows. With varying degrees of depth and intensity, the Italians underwent a change of outlook as a result of their sojourn in the provinces. This change wore two aspects. In the first place men acquired an enhanced view of their own worth. In the second, they became acutely conscious of their present disabilities and came to the conclusion that their position as it now was, was ill-fitted to men such as they. Eventually, the acquisition of the citizenship came to be seen as the solution to this particular problem. Of those who came to this conclusion by far the most important were the nobles who ruled non-Roman Italy. It was they alone who were in a position to initiate and lead the agitation for the citizenship and then, when the Romans proved obdurate, to make war on them.

Notes

1. Livy 23.20.2; Diod. Sic. 37.18.1.

2. Sherwin-White (1973) pp. 96-133; Harris (1971) pp. 85-107; Humbert pp. 108-22; Gabba (1983) pp. 41-4; Laffi (1983) pp. 64-70. See further 1.2.

3. Cf. Livy 9.43.23.

4. Meaning of *negotiator*: Hatzfeld p. 4; Wilson pp. 4-6. Activities of *negotiatores*: Hatzfeld pp. 193-237. Africa: Wilson pp. 42-6. Sicily: Wilson pp. 19-22, 66; Frank, 'On the migration of Romans to Sicily', *AJP* 55, 1935 pp. 61-4. Spain: Gabba (1976) pp. 105-8; Wilson pp. 22-7; for a different view see Knapp pp. 151-8. East: Wilson pp. 86-9; Frank pp. 275-7; Cassola *passim*; Hatzfeld pp. 31-7, 44-50 and (prior to the second century) pp. 18-20, 241. In general see Gabba (1976) pp. 75-6; Wilson pp. 9-12; Nicolet pp. 357-75.

5. (1976) pp. 76-87.

6. On these questions see *passim* Badian (1968), (1972); Brunt (1965); Harris (1979); Hackl; Sherwin-White, *Roman Foreign Policy in the East*, London 1984. See also Sherwin-White, *JRS* 1955, p. 169, *JRS* 1980; Hatzfeld pp. 369-76; Gabba, 'Mario e Silla' in *Aufstieg und Niedergang der Romischenwelt*, Berlin/New York, 1972 vol. 1.1, pp. 772ff.

7. Badian (1968) pp. 47-8; Brunt (1965) pp. 121-34; Gabba (1976) p. 229, n. 112; Harris (1979) pp. 94-101.

8. Salmon (1962) pp. 112-13; Badian (1968) pp. 57-8, (1972) pp. 61-3, 81, 100; Broughton (1965) pp. 151-2; Gabba (1976) p. 229, n. 110, 111; Toynbee pp. 225-6, 355-8; Wilson pp. 4-6; Hatzfeld p. 219, 235; J.H. D'Arms, *Commerce and Social Standing in Ancient Rome*, Cambridge Mass., 1981 pp. 20-47; Ch. Meier, *Respublica Amissa*, Wiesbaden, 1966 p. 210.

9. Badian (1968) p. 18 has emphasised the importance of such a change for the Romans. I do not think we can deny that something similar must have befallen the Italians.

10. (1976) p. 77. Cf. Ilari p. 13 and Hatzfeld p. 244.

11. Italici/Ῥωμαῖοι : Gabba (1976) p. 229, ns. 111, 112; Wilson p. 94; Hatzfeld pp. 8-9, 242-4; Ilari pp. 3-6. Language: Wilson p. 116; Hatzfeld pp. 337-40. *conventus/collegia*: Wilson pp. 13-14, 76, 117-18, 168-9; Frank p. 276; Cassola pp. 314-17, 320; Nicolet p. 354; Hatzfeld pp. 257-81. Relations between Italici and natives and privileges enjoyed by former: Hatzfeld pp. 291-326. In general see Brizzi pp. 128-30; Harris (1979) p. 95 and the very important remarks of Hatzfeld p. 244.

12. Sources: Greenidge and Clay pp. 168-9 with Athenaeus 5. 213b. Those who, according to Athenaeus, doffed the toga and disguised themselves in Greek dress were most probably Italiote Greeks and freedmen of Eastern origin (Frank p. 278). We may legitimately infer from this that all other Italians had likewise assumed the toga. We may also infer that these Italians did not put on Greek dress simply because

they could not pass as residents of a Greek state. Our sources mostly speak of a massacre of Roman citizens. Since the Italians had recently become such (4.1) we would expect to find them among the victims and this is confirmed by Appian (cf. Cuff *passim*). However, in view of this lateness in the change of status, we must assume that it was their previous behaviour which caused the natives to turn against the Italians and Appian does provide evidence for the detestation they aroused. It would be absurd to suppose that the mere assumption of the citizenship led to a massacre on such a scale. Cf. also the comments of Harris (1979) pp. 96-7 and Ilari p. 3.

13. Cf. Hatzfeld p. 244.

14. It should be noted however, that by then the Latins had, by and large, got what they wanted. See 2.2.

15. Wilson p. 88; Hatzfeld p. 255; Harris (1971) p. 170. Cf. n. 4 and 2.2, 3.2.

16. *Pagus*: Gabba (1972) pp. 78-81. Lucania: Magaldi pp. 12-13, 47-63, 66, 271-6, 300-2. Samnium: Gabba (1976) p. 220, n. 46; Salmon (1967) p. 317; Hatzfeld p. 240. Picenum: Laffi (1975) pp. XI-LV. Marsi: Letta p. 95; Letta and d'Amato no. 107.

17. Campania: Gabba (1976) pp. 222-3; Castrèn pp. 38-46; Wilson pp. 89-91, 105-6, 108-11, 152-4; Frank p. 276; Fredericksen *passim*. Apulia: Frank p. 275; Brunt (1971) pp. 366-70; Wilson p. 119. See also the remarks of Hatzfeld pp. 238-42; Broughton (1965) p. 155; Sherwin-White, *JRS* 1955, p. 169. On the rebel campaigns see 3.2.

18. Gabba (1976) p. 220, n. 46, 222. Since Plutarch (*Sulla* 29) describes Pontius Telesinus in terms similar to those he uses of Poppaedius Silo, he, too, could have seen foreign service but it is more likely he gained his experience in the Social War. See Appendix II.

19. Brunt (1971) pp. 422-34; Ilari pp. 57-85, 88-9, 137-9; Knapp pp. 147-50.

20. Livy 2.54.1, 8.2.4, 29.3.5, 30.16.12; Plut. *Sert.* 4, *Sulla* 25. Although this last is dated after the Social War it is close enough to our period to allow it to be used here, cf. Ilari p. 79.

21. On this see 1.2.

22. Diod. Sic. 37.15; Vell. Pat. 2.15.2 with Gabba (1972) p. 81; Toynbee p. 110; Galsterer p. 149.

23. See, for example, Gabba (1976) p. 75; Salmon (1962) p. 108.

24. Cf. 2.1, 3.1, 2. I do not, of course, mean to imply that no inter-mingling between Italians and natives took place, cf. e.g. Gabba (1976) pp. 107-8. By way of comparison we may point out that a complex variety of motives inspired the principal actors in the Williamite Wars in seventeenth-century Ireland. It is doubtful if the average Irish peasant understood the half of them but one issue he could grasp: his betters were asking him to fight for a Catholic king and so he responded enthusiastically to their call to arms, see E. Curtis, *A History of Ireland,* London, 1964, pp. 264-74.

25. Toynbee pp. 133-5.

26. Keaveney, *Crit. Stor.* (1984) pp. 357-67. Of wanton ill treatment of the Italians there appears to be no trace. The instance cited by Toynbee p. 113, n. 2 (Livy 44.1.5) seems to refer to Greek allies.

27. App. B.C. 1.7 with C. Nicolet, 'Le stipendium des allies Italiens avant la guerre Sociale', *PBSR* 46, 1978 pp. 1-11.

28. Vell. Pat. 2.15.2; App. B.C. 1.7 with Brunt (1971) pp. 677-86 and Ilari pp. 87-103, 158-73. See also J.W. Rich 'The supposed Roman manpower shortage of the later second century BC' *Historia* 32, 1983, pp. 321-3.

29. See Goehler pp. 50-1 and McDonald (1939) p. 133, n. 56 to whose list add *ILLR* 573. On the significance of the incident in Livy 41.13.7-8 see below. Salmon (1967) p. 308 and (1982) p. 126 seems to be mistaken.

30. Vell. Pat. 2.15.2; Eutrop. 4.12.2; Livy 42.4.4 (cf. 10.46.8); Letta and d'Amato no. 51; *ILS* 20-2, 6131. Cf. Salmon (1967) p. 308; Badian (1958) p. 151; Gabba (1976) p. 76; Ilari p. 19, n. 34; Bodei Giglioni pp. 72-6 and further 2.1.

31. See 1.2.

32. It is true that a commander had absolute power over all soldiers he commanded but there appears to have been a distinct tendency to single out non-Romans for difficult tasks. See next note.

33. Livy 41.13.7, 45.35.5-7. Cf. Shatzman pp. 202-4 and n. 29 above.

34. Vell. Pat. 2.15.2 with Sherwin-White (1973) pp. 122-3 and Salmon (1967) p. 308.

1.2

Romans and Italians at Home

In our previous chapter we made a casual reference or two to the contemporary situation in Italy. It is time now for it to claim our full attention. At the outset it may be stated that what we shall eventually find closely parallels what we found abroad: the Italians gradually begin to see themselves as the equals of the Romans and start to chafe under their present disabilities. Obviously the men who returned from the provinces armed with a new and disturbing perspective on the world played their part in creating this situation but I believe it owes just as much to conditions in Italy itself. In my view four diverse phenomena characteristic of the history of the period interacted to create the new mood. These were: the Romanisation of Italy, the survival of local patriotism, the growth of pan-Italianism and the changing character of Roman rule in the peninsula. I propose to say something about each of these in turn and I shall then try to demonstrate how they combined to produce the effect I have claimed for them.

By Romanisation we mean that process whereby the different peoples of Italy put off their own peculiar identities and assumed that of Rome.[1] A number of factors gave rise to the process. In the first instance, there is the simple fact of Rome's position of political dominance which naturally made of her the focus for Italian attention. This meant that in their external relations the concern of the Italians would be in a large measure with Rome. For them 'foreign affairs' would, to a considerable degree, mean their dealings with Rome and it was certainly through her that they approached the world beyond Italy. I do not of course, mean to imply that the Italian nations had no contact with each other or that those contacts were not important — we shall see shortly

21

that they were — but there seems to be little doubt that Rome bulked larger on the horizon for them than did any of their immediate neighbours. Thus, it follows that Rome would be, for them, the primary external influence.

The second factor to be considered is the ubiquity of the Romans in Italy. A solid block of Roman territory stretched from north Campania to south Etruria and north-east from Rome along the Via Flaminia to Picenum and Ariminum. Outside of this area Romans were to be found in pockets since many lived on confiscated land or resided in Italian towns. Latin colonies, culturally speaking Roman, are of especial importance in this regard. Non-Romans admitted to such foundations would rapidly acquire a veneer of Roman manners and, more significantly, the colonies would expose those in the neighbourhood to things Roman. Again, the extensive road building of the second century will have facilitated the rapid diffusion of the Romans together with their culture and customs as they penetrated even into remote regions. These highways further aided the spread of Romanisation in that they rendered movement between main centres easier and also had on them Roman settlements.[2]

Finally we should be aware of what one scholar has called the 'scrambling of the population of Italy'. Whether because of forced transfer, or by reason of voluntary migration in search of economic betterment or simply for the purpose of business there was now a far greater intermingling of the peoples of Italy than heretofore. This intermingling will, of course, have been helped by the fact that all Italians enjoyed the privilege of *commercium* with Rome and some allies also shared, with the Latins, that of *conubium*. In addition it will also be remembered that the Latins had the *jus migrationis* which permitted them to settle on Roman territory and acquire the citizenship. Finally, it should be noted that the Italians exchanged these same privileges among themselves.[3]

This third factor explains why the need for a *lingua franca* was felt in Italy; the first demonstrates why Latin came to be chosen for the role while the second shows us how its spread was encouraged and facilitated. The Romans never consciously imposed their culture on others and made no effort to force those they ruled to adopt their tongue.[4] Nevertheless their magistrates did insist on conducting all public business with outsiders in Latin.[5] Furthermore, as we saw in the previous chapter, Latin was the language of the camp where the allies were called to serve. Again many Roman nobles had a patron-client relationship[6] with members of the ruling oligarchies of Italy and here, as in their dealings with those Romans resident in Italy, the allies would require a knowledge of Latin. Small wonder then, in these circumstances that the allies were obliged to acquire a mastery of the language of Rome as a matter of sheer practical necessity. As has been remarked by one scholar, a knowledge of Latin, like a knowledge of French in seventeenth- and eighteenth-century Europe, became a matter of social necessity. One cannot forbear from adding that this analogy might also lead us to suspect that a certain cachet was attached to such an accomplishment and that it might be regarded as a mark of sophistication in certain quarters to be able to converse in the language of the leading power of the day. It is almost unnecessary to add that, where allies of diverse tongues met, they would use Latin as their common second language and would not trouble to learn each others.[7]

A social phenomenon, spontaneous in origin, the spread of Latin is difficult to assess in detail. Nevertheless, it is possible to sketch it in outline with illustrative examples and to offer, as a result, some tentative conclusions as to its extent. A number of peoples such as the Vestini and the Marrucini used the Latin alphabet from the first as did some towns in Etruria, Umbria and Apulia. It also appears on the coins of the Frentani. The language itself was, as we might expect, especially strong in the districts near Rome where tongues such as Hernican were now extinct. It appears on Marsic inscriptions of the Gracchan age and on one or two of an earlier period. Indeed, it is fair to say that both the Marsi and the Picentes were heavily Latinised by the time of the Social War. In the case of the latter the process was, in fact, already well under way in the third century. In this context we may point out that the use of Latin on coins produced by the central Italian rebels indicates clearly that it was their official language. It would also seem that it had made extensive headway in southern (or Oscan) Campania.[8] Particularly noteworthy, perhaps, is the fact that much of early Latin literature was the creation of men who came from Italy and not from Rome itself. To mention no others, Ennius came from Rudiae, while Plautus was a native of Umbria. For the talented man, be he orator, poet or dramatist, Latin appears to have been regarded as his natural vehicle of expression. Not only did patronage, if he required it, lie in the hands of Romans but Latin, with its dominance assured and well on the way towards being an international language, could offer him an audience which his native tongue could not reach.[9]

How extensive, then, was this Latinisation? Outside of the areas we have mentioned as being especially Latinised its progress was probably fairly slow and we may also beg leave to doubt if within them it spread uniformly. Certainly other languages such as Etruscan, Oscan or Messapic continued to be strong[10] and even where Latin was the official tongue other languages continued to be used informally. So much for the regional view. Looking at the matter in terms of class, we may safely say that, like the *literati*, many of the upper classes were (or were fast becoming) bilingual. The reasons for their acquiring Latin, which we have outlined above, were I believe sufficiently compelling to ensure that this would be so. It also seems safe to say that, as a consequence of military service or contact with Romans in Italy, members of the lower classes will have got some knowledge of Latin. The degree of competence achieved must obviously have varied from individual to individual.

The general conclusion would seem to be that Latin was now widely diffused. Where it was not in everyday use it was probably understood by the upper classes at least.

Another way in which Romanisation manifested itself was in the adoption by the allies of Roman titles for their magistrates or in the embracing, on their part, of Roman constitutional forms. For instance, Falerii uses Latin titles, a tribunate is found at Teanum Sidicinum and the extensive imitation of Roman models at Bantia is often commented upon. Allied states, too, showed at times a willingness to adopt Roman laws. It has been pointed out that while evidence for such phenomena is somewhat scarce, it does show a wide geographical diffusion. We find examples as far north as Etruria and Umbria and as far south as Lucania.[11]

To close our brief survey of Romanisation we may pose an intriguing question. Since foreigners found it difficult to tell Romans and Italians apart it behoves us to ask how far the appearance of the Italians themselves and of the world in which they lived had begun to assume a Roman cast. There are, in fact, some indications that such a thing was happening though not, perhaps, as many as some have thought. P.A. Brunt seems to believe that national dress disappeared in Samnium, Lucania and Bruttium. He also appears to argue that the toga was widely worn.[12] The evidence will not bear the weight of such an interpretation. Our source for the disappearance of national costume is

Strabo 6.1.2 who also tells us of the end of national speech and armour. However, Strabo is not talking of the situation as it was in the second century but of that near his own day.[13] Indeed it would be rash to say that the processes which eventually led to what we find in Strabo had made any great headway prior to 90. Oscan was yet strong and we shall soon discover that a distinctive national life still flourished in these areas. It requires no great effort of imagination to see that it was the Social War, with its bloodshed and its crushing of national vitality, which destroyed native culture and left the way open for its replacement by Roman.[14] The toga was, of course, the characteristic dress of the Romans and the hallmark of the Roman citizen who alone might wear it. However, the term *togatus* could also be applied to the Italians in recognition of the fact that they shared a common identity with the Romans. Bearing these two facts in mind we may beg leave to doubt that many Italians assumed the toga and, unlike Brunt, we would not take *togati* in Sall. *Jug.* 21.2 literally but rather as an equivalent to 'civilians'.[15]

With regard to other matters we are on surer ground. There is evidence, for instance, of a fairly widespread adoption of Roman money and weights and measures in Italy.[16] Not all native coins disappeared but silver did tend to give way before Roman issues.[17] In the second half of the century we witness extensive building programmes in certain Italian towns, financed partly by the profits of trade and partly from the viritane distribution of booty. It has been suggested that the Italians took their cue from Rome in these matters and that many new temples owe much to her example. This is especially true of Latin Italy but Roman influence has been detected elsewhere as well.[18]

Despite the levelling process we have just been describing, particularism continued to flourish in Italy. The peoples of the peninsula still had a keen awareness of their own separate identities. They knew perfectly well the ways in which they differed from each other and from the Romans. When somebody said, 'no triumph over the Marsi or without the Marsi' he obviously knew that the Marsi were a people in their own right and that one of their distinguishing features was their warlike nature. A meeting with one of their snake charmers would not I think, have done anything to lessen the impression of distinctness.[19] For their part the Romans knew full well that, although they were related to the Italians, they were by no means identical with them. Thus, Cato, in his *Origines*, was at pains to trace the history of the individual nations of the peninsula. Again, Tiberius Gracchus and Scipio Aemilianus, in their different ways, recognised that Rome had become great not just because of the Romans but also because of other peoples, namely the Italians.[20] Those who complained in 91 that they had fought to gain an empire for another would hardly have dissented from this viewpoint.

Nor should we make the mistake of supposing that the Italians were dependent on people like Cato for a knowledge of their past. They were perfectly capable of keeping alive their own myths, traditions and history. For example, Interamna Nahars preserved the story of its origin, Etruscans and Sabini had native historians and some towns in Latium possessed historical records.[21] A lively sense of the past seems to have been particularly strong in Samnium. We know less about Lucania but it is possible that a similar situation prevailed there. Their life-style resembled that of the Samnites, they too inherited a legacy of grievance and their behaviour in the Social War closely parallels that of the Samnites.[22] At any rate, so far as the latter are concerned, we do know that many of their leaders in the Social War belonged to families which had been prominent in the wars of the fourth century. Thus, Marius Egnatius was descended from Gellius Egnatius, the leader of the confederates at Sentinum and C. Papius Mutilus was related to Papius Brutulus who also took part in the fourth century wars. Likewise, Pontius Telesinus was a descendant of the victor of the Caudine Forks. Since these men belonged to the leading families of their nation, I find it impossible to believe that, as old established nobles, they did not, with all the pride of born aristocrats, keep green the memory of the heroic deeds of their ancestors and that they were not inspired by them when they, in turn, went to do battle with the traditional enemy.[23]

Local patriotism shows itself in other ways too. For instance, E.T. Salmon draws our attention to what appears to be a revival of native speech and culture among the Paeligni.[24] A more important manifestation of this spirit, though, is to be found in the building programme to which we referred earlier. As we saw there are Roman elements present in the styles but many non-Roman elements have been detected as well. Above all, however, the buildings are an expression of pride in one's native place. Those whose patriotism led them to cherish (and sometimes concoct) myths about their origins gladly adorned their homelands with monumental structures.[25]

It is not difficult to account for the persistence of this state of affairs despite all the inroads made by Romanisation. The reasons are chiefly three. In the first place, although Romanisation was undoubtedly making much headway it had simply not yet reached the point where it could supplant native cultures. That would have to wait for the day when all Italians were Roman citizens. Secondly, possession of a distinctive language may not ensure the existence of a national sentiment but it does erect an obvious barrier between peoples and, as we have seen, some of the native tongues of Italy still retained their vigour. Finally, the very nature of the ties which bound the Italians to Rome was a constant reminder to them that they were different. The world was made up of two kinds of people: the Romans and the others. In a famous passage (*de Leg.* 2.5) Cicero tells that every man had two *patriae*, his native place and Rome. If such a sentiment could be voiced long after the Social War, then it is not, I think, straining credulity to suggest that in the days before enfranchisement a man's attachment to his home place will have been all the stronger. It is, I believe, generally agreed that it would be incorrect to speak of such a feeling as 'nationalism' in the sense that we understand it except, perhaps, in the case of the Samnites and Lucanians. But our survey does amply illustrate that, in many communities in Italy, there was a real awareness of the possession of an individual character, a consciousness of uniqueness and a sturdy sense of independence.[26]

When Cicero spoke of a man's two *patriae* he neglected to mention a third focus for his loyalty: Italy.[27] In our period this loyalty reaches its finest flowering at the time of the Social War when the rebels created a state far different from that of Rome. Each rebel nation, while retaining its own independence, gave its allegiance to a new federal state which was governed by men chosen from among all the insurgents. The sophistication of the war machine which was created, the remarkable degree of co-operation which was shown, the speed with which men of one nation went to the aid of another are all eloquent testimony to the existence of a common feeling and a mutual trust. And these feelings were rooted in a shared consciousness that all held in common one thing: they were all Italians. Hence they gave their allegiance to Italy and so they named their state, Italia.[28]

Long before this full blooded and vigorous expression, however, we catch glimpses of pan-Italic sentiment at work.

Thus, it has been suggested that the Celtic and Epirote assaults prior to 265 may have awakened some primitive notion of a loyalty towards Italy among her inhabitants. It has been doubted if such feelings played much part in the first Punic War but we may note that the Mamertines, at least, were prepared to claim help from Rome on the grounds of kinship.[29] Be that as it may, we do know from Polybius that, in the Gallic invasion of 225, the Italians were keenly aware that the threat was to their common homeland.[30] And, in the second Punic War, we find the Romans appealing to the Italians not to allow barbarous foreigners to lord it over Italy.[31] Further, although we have no evidence, it is not improbable that similar thoughts ran through the minds of those who helped Marius repel the Germanic invaders. Thus, it is tolerably clear that, in these wars, the Italians could regard themselves as fighting by the side of Rome to defend Italy, the country to which they all belonged.[32]

With the absence of warfare in Italy for most of the second century the feeling that the men of that land shared certain characteristics and interests manifested itself in other ways. We have already seen, for instance, how people as different as Cato and Tiberius Gracchus showed an awareness of the importance of the nations who lived there. We remember, too, the great number of Italici who went abroad either as soldiers or traders. As they came to realise the difference between themselves and the natives they not only identified with the Romans, as we saw, but will also have come to an increased awareness that they all belonged to a land of their own called Italy. And, now, as in the past, comradeship in arms brought the various peoples of Italy together. The mingling of men in a common service cannot but have fostered the growth of a common Italian identity and will have served to implant in the leaders of the diverse nations of Italy a sense of community.[33]

Pan-Italianism was, therefore, Rome's creation. With her at their head the Italians came to see themselves as fighting for a common home-land and had this sense of identity confirmed by mingling in her armies. Arguably, one of the most striking features of our period is the way in which this creature of Rome's turned against her when it reached its full maturity. We cannot, however, understand how this came about until we have examined the fourth, and last, of the phenomena which I believe shaped the mood of Italy at this time. I refer to the changing character of Roman rule.

As we know, the Italians were, in the final analysis, subjects of Rome. Nevertheless we saw that they were allowed a fair measure of independence in running their own affairs. In other words, Rome was prepared up to a point, to recognise and respect their technical position as her allies. Their sovereignty was not interfered with where it did not clash with their overlords' interests. However, the ancient evidence permits us to claim that, in this period, the central authority at Rome increasingly encroached upon local autonomy. This tendency may be traced back to the second Punic War when Rome was obliged to take far reaching decisions without consulting those who were, formally, in alliance with her. The habit of authoritarianism thus acquired was never afterwards lost.[34] Before all else, the senate regarded it as its right to intervene in any part of the peninsula when public safety and order was threatened or seemed to be threatened. Thus, in 196, we find the praetor Glabrio proceeding against a slave revolt which had broken out in Etruria. The famous suppression of the Bacchic conspiracy which took place ten years later is probably the best known of such measures taken by the senate. But Roman overseeing of the business of Italy extended far beyond the stamping out of *conjuratio*. By a natural application of the basic principle that the well being of Rome and those in alliance with her was Rome's vital concern, it tended gradually to spread to most departments of provincial Italian life. So, the Romans were ready at all times to offer arbitration when disputes arose between states. We know, for instance, that the towns of Pisa and Luna referred such a dispute to them. They were equally ready to offer their services when factional squabbles broke out within a state and they were, if it should prove necessary, quite prepared to use force to compose the quarrel. Garrisons were sent to allied towns which asked for them in moments of danger and help was also provided in time of natural disaster. We know of measures taken against a locust plague in Apulia and of aid given to rebuild towns. As one might expect from the Romans, this concern for the common weal also found expression in the religious and moral spheres as well as the legal. During a plague a supplication was decreed for all Italy and, at another time, we hear of measures taken for the removal of a hermaphrodite from Umbria. In 161, a sumptuary law, the lex Fannia, was passed. Eighteen years later, another, the lex Didia, specifically bound all Italy since Italians claimed the lex Fannia did not apply to them. Earlier, in 193, the lex Sempronia applied the Roman law of usury to Italians.[35] Outside of these areas there are two other spheres in which the Romans made their presence felt. In the first instance, they were wont to dump their state prisoners on Italian towns, often with elaborate instructions as to how they were to be managed and some of these people were little better than rogues and scoundrels. The second instance is even more striking and more serious. Rome's servants now imported into Italy the kind of practices they were only too fond of indulging in abroad. To put it briefly: some Roman magistrates did not hesitate to mistreat their Italian allies of long standing in the way they did overseas provincials. Looting of temples, extortion of money and acts of violence against individuals are all well attested.[36.]

Looking at this evidence two questions naturally pose themselves. Does it allow us to say that the Romans had become oppressive overlords and are we entitled to claim the Italians saw them as such? A.J. Toynbee answered the first question in the affirmative and observed that although the juridicial position of the Italians remained the same, their actual position had considerably worsened.[37] I am not convinced, however, that the matter is quite as simple as that. Roman overlordship had both its benign and its malignant aspects. I doubt if the ruling aristocrats felt themselves particularly oppressed when disturbances, which could have cost them their position, were ended by direct action from Rome. Nor is it implausible to suggest that material aid in time of crisis was warmly received. We might also observe that if people ask for arbitration then it seems logical to assume they want it. On the other hand, arbitration was not without its risks since it was not unknown for an arbitrator to hand down an unfair decision. It would seem too, that state prisoners were not particularly welcome. At any rate Spoletium refused to have one individual but Iguvium, it appears, was then obliged to take him. By the same token, if Rome sometimes imposed her laws it is by no means certain the Italians had lost completely their power to accept or reject such legislation.[38] The prominence given to a demand for *provocatio*, when the Italians first began to bestir themselves, amply demonstrates how they felt about magisterial misbehaviour. Yet, once more, we have to remind ourselves that the senate tried to curb such excesses.[39]

It hardly needs to be said that the picture is not really as simple as Toynbee thought and indeed it is full of contradictions. In order, therefore, to arrive at a just estimate of the nature of Roman rule at this time I propose to examine two contrasting pieces of evidence which, I believe, hold the key to the problem. Of the postscript to the Bacchanalian decree A.H. MacDonald says, '(it) has a tone of depreciation. The consuls, it would appear, might communicate the decree to the allies, but they would not dictate its execution or do more than suggest the penalty with some embarassment, for they recognised this lay within the allies' autonomous jurisdiction.'[40] I feel it would be dangerous to regard this deference entirely as an empty formula or as a meaningless relic of a state of affairs which had long since passed. It is, after all, of a piece with the consultation with Spoletium in the matter of the prisoners or the degree of freedom Italians still enjoyed in the adoption of Roman laws. One readily concedes that the Italians could be overawed by the majesty of Rome[41] and, in consequence, might very well hesitate to refuse such a request but this does not invalidate our thesis.[42] The very fact that the Romans showed a willingness to deal with the Italians as allies to be consulted and not as subjects to be commanded cannot but have been significant for both parties. Clearly Rome could still defer to the sensibilities of the Italians and conduct her business with them in the traditional fashion. That is to say she could still give some weight and due recognition to their legal position as her allies and they must have welcomed this.[43]

What an incident at Praeneste in 173 reveals stands in glaring contrast. Then the consul Postumius made an unprecedented demand on the inhabitants. He ordered the town to entertain him and provide transport animals at public expense. This was done because, when on a previous visit there as a private citizen the people had failed to treat him with what he thought was proper respect. The Praenestians, whether out of modesty or fear, complied. The success of Postumius immediately emboldened others and soon such requisitions became commonplace.[44]

Postumius represents a new and sinister development. Here we see depicted most vividly that arrogance with which some members of Rome's ruling class had become infected as a result of the possession of imperial power. Filled with this spirit and conscious of having been exalted above all others, they, with heedless disregard, trampled over all and sundry.[45] It is very revealing, too, that Postumius should soon find imitators. If actions like this could be attended with impunity then it was but natural that others would want to repeat them, even if they were not motivated by the same malignancy. Once a dangerous precedent had been set it was all too easy to follow it. The reaction of the Praenestians is hardly of less moment. Though subjected to outrage they did nothing. The most natural conclusion to draw from this is that rightly or wrongly, they felt that protest would be useless and would meet with no redress.

Thus, we see the existence of two distinct attitudes among the Romans: the traditional respects the standing of those they rule, the new treats it with contempt. The one recognises that the Italians have a certain measure of independence, the other brings home forcibly to them that they are in reality subjects. It is the co-existence, side by side, of these two disparate attitudes which, in my opinion, renders it unsafe for us just to characterise Roman overlordship as oppressive. Rather we must have recourse to a formula which, though not as simple, will reflect more accurately the actual state of affairs. The Romans were undoubtedly encroaching more and more on Italian independence. Without a doubt they were eating into the measure of autonomy which their subjects had traditionally enjoyed. On occasions such encroach-ment would be carried out along traditional lines; action would only be taken after due consultation with the other party. On others, it would simply disregard such niceties and ignore the rights and feelings of the subject. And we have seen enough, I think, to be able to claim that neither mode of procedure was predominant.[46]

Once we have recognised this we are in a position to gauge Italian reaction. I believe that, in essence, it would be the same as that evoked by the terms of their military service and that it sprang from a like cause. A sense of uncertainty must have taken hold of the Italians. On any given occasion one could not be sure the Romans would behave with equity and, if they did not, there was no guarantee that those who sought a remedy would find it. Undoubtedly certain aspects of Roman behaviour gave rise to great resentment and anger. Magisterial misbehaviour, for instance, caused a deal of bitterness and was, eventually, to become an important political issue. But, over and above this, Roman encroachment, whether it wore a benign or malignant aspect, was, by its very nature, detrimental to the Italians in the long run. However much certain individual manifestations may have been welcome, there is little doubt that the policy as a whole tended to undermine the independence of the Italian commun-ities. Their position was being eroded and they were being thrust further into subjection.

We may now proceed to the second part of our investigation namely, a consideration of how these four phenomena served to shape the outlook of Italy.

If people are beginning to behave like Romans then it seems reasonable to suppose that they consider themselves to be the equals of those whom they imitate. Naturally, the backwoods man feels a certain diffidence before the urban sophisticate. But the *domi nobiles* of Italy seem to have had a well developed sense of their own worth and so were untroubled by any such inhibitions. At the outbreak of war they sharply reminded the Romans they were their partners in empire-building. Cultural assimilation to one's rulers does not, it is true, necessarily guarantee the political loyalty of the subject. He may seek equality by demanding parity of status with his master in the same state but he may, just as easily, look for it by aspiring to complete independence. However, in the case of the allies, it is perfectly clear that it was the first alternative which was chosen. The process of Romanisation awoke a desire for the citizenship and not for independence and the allies only turned to war when it became clear it would not be fulfilled.[47]

We may claim, then, that where Romanisation was of any consequence its effect was to induce in the allies a desire to become Roman citizens. However, as is well known, the phenomenon did not work uniformly and evenly. J.H. Goehler p. 27 neatly focuses attention on this aspect of affairs by pointing out that a small town like Bantia slavishly copied Roman forms of government while the far more important Pompeii sternly held aloof. The Marsi and the Picentes may have been heavily Romanised but the Lucanians and Samnites were still largely untouched. In Umbria and northern Campania Romanisation seems to have made more progress than in Etruria and southern Campania.[48] Therefore it follows that Romanisation could not have been a factor everywhere in Italy in forming the desire for the citizenship. Indeed, many men, at first, did not want it at all. We can see this in the offer of *provocatio* which was made as an alternative when the idea of enfranchisement was first mooted. Some were perfectly content with their lot save only for the specific grievance of magisterial misbehaviour. The subsequent almost unanimous demand for the citizenship must, in part at least,[49] be attributed to the fact that the ideal of equality through enfranchisement gradually spead from its natural birthplace and fired even those who, to begin with, would not have considered themselves as Romans. Once the notion was born its attraction became obvious even to those who would not, perhaps, have thought of it for themselves or would not have dared to hope for its attainment.[50] A bright idea will always win adherents.

In the light of the foregoing remarks we may now see the importance which attaches to local independence and to Roman encroachments on it.[51] It is difficult to see how those who wanted the citizenship would bear with equanimity the circumscribing of the power they already enjoyed which was involved in so much of Roman intervention at this time. Those who aspire to rise higher can hardly be expected to welcome the erosion of their present position and their tempers will have been sharpened in consequence. Likewise, those who did not desire the citizenship obviously had a high estimation of their own worth and of the worth of the place to which they belonged. They would not have welcomed those who sought to diminish it, especially when such attempts often involved brutal and arbitrary acts. The outraging of local pride should not be underestimated as a factor in impelling the Italians to seek privileges from the Romans. And when it became clear that the universal demand for enfranchisement was going to be ignored by the Romans then local patriotism, already strong, acquired an added dimension and an enhanced standing in Italian eyes. Being refused equality by assimilation they must needs fall back on their own resources and seek to obtain it by becoming independent. If they could not become Romans then they would be Italians and masters of their own destinies.[52] This is to be particularly noted in the case of the Samnites who, it will be remembered, still preserved the memory of their nation's long struggle against Rome. A people may cherish such traditions for several generations without finding in them any spur to contemporary action. When, however, there comes a time in which conditions appear to give them an immediate relevance then they will act as a stimulus. With the break from Rome approaching, the Samnites turned in on themselves as did the other Italian communities. They drew inspiration from their past and decided to renew the old struggle for independence. Some have branded Pontius Telesinus as an extremist who emerged in the dying days of the war but his position is no more than the logical culmination of a long existing tradition of local separatism, the consciousness of which had been inevitably sharpened by war. It is purely the accident of history that he was called upon to enunciate it for the last time.[53]

But, however much each nation asserted its individuality, all were acutely conscious that they did not stand alone and that there were bonds which tied them to their neighbours. All were Italians and all belonged to the common land of Italy. Thus they acted in concert when agitating for the citizenship and then in prosecuting the war. Regional patriotism presented no obstacle whatsoever to the pan-Italic ideal. As I stated a little earlier Rome's role in creating this ideal was that of Frankenstein who saw his creature eventually turn against himself.[54] There should be little difficulty now in appreciating why this should be so. For as long as the Italians believed that the interests of Rome and their own interests were the same then they were content that she should stand at their head as their leader in war and peace. But once a divergence occurred, once it became clear that the Italians were being asked to fight wars for small rewards and were further having their legitimate requests refused then they began to question the nature of their relationship with Rome. And they did this precisely because she had taught them that they owed an allegiance to an entity known as Italy. As Italians they could no longer brook her overlordship of Italy. The time had come for them to take it upon themselves.[55]

Notes

1. General surveys of Romanisation are few but particular import-ance attaches to Salmon (1982) which completely supersedes his 'The Beginnings of the Latin World', *Report of the Canadian Historical Ass.*, 1960. Brunt *JRS* (1965) pp. 97-101 has collected a good deal of information from various sources.
2. Devoto (1956) pp. 447-59; Magaldi pp. 195-6; Salmon (1967) pp. 313-4, (1982) pp. 99-100; Brunt *JRS* (1965) p. 99; Harris (1971) pp. 147-69, (1977) pp. 57-8; Nagle (1973) *passim* (and with caution); Goehler pp. 24-6.
3. Scrambling: Salmon (1967) pp. 310-11, 314, (1982) pp. 91-2; Galsterer p. 157. *Commercium*: Salmon (1967) p. 315. *Conubium*: Diod. Sic. 37.15.2; Dion. Hal. 6.1.1-3; Gaius 1.78-9, cf. Brizzi pp. 34-5. *Jus migrationis*: Humbert pp. 108-22. For the Italians see Galsterer p. 103 and Sherwin-White (1973) p. 113. I cannot agree with Salmon (1967) p. 314 that Gell. 16.11.2. shows the Marsi retaining some kind of racial purity. To me the passage suggests precisely the opposite. For some further remarks on factors aiding the spread of Latin see Kaimio pp. 95-101.
4. Goehler pp. 23-4. Cf. Salmon (1982) pp. 175-6.
5. Val. Max. 2.2.2. I do not know why Brunt *JRS* (1965) pp. 98-9 cites this passage as evidence for the use of Latin as a *lingua franca*. To me

it shows rather Roman insensitivity and even arrogance in these matters. See Plut. *Cat. Maior* 12 with Brizzi p. 117, n. 16. Cf. also Salmon (1982) p. 200, n. 360 and n. 8 below.

6. On this see further below and 1.3.

7. Galsterer p. 149. See below on early Latin literature.

8. Wilson pp. 88-91; Whatmough p. 258; Devoto (1956) p. 448, 451-2; Brunt *JRS* (1965) pp. 99-100; Salmon (1982) pp. 121-5, 157-160; Galsterer p. 149; Torelli (1983) *passim*. One point, noted by Brunt, deserves comment. Latin inscriptions set up by, or at the behest of, Romans have been found in remote areas and Brunt takes this as evidence for the spread of Latin. This is not necessarily so. Latin was the language of official business. No more than the ambassadors (n. 5 above) those who set up these inscriptions would naturally use it, and just as the ambassadors could hardly expect the whole of a Greek audience, say, to understand them but would require interpreters so those who set up the inscriptions need not necessarily have similar expectations of those they addressed either. This evidence need indicate no more than the fact that one or two individuals in the area were acquainted with Latin.

9. Goehler p. 30. See Cic. *de Orat.* 3.43, *Brut.* 169-72. I am not fully persuaded by Badian (1970/71) p. 383 that all of Cicero's orators were citizens by the time they appeared in the Forum.

10. Etruscan: Harris (1971) pp. 169-84 (and pp. 184-7 for Umbrian); Kaimio *passim*. Oscan: Salmon (1967) pp. 112-13, 122-3, 395-7; Heurgon pp. 113-14; M. Lejeune, *L'anthroponymie Osque*, Paris, 1976. Messapic: Whatmough pp. 320-4.

11. Brunt *JRS* (1965) pp. 100-1; Harris (1971) pp. 187-92; Devoto (1956) pp. 454-5; Ilari p. 16; Gabba (1972) p. 82; Campanile and Letta pp. 25-8, 49-61. Cf. Cic. *Balb.* 20-1 and further below.

12. *JRS* (1965) p. 98. Whether or not he is right about the toga (see below) I do not think we should speak of, 'a common dress as symbol of a common status'. Both Italians and Romans knew there was no common status. We may further remark that, 'a privilege [which] consisted in finding soldiers for Rome's armies' was beginning in some quarters to be seen as a burden.

13. As Brunt himself, (1971) p. 354, is at some pains to point out.

14. Brunt himself, *JRS* (1965) p. 99, admits Latin could be absorbed within a generation. This is what happened with English in nineteenth-century Ireland after another catastrophe, the Famine. On Etruscan costume see Harris (1977) p. 62, n. 33.

15. Ilari p. 4, n. 11; Goehler p. 32; Paul on Sall. *Jug.* 21.2 Cf. Daremberg-Saglio and *RE* 'toga'.

16. Crawford (1983) pp. 47-50.

17. See Magaldi p. 200-3 or Salmon (1982) p. 99 rather than Salmon (1967) p. 304, n. 2. See also Heurgon pp. 113-21.

18. Salmon (1982) pp. 100-17; Gabba (1976) p. 76; Gros pp. 21-33, 41-56; Bodei Giglioni pp. 68-76; Coarelli *passim*.

19. App. *B.C.* 1.45. Cf. Letta pp. 91-8.

20. Cato: Klingner pp. 20-3. Scipio and Gracchus: App. *B.C.* 1.9, 19. This view of Tiberius is controversial — see Richardson pp. 1-6 and further 2.1.

21. Salmon (1982) pp. 157-8.

22. For the life-style see Magaldi. Confiscations must have left a legacy of bitterness, see Frank pp. 112-13; Nagle (1973) pp. 374-7.

23. de Sanctis, *Scritti minori*, Rome, 1973 vol. 3 pp. 186-202. Cf. also Gabba (1976) p. 220, n. 46, 238, n. 212; Salmon (1967) p. 225, n. 2, 315-16.

24. (1982) p. 129. I draw attention once more (cf. above) to the survival of national costume.

25. Salmon (1982) p. 117; Gros p. 32, 49-50; Gabba (1972) pp. 106-7; Bodei Giglioni pp. 72-6; Wiseman (1983) pp. 299-307; Coarelli pp. 217-19.

26. See further the remarks of Salmon (1982) p. 125, 157-8. Brunt *JRS* (1965) is not satisfactory on this point. He says (p. 102) that of 'independence which belonged to the dim past ... outside Etruria there was probably no coherent record'. This ignores the evidence from Samnium and, although he alludes to it (p. 96), Brunt fails to see the possible significance of the long resistance in that quarter. Furthermore, in my view, he does not offer (p. 96) an adequate explanation as to why these putative Etrurian independents played such a small part in the Social War especially as there is no evidence for pro- or anti-Roman factions in the area. Indeed, the whole notion of a living traditional memory of independence there seems insecurely based since *ILS* 212 on which it rests appears to be, in fact, an antiquarian record.

27. For the word *Italia* and its history see Klinger *passim* and G. Radke, 'Italia: Beobachtungen zu der Geschichte eines Landesnamens', *Romanitas* 10, 1967 pp. 35-51. Catalano *passim* argues for the view that the concept of Italia had already taken root in the third century. Galsterer pp. 37-41 believes that the *ager Romanus* was officially known as Italia but I find this unconvincing since it seems to be based on a somewhat narrow interpretation of the sources.

28. A full discussion of the rebel state will be found in 3.1 where I hope to make clear why I believe Salmon (1982) p. 129 is preferable to Brunt *JRS* (1965) pp. 97-8 on this matter.

29. Salmon (1982) pp. 73-6. Cf. Polyb. 1.10.2.

30. Polyb. 2.23.12, cf. 2.31.7. See further Harris (1971) pp. 130-1.

31. Livy 23.5.4-15, 24.47.5. Cf. Polyb. 3.90.12-14. The fact that such appeals sometimes fell on deaf ears obviously does not mean that those who made them thought they were wasting their time doing so. They were enunciating sentiments to which many but not all Italians subscribed. Cf. Harris (1971) pp. 131-2; Salmon (1967) pp. 294-300, (1982) pp. 80-4 (perhaps underestimating the strength of pan-Italianism though rightly emphasising its roots in practical considerations).

32. On this see Klinger pp. 17-18 and Badian (1958) pp. 30-2, 144-5 or (with caution) Goehler pp. 31-8 and Brunt *JRS* (1965) p. 98.

33. Klinger p. 18, 20-3; Galsterer pp. 130-1, 150; Gabba (1976) p. 28, 36.

34. Salmon (1982) pp. 83-4, 92-3; Goehler pp. 22-3.

35. *Conjuratio*, arbitration, aid: McDonald (1939) p. 131, (1944) pp. 13-15, 18, 25-33. Religion and morals: Livy 39.22.5, 40.19.5; Pliny *NH* 10.139; Macrob. 3.17.6. Usury: Goehler pp. 53-4. W.V. Harris, 'Was

Roman law imposed on the Italian allies?', *Historia* 21, 1972 pp. 639-45 does not appear to me to be fully convincing because (a) he admits Roman jurisdiction in certain criminal matters, (b) allows it in the civil sphere in the case of the lex Sempronia, (c) while he is probably right about the lex Furia and the lex Appuleia de sponsu he is less persuasive with regard to the lex Fannia de sumptu. Making all due allowances for the right of the Italians to accept or reject Roman laws (see n. 11 and further below) the evidence would seem to indicate that, where it was thought necessary, the Romans did not hesitate to impose on them civil and criminal legislation.

36. Prisoners: to the list in Salmon (1967) p. 315, n. 3 add Cerinius in Ardea and the Carthaginians in Setia (Livy 32.6.5, 39.19.2) — these two with detailed instructions for confinement, Oxynta in Venusia, the Cretan who made Caesar an offer and Agamemnon in Asculum (3.2. and Appendix II). The last two were almost certainly common criminals. Roman misbehaviour: Toynbee p. 608-45. I am somewhat sceptical about Salmon's claim, (1967) p. 326, that Oscan speakers may have been especially singled out for such treatment as an act of deliberate policy.

37. pp. 106-15.

38. Galsterer pp. 131-4. The proposal to change the balloting laws in Arpinum (Cic. *de Leg.* 3.36) seems to have originated in the town itself and not at Rome although the latter was obviously the inspiration for it, cf. n. 11.

39. Goehler pp. 59-60; Galsterer p. 168. Cf. 2.1.

40. (1939) p. 131.

41. Polyb. 3.90.14.

42. As Harris (1971) p. 110 points out the occasion of the reprimand to Tibur (Bruns[7] p. 171) is quite unknown and it need not have sinister implications.

43. Cf. Badian (1958) pp. 141-4.

44. Livy 42.1.7-12.

45. Salmon (1967) p. 325, n. 3, Cf. 2.3.

46. See further the remarks of Harris (1971) pp. 107-13.

47. Harris (1971) pp. 112-13 is not the only scholar to comment on the stability of Italy for much of the second century. The sentiments of the heavily Romanised Pontius Telesinus (Vell. Pat. 2.27.2.) do not invalidate what has been said in the text. See further below.

We may also remark that the close cultural links which the Latins already had with Rome would naturally dispose them to see the citizenship as the most logical means of achieving equality. Indeed, awareness of the links they had with the Romans may, in part at least, explain why they conceived a desire for enfranchisement before many other Italians did. We should also remember that they, like the allies, could be goaded to the point of rebellion. On all of this see 2.1.

48. Harris (1971) p. 192; Salmon (1967) pp. 314-16; Letta pp. 87-104.

49. The reader must, of course, bear steadily in mind what was said in 1.1.

50. In general on the advantages of the citizenship see Salmon (1982) p. 126.

51. In my opinion, Brunt *JRS* (1965) pp. 101-2 does not see this.

52. See further Gabba (1976) p. 75, 100-1 although the evidence does not support his contentions about Campania.

53. Vell. Pat. 2.27.2. Brunt *JRS* (1965) p. 97 appears to doubt the historicity of this account but I do not find his arguments convincing. He wonders how the story might be transmitted to a Roman author and says it is 'very probably a fiction drawn from Sulla's *Memoirs* where hostility will have been shown to the Samnites'. In the first place it should be said that not everybody would accept that Sulla was particularly hostile to the Samnites, Cf. Keaveney *Crit. Stor.* (1982) pp. 529-31. More important, perhaps, we have no real means of knowing if the *Memoirs* are the source of the story. Yet we do know that Velleius was well informed about the Samnites (2.16.2-3), that some of them did survive the battle, cf. Keaveney (1983) p. 182 and that wolf-imagery was much in men's minds at this time, cf. 3.1. Therefore it is not straining credulity to suggest that Velleius drew his information from a Samnite source.

54. Brunt *JRS* (1965) p. 98 does not appear to give due weight to this point.

55. In the case of the Latins this picture must be qualified somewhat. For such qualifications see 2.1,2.

1.3

Conclusion: the Loosening of Ties

If we were to sum up, in broad terms, what we have been discussing in our two previous chapters we might do so as follows. The second century was a period which witnessed great changes in the Roman world[1] and inevitably the people of Italy were affected. The conditions under which they lived, whether at home or abroad, were such as to give them an enhanced view of their own worth. This naturally bred in them a discontent with their present position and sharpened their awareness of how even that was being undermined. They therefore sought amelioration and, conscious of what they had in common with the Romans, they aspired to be equal with them. This, of course, meant they would seek first the citizenship. But, by 91, the allies at any rate had come to the conclusion that only by independence could the cherished equality be gained, and so they rose in revolt. Therefore, one of the things we have been witnessing is the loosening of the ties which bound the peoples of Italy to Rome.[2] Barely perceptible at first — and, we may say, for a long time reversible — this loosening continued until for some the bonds fell away entirely.

Many of the leading Italian families stood as clients to their Roman counterparts. Both parties exchanged *hospitium*, sometimes intermarried and, above all, recognised that they had mutual obligations to each other.[3] The Italians, whether individually or collectively, would expect their patrons to defend their interests at Rome. For example, we shall shortly see them calling on Scipio Aemilianus to oppose the Gracchan land commission. It is said too that the younger Drusus introduced his proposals for enfranchisement at the urging of the allies.[4] The Italian could also turn to his patron for a solution to problems immediately

40

affecting his own state. For instance, that arbitration of internal quarrels we noted earlier was undertaken by a patron. In return, the Italian client, like his Roman counterpart, was expected to maintain the *dignitas* of his patron and aid his advancement in every possible way. In 205 the elder Scipio successfully appealed to the Italians for aid in mounting his expedition against Carthage. Again, in 109, when Mamilius introduced a bill of indictment Roman patrons organised their Italian clients to help in resisting it. The troubled period we are about to review will also furnish several instances where Italians were used as agents of physical intimidation.[5]

The advantage to Rome from such a system is obvious. To govern an empire with Italy disaffected was plainly impossible. It was therefore in her interest to have Italy ruled by régimes composed of men who were not only contented with their lot but were bound to her by ties of personal loyalty. And such régimes were usually oligarchic. As early as 296 we find the Romans intervening to protect just such a government from a popular movement. It is true that in the second Punic War it was not unknown for the commons in some instances to remain loyal while the ruling élite threw in its lot with the Carthaginians but it is safe to say that in the second century non-Roman Italy was largely governed by small groups of aristocrats, who willingly accepted the overlordship of Rome.[6]

We may claim, then, with reasonable confidence that the greatest service the Romans could render these friends of theirs was the provision of support to protect their position against external and internal threat. But it is precisely here that we can first detect a weakness in the system. For most of the second century no such threats existed. Italy was free from foreign invaders and within nothing occurred which might present a serious threat to her rulers. We certainly hear of slave rebellions, brigandage and cases of mass poisoning but these should be seen as menacing society as a whole and not the governing class exclusively. Certainly the Bacchic conspiracy did, at a time of social unrest, have the potential to develop into a mass movement but it appears to have been an isolated phenomenon.[7] What seems to be totally lacking is any consistent and serious opposition which might threaten to topple the ruling régimes. The ruled maintain their habitual and traditional allegiance and are not to be seduced from it. We gauge the hold the aristocrats had over their subjects from the fact that they were able to infect them with their own enthusiasm for the citizenship and marshal their support when they began to lobby for it. Then, when they called upon them to go to war, the call was answered. In the light of such displays of confidence, it is not straining credulity to suggest that the oligarchs had come to the belief that they might possibly exist without the support of Rome. Likewise, in the long period of freedom from external threats, they seem to have acquired the notion that they might meet such threats in the future without the aid of Rome, if that were necessary. We have seen how pan-Italianism had shown the Italians that they had certain interests in common and it would be surprising if they did not come to the conclusion that they could act in concert for their own defence. I doubt if this belief was shaken by the Germanic invasions. Rather, it would appear that for the allies, at any rate, it was strengthened. Ten years later they furnished the clearest proof of their conviction that they could do without Rome. Indeed, so far from regarding the Romans as their natural protectors, the Italian oligarchs began to look upon them as exploiters. In times past when Rome called for troops she could, with a good degree of plausibility, claim that she and the Italians were acting together to defend their common homeland. Now, however, these troops were being used abroad almost exclusively for the benefit of Rome alone and we saw how the resentment at this state of affairs was loudly voiced in 91. The fundamental interests of the Romans and the Italians were beginning to diverge.

One scholar has suggested that, 'the discrepancy between the equality enjoyed in private life by the Italian upper classes and the political disadvantages under which they laboured may account for the bitterness manifested by the *socii* in 90'.[8] There is plainly much truth in this contention. To be intimate with, and be treated with respect by, the great at Rome in the social sphere, and yet to be consistently denied that equality they so ardently sought in the political, cannot but have been galling to men who were now imbued with a strong sense of their own worth. But we should not forget either that Roman encroachments on the traditional freedoms enjoyed by Italians tended to undermine their actual status. This must then have inevitably led to the realisation that the whole patron-client relationship was showing signs of becoming debased and was in danger of turning into that of master and servant with the consequent disenchantment of the client. And dissatisfaction with clientage could also arise for yet another reason. It failed to get many Italians what they wanted, namely, the citizenship. To enlist their patrons' support for their cause was for a long time the only way in which those who lacked the franchise could hope to obtain it. Men of *auctoritas* would have to labour on their clients' behalf at Rome since they could not act for themselves. Here Italian efforts were attended with a conspicuous lack of success. The widespread indifference or hostility to their aspirations which we shall soon encounter among the Romans bear testimony to this. Even more eloquent, perhaps, is the fate of those like the younger Drusus who did embrace the cause of enfranchisement.

Now, it must be emphasised that this loosening of ties, of which we speak, affected all Italians, Latins as well as allies. There is abundant evidence to suggest that with an enhanced sense of their own worth they, too, grew wearied of their present status and sought to change it. We may safely say, also, that they shared in the nascent pan-Italic sentiment. In view of their already close connection with Rome they, like the allies, thought of the citizenship as the natural remedy for their condition and played a conspicuous part in early efforts to get it and when they appeared to be balked they wavered in their allegiance for a little time.[9]

Yet there came a day when the paths of the Latins and the allies diverged. At last we reach a time when the ties which bound the allies to Rome snapped altogether. A moment had arrived when they decided that if Rome would not grant them the equality they desired then they would establish it for themselves. If this should mean breaking the links which joined them to the Romans then they were willing to pay the price for such links now had no meaning for them. When measured against what they now sought they were as nothing.[10] In contrast, the Latins who had once been so forward in making the same demands now remained steadfastly by the side of the Romans. Logically their actions in the Gracchan period should eventually have led them to the same position as the allies a generation later. But they did not. Their wavering loyalty ought to have broken. But it did not. Self-evidently our task must now be to discover why it was that the processes we have been discussing in these chapters which, if unchecked could ultimately lead to rebellion, were halted in the case of the Latins but continued for the allies until they reached their climax in the Social War. We know that there were some elements in the contemporary situation which drew men to Rome while others tended to set them apart from her. We have now to ask why the first came to predominate for the Latins while the second did so for the allies.

Notes

1. A point emphasised by Earl (1967) p. 17. See McDonald (1939) and (1944) *passim.*
2. In general on Roman control of Italy see Galsterer pp. 10-11.
3. Badian (1958) pp. 11-13; Salmon (1967) pp. 328-30; Wiseman (1971) pp. 54-5; Letta pp. 99-100, cf. Letta and d'Amato no. 130.
4. See 2.1, 2.
5. Livy 28.45.13-14; Sall. *Jug.* 40 (misunderstood, I think, by Paul *ad loc.*). See Galsterer pp. 138-42; Badian (1958) pp. 159-63; Salmon (1967) p. 322.
6. Badian (1958) pp. 147-8; Brizzi pp. 33-7, 277; Letta pp. 99-100; Galsterer pp. 142-51; Harris (1971) pp. 129-44.
7. McDonald (1939) pp. 130-1, (1944) pp.13-15.
8. Wiseman (1971) p. 63. It will, I trust, be clear from what is said in this chapter why I cannot accept his other contention that the social ties which bound Italians to Romans were not relevant to the contemporary political situation.
9. See 2.1.
10. Cf. Gabba (1976) p. 237, n. 209.

Part Two
The Alienation of Italy

2.1

The Gracchan Crisis and the Great Refusal

In 125, one of the consuls Fulvius Flaccus proposed the Italians be given the citizenship. Those among them who did not want it might have instead the right of *provocatio*. Flaccus had an ulterior motive for making this offer. Under the lex Sempronia of Tiberius Gracchus a commission was set up to enquire into men's titles and those, whether Roman or Italian, who had alienated public land were to be forced to yield it up. Flaccus himself was one of these commissioners and he and his colleagues had to face the unpalatable fact that Italian resistance was so effective as to bring their work to a virtual standstill. In order, therefore, to break the deadlock he brought forward his proposals on the understanding that the Italians would then be more accommodating in the matter of the land. Many in Italy, we are told, were agreeable to this since it seemed to be a satisfactory arrangement. In the senate, however, fierce resistance was aroused and the fathers rid themselves of the nuisance by despatching the consul on campaign before he could proceed with his legislation.[1]

In the same year the Latin colony of Fregellae revolted but the uprising was crushed and the city razed to the ground. It is generally believed the revolt was in some way connected with the contemporary activities of Flaccus.[2] In 123 Flaccus was back in Rome and lent his support to his political ally C. Gracchus who had just entered on his first tribunate and was unveiling his legislative programme.[3] During his second tribunate, 122, Gracchus revealed what he had in mind for the Italians. The Latins should be admitted to the full citizenship while the allies would receive Latin status.[4] A counter proposal emanated from his opponents. The elder Drusus who had been detailed to

47

outbid the tribune in popularity offered the Latins the right of *provocatio* at home and abroad. When Gracchus perished his scheme died with him and, presumably because the senate now saw no need for it, Drusus' plan was likewise allowed to be forgotten.[5] A generation was to pass before another Roman was to attempt a major change in the status of the Italians.

It is generally assumed that Flaccus was the first Roman to offer the citizenship to the Italians. Recently, however, J.S. Richardson has argued that this distinction belongs to Tiberius Gracchus.[6] He begins from the not unreasonable assumption that Tiberius intended to give land to Italians as well as citizens. Although there has been scholarly controversy on this point it seems to me that Richardson is right to take the view he does.[7] It is certainly not inconsistent with the general thrust of Tiberius' policy with its concern for manpower. More important, perhaps, it is supported by Appian whose evidence, in my view, cannot easily be explained away.[8]

Now we happen to know that by 111 the *ager publicus* which the commissioners had distributed was made *privatus*. This, Richardson claims, causes difficulties. Land in Italy fell into the category of *res mancipi* which meant it could only be transferred to another citizen or to someone possessing *commercium*. For Richardson this latter category means the Latins alone. So Richardson concludes that, in order to transfer *ager publicus* to the allies Tiberius would have to make citizens of them. Ancient evidence for such a scheme is to be found, he believes, in Vell. Pat. 2.2.2 and Cic. *Rep.* 1.31, 3.41.

To me this hypothesis carries less than total conviction. Our knowledge of Roman land tenure prior to 90 may be less full than we would wish but we do know enough to make it reasonably certain that Tiberius would not necessarily have to have recourse to the sort of device Richardson envisages. Furthermore, neither Velleius nor Cicero, whether taken singly or together, prove that he in fact did so.

In the first place, it may be observed that it is unlikely that only the Latins enjoyed the right of *commercium* for, as we have seen, other Italians also appear to have shared in it.[9] Again it would appear that *peregrini* could own property and have their rights fully protected even though they could not hold it *ex jure Quiritium*.[10] We should also bear in mind that there is some reason to believe that rules governing transfer of property which prevailed in private law were not necessarily applicable to the public land. In other words, the state was not bound by the same constraints as were individuals.[11] We certainly know of a number of cases where foreigners did get Roman land. For example, Onesimus became a *socius* and the senate gave him 200 *jugera* of *ager publicus*. We do not know under what terms he held this land but it is surely not without significance that his treatment, and Livy's description of it, differs not one whit from that of cases where *civitas* and land were given together.[12] Furthermore, it is well known that non-citizens (*incolae*) resided in Roman colonies. While their position was obviously less privileged than that of citizens it seems to me unlikely that some provision should not be made for safeguarding their property rights.[13] Finally, there is the viritane allotment of 173 to consider. The very fact that Livy specifically states that Romans got 10 *jugera* while Italians got three would appear to me to indicate decisively that the latter received land without becoming citizens.[14] Thus, if we bear in mind that non-Romans could receive from the state Roman land outright and that machinery appeared to exist to safeguard their rights, then we can see that Tiberius, in support of his schemes, will not have been compelled to offer citizenship with his allotments.[15]

Nor do our sources lend support to the idea that he had such a plan. We must first of all scrutinise Velleius' words (2.2.2): *pollicitusque toti Italiae civitatem, simul etiam promulgatis agrariis legibus*. These words interpreted strictly, would appear to mean that Tiberius promised citizenship at the same time as he actually promulgated his land bill. That is to say, while the land bill was a concrete reality, the citizenship was no more than a vague promise. The passage hardly supports the theory that a bill was now brought forward for the latter. It therefore follows that Tiberius, as depicted by Velleius, did not attach to enfranchisement the importance Richardson supposes he did. At the very best it was something to be dealt with at an unspecified future date, and even this is open to doubt. In view of the furore caused when others tried to give the Italians the citizenship we should expect to hear more of Tiberius' alleged scheme if he had indeed made it public. Yet Velleius is the only author to make explicit mention of it and so there must always be a suspicion that he may have confused Tiberius with his brother.

I do not believe either that Cicero's somewhat enigmatic words can be taken to refer to the granting of citizenship by a law of Tiberius. Laelius, as portrayed in the dialogue, accuses

Tiberius of neglecting and violating the treaty rights of the allies. Richardson believes that what is in question is that Gracchus was enfranchising members of the allied communities without the consent of their rulers which was a breach of the treaties they had with Rome. For a number of reasons this seems unlikely. Richardson compares this situation with that which prevailed in 187 and 177 when the Italians tried to get back some of their citizens who had migrated to Rome. But there is nothing in our sources to suggest that those who were entitled to exercise the *jus migrationis* then had to seek the permission of their rulers to do so. In the case of the others, of course, the question simply did not arise. Indeed, at that time, it was not the acquisition of citizenship *per se* which worried the oligarchs but the drain on manpower. It may very well be, I admit, that things were different in 133 and that they were now worried about the change in the status of their people. But, then, we should have to explain why it was that when the Italians found a champion in Scipio he concerned himself solely with the land question and did nothing about the citizenship.[16] The case of Balbus of Gades which Richardson invokes is not helpful to his thesis since it seems to show that a state could not hinder an individual from accepting Rome citizenship and, so, if Tiberius really were making such grants he would be perfectly entitled to do so.[17] Moreover, the nature of the passages is such as to preclude them from offering unequivocal support to any particular theory. In due course we shall see that there is one other interpretation which is at least as plausible as that of Richardson. We must therefore conclude that the evidence of Velleius and Cicero does not overthrow the explicit statement of Appian that Flaccus was the first to excite among the Italians the desire for Roman citizenship.[18]

But what exactly does Appian mean by this? Is he telling us that Flaccus implanted in the heads of the Italians notions they had never before entertained or is he saying he taught them that dreams they already cherished might become a reality? To answer these questions we must try and discover if the Italians manifested any desire for the citizenship prior to 125.

We have already remarked that one of the notable features of life in Italy in the second century is the migratory habits of her inhabitants. Within the country itself there is a movement which parallels the contemporary diffusion of Italians over the Mediterranean basin.[19] For instance, Sabellians appear to have made their way towards Latin colonies.[20] We shall have much to say a little later about the 4,000 families who settled in Fregellae. Of more immediate interest to us here is the behaviour of certain people from Ferentinum. They were apparently so anxious to obtain the citizenship that they were prepared to enrol themselves in the usually unpopular Roman coast-guard colonies. *Civitas* was their primary aim since some of them began to conduct themselves as citizens before they had actually taken up residence there. This kind of thing opened up the possibility that people would enrol simply to become citizens and then not bother to go to the colonies. Alerted to the danger, the senate ruled that people in this position could not be regarded as citizens.[21]

This tendency of the Italians to wander from home, would, if it were on a large scale, bring with it problems for those who ruled their communities. The pride of the nobility would ill-brook this debilitation of the strength of their respective nations and the consequent weakening of their own position and importance. More immediately, remembering the severe reaction of Rome when, in the period 209-204, twelve Latin colonies failed to produce the troops required of them, they would be afraid this haemorrhage would prevent them from fulfilling their military obligations.[22]

For the Latins, at least, the problem had, by 187, become acute and they sent representatives to Rome complaining that a great number of their citizens had moved to the city and been enrolled in the census there. Although these people were perfectly entitled to exercise the *jus migrationis* in this way, the Romans, who clearly recognised the problems faced by the Latins, were prepared to give the complaints a sympathetic hearing. They ordered the repatriation of anybody who had been registered — or who was the son of somebody so registered — as a citizen of a Latin state since 204 upon that state producing proof of such registration. The praetor Culleo was given the job of flushing out the culprits and the task was performed so thoroughly that 12,000 Latins were expelled.[23] It would also appear that measures were taken to check emigration in the future. There is reason to believe that it was now that a well known curb on the *jus migrationis* was introduced. Henceforth a Latin might quit his native place only if he left a son behind him in his stead.[24]

The effectiveness of the expulsion and of the circumscribing of the *jus migrationis* may be gauged from the fact that representatives of the Latins were back in Rome in 178 pestering the consuls and censors with the same complaints as a decade previously. Eventually, in the next year, they obtained an audience with the senate where they claimed that large numbers of their citizens had decamped to Rome — a circumstance which instantly arouses the suspicion that some, at least, of those expelled had simply crept back once the fuss had died down. Moreover, the ambassadors reported that resort was being had to legal subterfuge in order to dodge the requirement to leave a son at home. Some people gave their sons as slaves to Roman citizens who then manumitted them, thus making them citizens too. Others, who were childless, simply adopted someone as a son. Indeed there were even those who couldn't be bothered to make gestures like these but boldly made their way to Rome regardless. Present with the Latins on this occasion were delegates from the Samnites and Paelignians who had a worry of their own. They declared that 4,000 families from their areas had decamped to Fregellae. The ambassadors now requested that all wandering *socios* (Livy's term) be ordered to return where they belonged. Manumission or adoption for the purpose of acquiring citizenship should be forbidden and anybody who acquired citizenship in this way should not be regarded as a Roman. The senate acceded to these requests.

Now the measures taken with regard to manumission and adoption obviously apply only to the Latins but could the decision to expel *socios* apply to the allies as well? It is useless to try and answer this question by reference to the terminology Livy uses to describe the complainants but a close examination of his narrative sequence may prove more profitable. The *legationes socium nominis Latini* are admitted to the senate where they complain that their citizens are censed in Rome and that many had actually moved there. Next come the Samnites and Paelignians with their complaint about Fregellae. Then follows the exposition of how the *jus migrationis* is being abused and finally the senate's ruling is given. Although the bulk of the passage is taken up with Latin grievances it is, I think, clear that all Italian delegations had been received together and made their case together. Certainly the presence of the Samnites and Paelignians, at the same time as the Latins, is unambiguously attested and, in this context, we may note especially the force of *quoque* in 41.8.8. This is, of course, what we should expect for all Italians were concerned with the same basic problem; migration of population. So, Livy is portraying all parties as making the same representations. It would therefore follow that the recommendations for a solution must have come from all the delegates and were intended to remedy all of their discontents. The order for expulsion must then be seen as applying not only to the Latins but also to the allies. While the emigrants in Fregellae would have been the main victims among the allies there are likely to have been many at Rome who would be affected as well since, even as early as 187, the city was full of foreigners.[25]

The consul Claudius then passed a law *de sociis* which ordered those Italians who had themselves been registered, or whose ancestors had been registered, in an Italian community before 189 to return home before 1 November. The praetor Mummius was given the job of seeing that this was done. The senate also laid down that any magistrate to whom a slave was brought for manumission must extract an oath from the master to the effect that this was not being done for the purpose of a fraudulent acquisition of the citizenship. Yet the expulsion order seems to have been carried out rather halfheartedly or, at any rate, was successfully evaded, since, in 173, the consul Albinus was obliged to proclaim that those whom Claudius had ordered to return should do so. This had some effect for we are told that the number of Roman citizens in this census was now somewhat smaller.[26]

We hear no more of efforts to rid Rome of Italians until the exclusion act of Pennus. This law was passed by the tribune in 126 and had as its aim the expulsion of all foreigners from Rome.[27] Conventionally this is seen as a response to the enfranchisement proposals of Flaccus. The Italians had come to the capital in droves to support him and measures had to be taken to counter the menace.[28] Recently, however, it has been demonstrated that this theory presents serious difficulties. Flaccus cannot have formally promulgated his bill until the 1 January at the earliest and Pennus had ceased to be tribune in the preceding December. Further, it is known that C. Gracchus made a speech attacking Pennus' act. Now if this is not a retrospective assault made in 125 or 124,[29] then the speech must have been made early in 126 before Gracchus departed for Sardinia. And there are other objections which may be raised. It is, of course, very likely that Flaccus' plans were already known before he entered office and that he had been advertising them in the course of 126.[30] However, this will hardly have provoked an influx of Italians in that year. Their arrival would be too early for their moment would only come when a bill was actually promulgated. For economic reasons alone, it is improbable they would spend several months at Rome especially since it was to no purpose. In fact, our sources contain no explicit mention of an Italian influx in either 126 or 125. It is simply an inference from the existence of an expulsion act and it is an inference which I believe to be mistaken. As I shall attempt to demonstrate in a moment, a more likely occasion for Pennus' act may be found. But, if the Italians were not actually present and Flaccus' intentions were well known, it could still be argued that the tribune's law was antici-patory; he foresaw the consequences of the scheme and intended to forestall the trouble which lay ahead. This, however, seems to me to attribute to him altogether too much prescience and does not explain why we find Fannius[31] failing to follow his allegedly successful example a little later.[32]

If it is hard to establish a direct connection between Pennus' act and Flaccus' projected bill, a case can, in my opinion, be made for seeing it in the context of those efforts which had been made earlier in the century to deal with the twin problems of migration and the assumption of the citizenship. It can be viewed as part of a pattern of legislation which began in 187. First of all, we should recognise that an act to rid the city of resident aliens need not be regarded as being in any way unusual at this time. We have seen how ineffective previous expulsion orders had been. When the fuss died down, migration resumed. The fact that our sources of information dry up shortly after 173 obviously prevents us from knowing what happened next. But, in view of what did take place in the previous decade or so, we may safely assume that it was unlikely that the last decree we hear of succeeded in solving the problem. For that matter if there were others, knowledge of which is now lost to us, it is equally improb-able that they provided a permanent remedy. Then, in the light of what we do know, we must conclude that things went on pretty much as before and Italians continued to flock to Rome. We saw that as early as 187 the city was full of foreigners and by 122 there is evidence to suggest the Roman plebs had begun to genuinely fear they could be crowded out by the Latins.[33] It can, therefore, be argued that Pennus' act was the latest in a series designed to deal with a long standing problem which was felt once more to have grown intolerable.

Now, if Pennus' aim had been merely to clear a potentially dangerous mob from Rome then it ought to have been a relatively simple operation. Italians, newly arrived in town and congregating in large numbers, would have been readily identifiable and easily dealt with. He need do no more than Fannius was to do and bar undesirables temporarily from the city's environs.[34] However, there is reason to believe that a more extensive and far-reaching operation was mounted and one which resembled those made on previous occasions when efforts had been made to rid Rome of Italians. Our source is Val. Max. 3.4.5. According to this account a dark secret was revealed at this time. It was discovered that the consul for 130, M. Perperna who was now dead, had never been a Roman citizen at all. Investigations made under Pennus' act showed that his father, who still lived, was in reality an Italian. Some of the details as given by Valerius are wrong and it has been argued (although not conclusively in my view) that a fraud had not, in fact, been perpetrated[35] but, so far as I am aware, nobody has tried to overthrow or even much remarked on what is, from our point of view, the most interesting feature of the story: Valerius depicts Italians as making application for the return of one of their number under the law. It will be recalled that this was precisely the kind of thing which had happened in 187 and 177. Upon furnishing proof that somebody had been registered with them after a certain date, a state could then reclaim him from Rome. It would appear, therefore, that Pennus was not concerned with a temporary influx but with permanent residents.[36] It has been suggested that Gracchus' speech against Pennus' act was a plea for generosity in the matter of the citizenship and the surviving fragment is therefore to be taken as warning against the pursuit of a narrow policy in this sphere.[37] While this is probably true, it does not necessarily follow that Gracchus was urging his audience to choose the path of Flaccus rather than the alleged one of Pennus. In the present state of our knowledge it is equally legitimate to suggest he was simply asking that Italians now resident in Rome be left in peace.[38]

It would seem then that we have abundant evidence that long before 125 Italians had been actively seeking the citizenship. The difficulty lies in interpreting such evidence since we are nowhere explicitly told to what stratum of society these people belonged nor do we learn anything of their motives.[39] Recourse must, therefore, be had to reasoned conjecture and inference. In view of the large numbers involved it seems safe to assume that very many must have belonged to the lower orders. If that is so then we must agree with E. Badian that their objectives were fairly limited. They looked for economic betterment and wished to escape conscription. Those oligarchs who sought the citizenship in 125 wanted to achieve equality of status with the Romans[40] but it is unlikely that those who flocked to Rome early in the century (in 187, for instance) professed this sentiment. For one thing, it may have been too early for such a notion to have wide currency. For another, it is doubtful if the lower classes could have formulated the idea for themselves. We know that they came to share their masters' sense of grievance but they are unlikely to have had a sophisticated response to their situation.[41] The remedy for present ills would have to be formulated by their overlords. The notion that one should seek the citizenship because it conferred equality can hardly have become a universal ideal until the oligarchs, in pursuit of their own campaign, made it so.

Yet, we are not justified in concluding as Badian does, that there is no connection between these events and what is revealed to us in 125. Nobody would deny, I think, that those who went to Fregellae looked only for material benefit; there was no hope for the Roman citizenship and the chances of achieving Latin status were not much better.[42] On the other hand, the behaviour of the men of Ferentinum and the sacrifices they were prepared to make strongly suggests they sought the citizenship purely for its own sake.

I would argue that if the picture I have painted of the Italian position in our first section has any verisimilitude at all then the factors which I believe led to a desire for equality must have begun to weigh at some time prior to 125. The alternative is to make the unlikely supposition that there was something peculiar about conditions in the 120s which would induce the Italians to suddenly want what they had not previously sought and to want it so badly that they were prepared to make substantial sacrifices in order to get it. Why should citizenship all at once become so dear that they would part with their land for it? Naturally the processes I have described will not have worked everywhere with equal swiftness and equal effect but we have good reason to believe that they had a particularly potent effect in the case of the Latins and it is precisely our knowledge of their earlier assumptions of the citizenship which allows us to trace, in outline, the development in their outlook. It will not have escaped notice that the Latins played the principal Italian part in the events of 187 and 177. They were the ones who made the loudest noise and

Smith suggests that a possible reason for the establishment of large Roman colonies at Mutina and Parma in 183 was to allow Latins, hungry for the citizenship, to acquire it.[43] That the Latins continued to press at the gates of Rome is amply demonstrated by the vision conjured up by Fannius for the edification of the plebs in 122. Certainly they were to the fore in the agitation in the time of Flaccus and Gracchus. If, as has been plausibly conjectured, their lands were particularly threatened by the activities of the Gracchan commissioners[44] then they were obviously in a position to put especial pressure on Flaccus. And it was one of their colonies, Fregellae, which rebelled when Flaccus failed to carry through his proposals. Moreover, as we shall soon learn, both Gracchus and his opponents showed a marked regard for them in the matter of legislation — an undoubted tribute to the strength of feeling which had been manifested.[45]

The argument can, doubtless, be advanced that the prominence of the Latins, in 187 and 177 and again in the 120s is purely coincidental. However, it does not have much to commend it. I would argue that what we are witnessing is a continuous and uninterrupted movement.[46] which (for us) begins in 187 and culminates in the time of Gracchus. The Latin desire for the citizenship is constant and unwavering over this long period of time. The difference between its beginning and its end lies solely in the development of the character of that desire. What had begun as something spontaneous with limited — largely economic — objectives ended as a carefully orchestrated political campaign with a sophisticated aim: the citizenship for the equality of status it could give. The movement begins by reflecting the aspirations of the common man but it ends by mirroring the aims and ambitions of the oligarchs. This suggests to me that when the rulers of the Latins set about lobbying for the citizenship for their own ends they naturally harnessed the energies of their inferiors and bent them in a direction beneficial to themselves. Capitalising on their natural position of dominance they were easily able to persuade their subjects to support them when they decided that an already widespread desire of long standing should now acquire a broader dimension.

We are less well informed about the allies. There is, however, some reason to suspect that among their commons there were those who imitated the Latins and contrived to obtain the citizenship — in their case an illegal act. We dwelt at some length on the subterfuges employed by the Latins to circumvent restrictions and it is not straining credulity to suggest that allies had recourse to similar devices. The nature of the Roman census left it wide open to abuse as it merely recorded that a man behaved as a citizen; it did not actually guarantee that he really was one. To further facilitate the unscrupulous, the Romans, as we have learned from what happened in 187 for instance, were reluctant to pry into such matters unless forced.[47] It would therefore require a great deal of faith to believe that nobody took advantage of a situation like this and we do happen to know that Livy 41.8.6-12 seems to indicate that allies were among those who had usurped the citizenship by 177. Indeed, if we believe that Valerius tells us, the elder Perperna provides a spectacular illustration of what a man of parts could achieve.[48] Thus, when the allied upper classes began, like their Latin counterparts, to rally their subjects in support of their own bid for enfranchisement, it is not beyond the bounds of possibility that they, too, were calling on men, some of whom at any rate, had already manifested a desire for the citizenship.[49]

In my view, then, the demand for citizenship, in the time of Flaccus and Gracchus, represents a coming together of two strata of Italian society. Oligarchs, who had indeed desired the citizenship but lacked the means to acquire it until Flaccus gave it to them, now enlisted in their cause men who had long shown both the will and the ability to obtain it.[50] When Appian speaks, then, of Flaccus having been the first to inspire the Italians with the desire for citizenship it should not be taken to mean he literally gave them ideas they had never had before. Rather, he showed the oligarchs that what they had hitherto looked upon as a dream could become a reality. As Badian has emphasised, Flaccus introduced the Italian question into Roman politics.[51] In effect, this means he taught the Italians — since they seem to have been unable to make the discovery for themselves — how they might put pressure on the Romans to grant them the citizenship. They had something Flaccus wanted and he, in turn, seemed to have the power to get something they wanted. Hence his initiative and hence the claim that he awoke a desire in their hearts.

The connection between the activities of the Gracchan land commission and the Italian demand for the citizenship is explicit in our sources. As the triumvirs set about their task they soon discovered that it was not always completely clear what was *ager publicus* which might be resumed and what was not. Sometimes it was difficult to distinguish land legitimately held from land which had been illegally encroached upon. We hear, for instance, that surveys had not been properly carried out and that title deeds could be ambiguous or had simply been lost altogether. The commission, however, had the power of adjudication and it was used freely to cut through the difficulties and reclaim land whose status was dubious. Both Roman and Italian *possessores* were affected but it would appear that the latter were particularly harshly treated. As we might expect, this caused resentment among those who felt they were being deprived of what was rightfully theirs. The actions of the triumvirs, we are told, had dangerously unsettled the Latins and the allies.[52]

Protest took an effective form in 129 when the Italians found a champion in Scipio Aemilianus.[53] Arguably he represents, at its best, that type of Roman who believed in dealing with the Italians in the traditional manner. He shows an attitude both benevolent and paternalistic. One finds it difficult to imagine him engaging in the kind of wanton cruelty now practised in Italy by certain Roman magistrates but, at the same time, he gave the Italians a sharp reminder of their position at the siege of Numantia when he, as he was perfectly entitled to do, visited heavier punishments on them than on the Romans. Therefore, it is safe to say that Scipio would abhor the notion of any change in the status of Rome's Italian subjects but would, also, insist that they be treated with perfect correctness. Rome should live up strictly to its obligations to them under the present arrangements. Treaties must be scrupulously observed and the Romans at all times should proceed with justice and equity. He was plainly conscious of the fact that those who aided Rome in her wars should not be subjected to wanton disturbance nor should they be alienated. We may suppose the Italians were aware of this when they sought his help. At any rate, Scipio gave that help willingly.

He seems to have argued that, in laying hands on Italian land, the commissioners were exceeding their competence because they were interfering with the treaties which bound the Italians to Rome. They were, in effect, meddling in international affairs. The senate accepted this argument and ruled that, in future, where the Italians objected to the activities of the land commission their cases should be decided upon by the consul. Tuditanus, who happened to be the consul present in Rome at this time, seems to have found these cases too much for him and went off on campaign. He was back, however, by 1 October and most likely was then obliged to give judgement. Unfortunately we are not told exactly what decisions Tuditanus and his successors reached but all the indications are that their operations were, in the main, unfavourable to the triumvirs. We hear of 'excuses' which were made by the landowners which had the effect of hindering the work. I take this to mean that the Italians, at the very least, were able to slow down the work of the commissioners and in many instances bring it to a halt by having recourse to the courts. Thus, although the commissioners could continue to reclaim what was indisputably *ager publicus* they now found it very hard indeed to do the same for most of the land occupied by the Italians. It is not difficult then to appreciate that the Gracchan programme was now in severe difficulties.[54]

In effect, the future of the land commission lay with the Italians. If the triumvirs wished to complete their task successfully they would have to win their consent. Therefore, Flaccus' move was a perfectly logical one. He would induce the Italians to withdraw their opposition by offering them something substantial in return. *Civitas* or the *jus provocationis* would be bartered for land.

As we know, this attempt failed and yet Italian opposition to the Gracchan land programme now seems to disappear from history. To account for this state of affairs in the period after the death of C. Gracchus is not difficult if we accept two recent suggestions. Then it would appear the commission was packed with optimate supporters and so did little. And even that little was brought to a halt when it was wound up, as has been argued, fairly soon after Gracchus' death.[55] But this does not explain why the opposition vanished even earlier. In my view this happened as a direct result of a deliberate act of policy by Caius himself.

His *lex agraria* seems to have been designed to supersede that of his brother. If we are agreed that it was to be a more comprehensive law than its predecessor then we should expect that, among other things, it would address itself to the task of removing ambiguities and anomalies in the previous legislation. Granted that this is true, then we can picture Gracchus taking steps to close the loophole Scipio had exploited. In other words, the land commission was to receive once more the necessary power to carry on its work. Inevitably this would arouse Italian ire but Flaccus had already shown how this might be quieted.[56] So Gracchus revived his friend's proposal in a modified form: the Latins would receive the citizenship while the allies would get Latin status. Once more land was to be bartered for status. Of course, we need not for a moment doubt that Gracchus saw Italian enfranchisement as something desirable in itself which natural justice demanded should be granted.[57] but, however motivated, it is difficult to escape the conclusion that Gracchus' proposal would have the same effect as Flaccus had envisaged for his. His declared aim of granting the citizenship would have made the Italians more accommodating in the matter of the land. Hence we hear of no further Italian opposition to the triumvirs.[58]

Self-evidently, those who obstructed the commissioners were the well to do. Only those with something substantial to lose would have mounted such a resistance. But, if those of us who believe that Tiberius Gracchus intended to distribute lands to the Italians are right, then the interests of the Italian aristocrats and those they ruled would be diametrically opposed. One would want what the other would not give. We might thus expect, in Italy, a division along class lines. Such, in fact, is what we find but the arena for the contest is Rome not Italy and it is swiftly aborted. We are told that great numbers flocked to the capital from the country, some to oppose and some to support Tiberius' bill. Accepting that there were Italians among them, then we may postulate that some magnates had successfully marshalled their retainers to oppose the measure while others found that the poor of their areas had elected to back the tribune.[59] Yet, as has been acutely observed, by the time we hear of protests against the working of the law there would seem to be unanimity between rich and poor.[60] A feature of Italian life which runs as a constant through our period now reasserted itself. I refer to the ingrained and habitual deference which the ordinary Italian showed towards his rulers.

The explanation for this abrupt change of attitude is not, perhaps, far to seek.[61] The support which Tiberius enjoyed in Italy was surely based on nothing more than a spontaneous outburst of undisciplined popular fervour. A glamorous leader had arisen who promised much and so it was natural that the Italian peasant should look to him and give him his allegiance with enthusiasm. But it is in the nature of such things to be fleeting and transient. With the death of Tiberius, the focus of their ardour and the leader who might direct their energies had vanished and it was but natural that, in the circumstances, enthusiasm for his cause should quickly wane and soon dissipate itself. It is true they could still hope for something from the land commission but when this faltered their disillusionment must have been complete since they had nobody to whom they might look for redress. In the circumstances the lower classes could do no other than return to the loyalty they had always given to those who, after all, were regarded as their natural masters. There is a possibility that these masters actively sought to woo those who had been alienated. It is not beyond the bounds of probability that, with the weight of their authority, they were able to misrepresent what was involved in Tiberius' scheme and so win back some of his erstwhile supporters. A primitive and ill-informed society would facilitate such a task. On the other hand, many of those who supported Tiberius probably knew exactly what he was about and might not be so easily swayed. Something more concrete would be required for them and here the suggestion of Greenidge is both likely and attractive. He argues that when the magnates struck their bargain with Flaccus they took care to spell out to their subjects what it would mean for them: land distribution would follow on enfranchisement.[62]

In adopting Flaccus' scheme of bartering land for status C. Gracchus naturally ensured that the Italian peasant would remain loyal to his master who, in turn, was supporting him as a consequence of the same scheme. Some of the lands now available to the commission would be given to the Italian lower classes and, in addition to viritane settlements, they were also to be admitted to his colonial foundations.[63] It is difficult to escape the conclusion that C. Gracchus deliberately aimed at conciliating all classes in order to ensure that the divisions which manifested themselves in his brother's time should not recur.

By satisfying all degrees in this fashion Gracchus could hope for the united and undivided support of Italy. The sequel shows that he was correct in his assumption. Even before he formally promulgated his bill Italians were conspicuous among his followers. At the election to his first tribunate a great crowd swarmed into the city to give him their backing.[64] We may emphasise once more that while Gracchus' Italian policy was in its essence disinterested he could not but profit by it in a practical way. Without doubt the newly enfranchised Latins would, in the future, express their gratitude by means of their votes but, more immediately, the vast crowds of Italians would provide rich opportunities for the exercise of personation and intimidation. His enemies knew this too and understandably they took fright at the prospect. When the approach of the day for voting on Gracchus' enfranchisement proposals brought with it the certainty of another influx of Italians ready to back their champion, they acted swiftly and decisively. The consul Fannius barred from the city and its immediate environs anybody who did not have a vote.[65]

This close connection between the twin problems of enfranchisement and land has led to the argument that the demand for the citizenship arose at this time purely as a result of an external factor which had nothing to do with the citizenship itself. It came about simply as a by-product of the activities of the agrarian commissioners. I find this difficult to accept. To me it appears more logical to speak of the problems of the triumvirs as providing the opportunity for the introduction of the citizenship question into Roman politics. Casting around for a means to break the deadlock Flaccus saw what the Italians wanted and resolved they should have it. The Italians' desire was not created by the land problem, it merely found in it a vehicle for its expression. Gracchus, in turn, pursued a policy which was simply a refinement of that of his predecessor: while taking care to conciliate the Italian commons he too offered the aristocrats a change in status in return for land.[66]

Appian tells us specifically why the Italians were prepared to make sacrifices for the citizenship. They wished to be partners in empire rather than subjects.[67] As a natural corollary to the theory I have just tried to combat Gabba denies the truth of this statement. He believes the citizenship was sought, not as end in itself, but for the protection it would afford against the violence of Roman magistrates. Indeed, many simply did not want it at all because it would mean sacrificing the advantages they enjoyed under the present arrangements. He finds support for these notions in the fact that both Flaccus and the lex Acilia offered the *jus provocationis* as an alternative to citizenship.[68] This seems to me to be a somewhat forced interpretation which puts undue stress on one part of our evidence at the expense of the other. Since the sources tell us that both citizenship and *provocatio* were on offer we have, I believe, no alternative but to accept that some wanted the former while others were prepared to settle for the latter. As to the relative size of the two groups we are largely in ignorance, but any attempt to divine the mood of Italy at this point must surely give due recognition to the existence of both. Now, if it is self-evident that those who wanted *provocatio* thought only of the solution of one particular problem then it appears to me equally self-evident that those who desired *civitas* looked beyond the confines of this one matter; they had acquired a broader perspective and were looking for an improvement in their position as a whole.[69] If this is so, then I see no reason why we should disbelieve Appian when he says the reason they wanted the citizenship was in order to become the equals of the Romans. That there should be such a division in Italian opinion at this time need not cause surprise. In 1.1,2 I outlined the factors which I believe led to a desire for equality which first of all expressed itself in a call for the citizenship. However, it should be self-evident, as we said there, that these factors can hardly have worked uniformly in space or in time. Some will surely have been relatively quick to conclude that the citizenship should be their goal while others would have been perfectly happy with something like *provocatio* which appeared to offer a solution to a limited, albeit pressing, problem. Gracchus' proposed legislation also recognised this division of sentiment in that it offered citizenship to the Latins, while granting Latin status to the rest. This latter clause was plainly designed to be attractive to those who did not want *civitas*. The measure also left open the possibility of future developments. With the growth of Italian political maturity those who did not desire citizenship immediately might do so later and the enhanced status Gracchus was offering would make their future incorporation all the easier.[70]

Thus far then we may claim to have discovered two widely differing Italian attitudes to the possibility of enfranchisement. But, there is a third and more extreme which reveals that certain people had reached a position which the rest of Italy was not to attain for a generation and it is illustrated for us in the revolt of Fregellae.

As I stated at the beginning of this section, the rebellion of Fregellae is often held to be connected with the contemporary political activity of Flaccus. This must be correct for, although no source specifically says why the town revolted, such evidence as we do possess strongly points to the failure of his proposals as leading to the uprising.[71] There were at Rome those who were prepared to believe not only that Flaccus had sown discontent among the Italians with his schemes (which was true enough) but that he had actually incited them to revolt. Gracchus fell under similar opprobium. He too was said to have stirred up rebellion and he was even charged with being a party to the conspiracy at Fregellae.[72] When we have discounted the more extreme accusations, this picture must still be substantially correct. It did not take much wit for a contemporary to see how the activities of the reformers had unsettled Rome's subjects. If Italy were excited in this way by the prospects Flaccus held out before it then it is not straining credulity to maintain that, in the prevailing climate, the blighting of such prospects could possibly lead to a violent reaction in certain quarters. That, I would suggest, is what happened at Fregellae. Then, as Flaccus was a man with many enemies, the malignant would be only too ready to see in an involuntary result of his activities an act of deliberate policy.

It is notorious that our sources for this incident are extremely meagre. Nevertheless, the labours of scholars have succeeded in producing a version of events which appears to be coherent in structure and plausible in content. As we know, a large number of Paeligni and Samnites emigrated to Fregellae in 177 and it is said they hoped to acquire the benefits of the *jus Latii.* Between then and 125 this element grew in numbers and it was these one time emigrants or, rather, their descendants who, disappointed in their hope of having their position regularised, organised the insurrection. In fact, there would appear to have been a split on social and ethnic lines in the town because most of the wealthy Latin nobility are thought to have remained loyal to Rome. The name of one of them, a certain Q. Numitorius Pullus, has been preserved. The rebellion itself was an isolated phenomenon since the notice of a contemporary uprising in Asculum may be safely discounted. Two explanations can be advanced for this failure of other states to join in and neither excludes the other. First of all, there was no widespread discontent which might induce them to do so. Secondly, the Fregellans were not popular with their fellow Italians. Their greedy garnering of bodies in 177 had caused resentment and there may have been other acts of selfishness in the interval to reinforce this sentiment. Such is the commonly accepted view of the events at Fregellae.[73] But, in my opinion, for all its apparent persuasiveness it is open to serious objection at every point and cannot, therefore, be accepted as a satisfactory version of those events.

To begin with, we cannot actually be sure the emigrants were still in Fregellae. There is, at least, the possibility that they could have been removed in the great clear out of 177. Assuming, however, they were still there we have no evidence whatsoever for disaffection among them. When they first arrived they could have had little expectation of acquiring Latin status and there is no real reason to suppose they had any now.[74] Thus, the existence of discontent among the emigrant community is no more than a conjecture. Certainly, in the absence of other evidence for a pool of discontent elsewhere, it would be a perfectly reasonable one to make. But when we do have such evidence it seems altogether more prudent to relate the rebellion of Fregellae to the situation it unquestionably depicts rather than to one which is merely hypothetical. We have already pointed to the prominence of the Latins in the events of this period. They may, it will be recalled, have been in a position to put special pressure on Flaccus because it was their lands which were particularly coveted by the triumvirs. Cicero, at any rate, specifically mentions them among those angered by the commission's activities and, for what it is worth, a scholiast says it was for their sakes that Scipio undertook to oppose the triumvirs. Most important of all, perhaps, is what we learn from Asconius. He says that the destruction of Fregellae had the effect of cowing the other Latins who were ill-disposed towards Rome.[75] All of this adds up to one thing: some at least of the Latins were seriously disaffected. As we saw, the Romans responded by proposing or enacting legislation in their favour. We shall have more to say about this shortly but here we may observe that such legislation demonstrates quite clearly how seriously the Romans viewed the situation. Thus, I can see no reason why Fregellae, as a Latin colony, should not share in the sense of grievance common to all Latins. Indeed, Asconius implies that such was, in fact, the case. Fregellae was one of a number of communities who harboured no friendly feelings towards Rome. What marked her off from the rest was the unfortunate manner in which she chose to express her ill-will. Moreover, there is reason to suppose that the revolt, so far from being orchestrated by the emigrant element, was, in fact, mounted by the ruling Latins. Pullus, we saw, is usually taken to illustrate a division along social and ethnic lines in the town: the Latins largely remained loyal while the others fell away. I would argue, however, that it might be more accurate to view his treachery as evidence for a split which occurred in the ruling class after the rebellion began.[76] We hear that, when all was done, he was able to convince the Romans that his services as a traitor outweighed the hurt he had done as a rebel. Pullus, then, would appear to have been a party to the revolt at its inception and had only latterly changed sides. In consequence, although we cannot speak with absolute certainty, the natural inference to be drawn from our sources when they are taken together with the general evidence for Latin grievances, would appear to be that Pullus, in joining the uprising, was merely imitating the example of other members of his class rather than making common cause with rebels sprung from the lower orders.[77]

Much of what I have had to say up to this point will, I hope, serve to call in question the notion that Fregellae was somehow isolated from the rest of Italy. There are other considerations which point in the same direction. The idea that Fregellae had many enemies appears to rest on a certain interpretation of what L. Papirius Fregellanus did in 177. According to this Papirius argued before the senate that neither the Italian emigrants in Rome nor the Samnites and Paelignians in Fregellae should be compelled to return home. This notion seems to me improbable and it receives no real support from our sources.[78] In any case, if resentment really was caused in 177, it is difficult to see why it should have lasted over 50 years especially as there is no evidence for further acts by the Fregellans which might have kept it alive in the intervening years. Moreover, it would surely be Samnites and Paelignians rather than fellow Latins who would feel such resentment. In which context, it is worth observing that now, as at the time of the Social War, old quarrels could possibly be forgotten as all united in pursuit of a common purpose.[79] This inevitably brings us to the alleged revolt at Asculum.[80] Plainly it would be absurd to take the story at its face value for the simple reason that, if Asculum really had rebelled, then it would assuredly have gone the way of Fregellae. Before we dismiss it completely though, we should at least consider the possibility that it represents a garbled version of a very real state of affairs. A generation later hotheads in Asculum precipitated war so it might not, perhaps, be totally impossible to visualise some present now who, like the Fregellans, meditated revolt but wisely shrank from the enterprise. We could then claim that our abbreviated source has simply misrepresented what really happened. While we have no definite proof that this was so, it seems to me that as a theory it is at least as plausible as that which would see in our notice a confusion with the famous incident which precipitated the Social War.

We are told Fregellae rebelled *sua sponte*[81] and this we must accept since we have no evidence for plots hatched with others and no other state actually joined in the rebellion. We are at liberty to draw two possible conclusions from this. We can see in the uprising a desperate gesture of defiance by a people who stood friendless and alone. The disappointment of their hopes had so enraged the Fregellans that, careless of the consequences, they could think only of striking a blow against Rome. As history furnishes numerous examples of such doomed enterprises and, as our sources for Fregellae are so slight, it is clearly not unreasonable to suggest that something of this order could have happened here. However, such information as we do possess leads me to believe that a different explanation may be more appropriate. We must, I believe, view the rebellion of Fregellae in the light of what has been said about the state of Italy in the preceding paragraph. Fregellae began her revolt fully conscious that other Italian states shared her sense of grievance. It would then follow that her expectation (or her hope) will have been that others would be inspired to follow her example spontaneously and join in the insurrection. In the event this proved to be a mistaken calculation since the time for a general Italian uprising had not yet come.[82]

It is in the Gracchan age therefore that we are permitted to see for the first time the consequences of the working out of those processes which I maintain led to the desire for equality. By then matters have come to a certain stage of development but they are still at a considerable distance from that universal call for enfranchisement which we encounter a generation later. Three levels of consciousness are detectable at this time. The most backward look for *provocatio* and no more.[83] The more sophisticated, however, want the citizenship. The Fregellans represent a third and more extreme position which anticipates what was to happen in the next generation. They sought the citizenship too but, unlike the others, took up arms when it was refused.[84] With them we may loosely bracket many other Latins and possibly Asculum. The strength of their desire and the level of their discontent were probably no less than those of Fregellae and they were differentiated from her only by their failure to follow where she attempted to lead. As I have been at some pains to emphasise it, I hope it will not have escaped notice that of all the Italians the Latins were at this time the most politically advanced. The factors I outlined 1.1,2 had evidently been swifter in inducing a change in them than in others. This state of affairs was to have certain important consequences which we shall ponder in due course.[85]

Here, we shall simply observe that, in studying the Gracchan period, we must at all times be prepared to give the recognition to the degrees of intensity with which men cherished their ambitions. We should also bear in mind that the frontiers between these different groups were not firmly fixed and that the distinctions between them were often blurred or unsettled. It has to be recognised that those who wanted much might not always be ready to exert themselves to gain it and might very well, in the final analysis, settle for less. This fluidity of attitude which is characteristic of the Italians at this time and which stands in such strong contrast to the rigidity they showed some 30 years later has already been glimpsed in the failure of other Italians to aid Fregellae even though they shared her grievances. The proposal of the elder Drusus to grant *provocatio* to the Latins brings it into even bolder relief. This was one of a number of measures which Drusus promulgated with the object of outbidding Gracchus in popularity. J.S. Reid found it puzzling and asked how could Drusus hope to achieve this aim when what Gracchus was offering was so much more comprehensive?[86] I think we must take it for granted that Drusus knew exactly what he was about and this leads to but one conclusion: from his reading of the situation he came to the realisation that by offering the bare minimum to one section of the Italians he could make them content. It is not improbable that there were some Latins who wanted *provocatio* only from the outset but it is also reasonable to suppose Drusus calculated that many who wished for citizenship would gladly take the lesser privilege if it were offered to them.[87] Nor will it have escaped notice that nothing at all was dangled before the allies. It may very well be that Drusus thought them too obdurate to be seduced but I doubt it. The comparatively modest advancement planned for them by Gracchus suggests rather that his opponent knew their desire for change was not sufficiently strong to lead them to make trouble. Hence no need was felt for concessions. The day when the allies would react with fury when balked was still far off.

Flaccus' proposal reveals for the historian the existence of a widespread desire for the citizenship among the peoples of Italy although it is, however, by no means unanimous or (in many cases) deeply felt. From the time the consul revealed his plans until the death of C. Gracchus the elevation of the political status of the Italians may, not unfairly, be described as one of the great issues of the day. But once the reformers had vanished from the scene it ceased to be so since the Italians for a long time lacked both the will and the means to pursue their objective. Yet, if the pair had failed to achieve their main aim their work had two momentous consequences. In the short term the agitation of these years led the Romans to the conclusion that something would have to be done to quiet the Latins and that that something was rather more than Drusus' modest proposal. It was nothing less than a provision whereby the most prominent Latins received the citizenship. In the long term the activities of Flaccus and Gracchus led directly to the Social War. If daggers were thrown into the Forum then dragons' teeth were sown in Italy. The Italians never forgot what they had been taught in these years: their ambitions were legitimate and it was proper for them to seek their realisation. These attitudes slowly hardened in the years after Gracchus' death until the continued Roman refusal to accept their validity could no longer be tolerated and the once passive subjects made a ferocious assault on their masters.

Notes

1. App. B.C. 1.21, 34; Val. Max. 9.5.1.
2. Liv. ep.60; Obsequens 30. See further below.
3. *MRR* 1.513-14.
4. App. B.C. 1.23; *ORF*[3] p. 144 with Gabba (1967) p. 79; Sherwin-White (1973) p. 137. Plutarch's evidence might be pressed to show the existence of more than one bill and could demonstrate a development in Gracchus' attitude to the Italian problem (*C. Gracch.* 5, 8, 9). However, it may be brought into harmony with Appian in the way suggested by Stockton pp. 238-9. Vell. Pat. 2.6.2 may be interpreted after the manner of Fraccaro apud Gabba (1967) pp. 68-9 or Greenidge (1904) p. 233 or it may be seen simply as inaccurate rhetoric (Stockton p. 157).

K. Meister, 'Die Bundesgenossengesetzgebung des Gaius Gracchus', *Chiron* 6, 1976 pp. 114-18 suggests that Gracchus wished to give the allies the *jus suffragii* to be exercised in the thirty-five tribes. This is not convincing. In the first instance, Meister does not explain why Gracchus should have had recourse to such a device. In the second, he appears to press too much out of Appian and ignores the possible distortions in Plutarch arising from his biographical preoccupations and methods of composition. Finally, as we have just seen above, Velleius does not necessarily have to be taken literally.

5. Keaveney *Crit. Stor.* (1984) pp. 368-70.
6. Toynbee p. 550 also held this view but Richardson, so far as I am aware, is the first to present a detailed argument for it. The notion that Scipio Aemilianus might have had such a plan is very unlikely, cf. Strachan-Davidson p. 21.
7. For instance, Greenidge (1904) p. 115 and Shochat pp. 25-45 hold this view while Earl (1963) pp. 20-1 and Badian (1958) pp. 169-71 reject it. Nagle (1970) pp. 373-94 thinks only Romans and Latins benefited but his interpretation of Appian appears strained.
8. See especially B.C. 1.13 and note Cuff *passim.*

9. Cf. 1.1, 2 and further Sherwin-White (1973) pp. 125-6.

10. Jolowicz pp. 280-1.

11. Jolowicz pp. 8-9, 156-7.

12. Livy 44.16.7, cf. 2.16.4-5, 26.21.9-13.

13. Tibiletti (1950) p. 217; Badian (1958) p. 171; Salmon (1969) pp. 25-6, 169 n. 29; Galsterer p. 42, 51, 53-6; Sherwin-White (1973) pp. 80-1.

14. Livy 42.4.3. Cf. Salmon (1982) p. 96, 199, n. 334 although I would not agree with him that Livy 6.4.4 is a parallel.

15. See also Catalano pp. 206-9 when considering these matters.

16. See further below on these points.

17. Cic. *Pro Balb.* 32 with the remarks of Reid (1878) pp. 16-19.

18. B.C. 1.34.

19. Cf. 1.1, 2.

20. Toynbee p. 337; Salmon (1967) p. 318.

21. Toynbee pp. 137-54; Smith (1954) pp. 18-20; Salmon (1969) p. 184, n. 165. It seems to me that Badian (1970/1) pp. 385-6 underestimates the importance of this incident. See further below.

22. Livy 41.8.7-8 with Toynbee pp. 137-8.

23. Livy 39.3.4-6 with Toynbee pp. 139-40. Livy 39.3.4, 6 shows that only Latins were involved.

24. It is believed, however, that this restriction could have been imposed already on Latin colonies founded since 265. It may, therefore, have been extended to all other colonies on this occasion. Discussions of the problem will be found in E.T. Salmon, 'Roman colonisation from the Second Punic War to the Gracchi', *JRS* 26, 1936 pp. 55-7; Toynbee p. 140; Humbert pp. 115-16.

25. Livy 41.8.6-12, cf. Toynbee pp. 140-1; Goehler p. 65; Tibiletti (1950) p. 204. Badian (1970/1) p. 391, n. 56 strangely claims that no Samnite delegation tried to get their people back. Letta pp. 89-90 simply denies the evidence of Livy. On the role of Fregellae it seems to me that Malcovati pp. 137-40 is preferable to Badian (1955) pp. 22-3. On Livy's terminology see Wegner pp. 95-104. Foreigners at Rome: Livy 39.3.6.

An alternative interpretation of Livy 41.8.6-8 which still leads to the same conclusion as in the text, could be that the *legationes socium nominis Latini* represent all the Italians and voice the universal complaint. The Samnites and Paelignians are then especially mentioned because they have a particular grievance of their own. *Censos* should, of course, apply only to the Latins but we have reasons to suspect fraud on the part of some allies and these will be discussed a little later.

26. Livy 41.9.9-12, 42.10.2-3. This failure to carry out the expulsions properly might indicate that the emigrants in Fregellae were left undisturbed.

27. Cic. *de Offic.* 3.47, cf. *Brut.* 109. Dating: *MRR* 1. 509, n. 2.

28. Gabba (1967) p. 67; Badian (1970/1) p. 388.

29. Something which is not beyond the bounds of possibility but does not upset our thesis, cf. n. 38.

30. Though we should, perhaps, consider the possibility that, from motives of prudence, he, like Sulpicius and Cinna after him, kept them concealed, cf. 4.1, 2.

31. See below.

32. I have here added to and amplified the arguments of Stockton pp. 94-5. It is a matter for regret that he does not appear to have realised their full significance. Like Brunt *JRS* (1965) p. 90 he takes, in my view, an excessively narrow and unimaginative view of the problem and denies that any context can be found for Pennus' measure. It does not appear to have occurred to him that, if we cannot connect the act with the activities of Flaccus, the existence of other earlier expulsion acts makes it incumbent on the historian to at least ask the sort of questions I now propose to discuss.

33. *ORF*[3] p. 144. Fannius is, of course, depicting an imaginary situation but it must have been one his hearers could easily envisage.

34. App. B.C. 1.23; Plut. *C. Gracch.* 12.

35. The most important discussions are in *MRR* 2. 160, n. 2; Badian (1970/1) p. 378; Harris (1971) pp. 322-3; M. Gelzer, *The Roman Nobility*, trs. R. Seager, Oxford, 1969 p. 33, n. 270, 51, n. 457. The following points may be noted:

(a) Valerius gets biographical details about the cos. 130 wrong; he is confused about what law is in operation; it is difficult to see why the Sabelli should want somebody who appears to be an Etrurian.

(b) The fact that the father of the cos. 130 behaved like a citizen does not make him one, cf. Cic. *Pro Arch.* 11.

(c) The omission of the cos. 92 from the list of the *cuncta nobilitas* in Cic. *Rab. Perd.* 21 has been attributed to the fact that Cicero knew of this incident. The alternative explanation, that his absence is due to the fact that his presumed son was a Sertorian, seems less plausible.

(d) If things fell out as Valerius says they did then the family's continued presence at Rome is to be attributed to powerful friends, cf. Galsterer p. 163; M. Reinhold, 'Usurpation of Status and Status Symbols in the Roman Empire', *Historia* 20, 1971 p. 278.

36. Bernardi p. 70 cites Plut. *C. Gracch.* 3 and 12 as proof that Pennus' bill failed. To me, however, they furnish an additional argument for declaring its purpose was not what it is usually thought to be.

37. *ORF*[3] p. 180. Cf. Greenidge (1904) p. 167; Badian (1970/1) p. 388.

38. This, of course, assumes it was made in 126. However, given that it would take time to flush out the guilty, then Gracchus could indeed have railed against the workings of the act on his return to Rome. In that case, there is a possible connection between Pennus' act and Flaccus' bill but not the direct one which is usually postulated. Gracchus is not attacking Pennus' act because it is an immediate and vicious response to his friend's proposal. Rather he is holding it up as a specimen of the kind of disastrous policy which Flaccus opposed and which he himself would shortly try to combat also.

39. For a selection of views see McDonald (1944) p. 21; Toynbee pp. 137-8; Badian (1970/1) pp. 385-7; G. de Sanctis, *Storia dei Romani*, Florence, 1969, vol. 4.1 pp. 547-8, 554.

40. What I assume here is argued in detail below.

41. See 1.1, 2.

42. While allies could become citizens of a Latin colony at its foundation (Toynbee p. 108) or when its numbers were augmented (Livy 33.24.8-9 with Tibiletti (1950) pp. 192-5) it does not appear that they

could automatically expect enrolment if they arrived at another time, cf.
Livy 32.2.6-7.
   43. (1954) p. 20.
   44. Badian (1970/1) pp. 396-7.
   45. A more detailed treatment of these matters will be found below.
   46. The expulsion acts were merely temporary interruptions.
   47. Cic. *Pro Arch.* 11, cf. Badian (1970/1) p. 387 and 2.3.
   48. I do not, of course, mean to suggest that many of his class
imitated his example. For one thing, detection would surely be
inevitable. For another, Roman tolerance might extend to one or two
individuals but hardly to a solid phalanx, cf. 2.3 and n. 35 above. We may
observe at this point, that this case bears no resemblance to those dealt
with by the lex Licinia Mucia.
   49. It should be noted that the ruling classes of Italy never manifested
hostility to the idea of acquiring the citizenship. When they tried to recall
their people it was for demographic reasons and not because they
resented their elevation in status. If it comes to that, the benefits that
flowed from the possession of citizenship — Salmon (1982) p. 126 and
McDonald (1944) p. 21 — from whatever motive it was originally
acquired must have been obvious to all. One wonders then how far the
appetites of the upper classes were whetted by seeing their own people
enjoying them.
   50. It should, I believe, be obvious why the upper classes could not
adopt the methods of the lower orders but would be obliged to have
recourse to political agitation.
   51. (1970/1) p. 389.
   52. App. B.C. 1.18 with Gabba (1967) pp. 55-8; Liv. ep. 59; Cic. *de
Rep.* 1.31. Cf. Toynbee pp. 546-54 and Ilari p. 19 n. 34.
   53. Stockton p. 92 suggests that it was only in 129 perhaps that the
commissioners began to interest themselves in non-Roman land. This is
unlikely in itself and seems to run contrary to App. B.C. 1.18. What we
are witnessing surely is muted protest gaining a voice when the Italians
found a champion, cf. 1.3, 2.2.
   54. App. B.C. 1.19, 21; Cic. *de Rep.* 1.31, 3.41; Liv. ep. 59; Dio fr. 84;
Schol. Bob. p. 118 St.; Plut. *C. Gracch.* 10 with Gabba (1967) pp. 59-62,
66; Strachan-Davidson p. 21; Last *CAH* 9 p. 44. For Scipio's attitude see
in addition Liv. ep. 57 and Vell. Pat. 2.4.4 with Badian (1958) p. 175.
Stockton pp. 43-4 appears to attribute purely 'party' political motives to
Scipio. This ignores part of our evidence and thus presents a distorted
picture. Hatred of the Gracchan commission need not necessarily
exclude other motivation as well. It is to be particularly noted that
Stockton does not seem to grasp why those who might favour the Italian
magnates on the land question could still oppose them on the franchise.
For a more balanced and mature assessment of Scipio see the sensitive
and careful analysis of Greenidge (1904) pp. 154-7.
   The paralysis depicted by Appian appears to accord ill with the
evidence of Liv. ep. 59 and Dio fr. 84 which seem to show the commission
both active and successful. However, the *seditiones* of the epitomator
probably refer simply to Appian's legal wrangles and their attendant ill-
will. Dio's picture of extensive ravaging should probably be taken as a

record of the commission's continuing proceedings against Romans which would not be affected by the new dispensation, cf. Hardy p. 39. I doubt if what he says holds good in the case of the Italians because then it would be difficult to see why Flaccus acted as he did.

55. Badian (1970/1) p. 399; R.D. Develin, 'The Dismantling of the Gracchan Agrarian Programme', *Antichthon* 13, 1979 pp. 48-50.

56. Gracchus' law: Greenidge and Clay p. 34 with Hardy p. 41 and Greenidge (1904) p. 209. Mention should also be made of the abundant evidence (Greenidge and Clay pp. 38-9) for Gracchus' colonial schemes in Italy. These schemes can hardly have left the Italians untouched.

57. Cf. e.g. Greenidge (1904) pp. 233-5.

58. It should also be borne in mind that the triumvirs may not have been quite as zealous as heretofore. The provision of corn doles may have done something to relieve the demand for land, cf. Cuff p. 183 and n. 63 below.

59. App. B.C. 1.10 with Gabba (1967) p. 29; Diod. Sic. 34/35.6.1. Cf. Nagle (1970) pp. 374-82. Badian (1958) p. 171, 175 does not give due weight to this point.

60. So Earl (1963) p. 21 — denied for no good reason by Stockton p. 43. I do not accept Earl's explanation of the phenomenon however.

61. Despite Badian (1958) p. 171, n. 7.

62. Greenidge (1904) p. 166; Stockton p. 44, 46. I find Schochat pp. 42-3 unconvincing.

63. App. B.C. 1.24 with Gabba (1967) p. 84 and Last *CAH* 9 p. 81. Some scholars, e.g. Hardy p. 41, think that Gracchus might not have allowed the triumvirs to renew their assault on Italian land for fear of the trouble it might cause. For two reasons this seems to me a little unlikely. Firstly, the sources (see n. 56), meagre as they are, do appear to imply that he gave them ample powers. Secondly, as I have tried to show above, it would be possible to resume land without necessarily antagonising the *possessores*.

64. Plut. *C. Gracch.* 3 with Badian (1958) p. 181.

65. App. B.C. 1.23; Plut. *C. Gracch.* 12. Cf. Stockton p. 158 and Greenidge (1904) p. 166.

66. The view I have tried to refute here is that of Gabba (1976) p. 71. He recognises, (1976) p. 217, n. 11, the difficulties Fregellae poses for his thesis but his attempt to explain it away as an isolated phenomenon is not acceptable. See below.

67. B.C. 1.34.

68. We might add that Drusus offered only *provocatio* to the Latins in his proposed legislation. The implication of this will be considered shortly.

69. It is most likely that in some places only individuals would want the citizenship while in others whole communities would be involved, cf. Badian (1970/1) pp. 391-2; Hardy pp. 36-40.

70. Greenidge (1904) pp. 233-5. On precedents for Gracchus' proposals see Badian (1958) p. 186.

71. Greenidge (1904) pp. 169-70; Gabba (1976) p. 217, n. 11; Carcopino (1929) p. 12.

72. Plut. *C. Gracch.* 3,10; *de Vir. Illust.* 65. Cf. App. B.C. 1.34.

73. With varying degrees of emphasis and, with a greater or lesser amount of detail, this is the view maintained by Stockton pp. 96-7; Gabba (1976) p. 217, n. 11; Carcopino (1929) p. 12; Badian (1970/1) pp. 389-91.

74. See n. 26, 42 and Goehler p. 65.

75. Cic. *de Rep.* 1.31; Schol. Bob. p. 118 St.; Asc. 17C.

76. Sources for Pullus: Cic. *de Fin.* 5.62, *Phil.* 3.17, *de Inv.* 2.105.

77. There is certainly nothing in our three sources which would imply that Pullus was a traitor to anybody save fellow Latins. Furthermore, given the state of our evidence, the theory that all classes were united at the start of the revolt is at least as plausible as that which postulates they were split.

78. On this see Malcovati pp. 138-40 against Badian (1955) p. 22-3, (1970/1) p. 391.

79. App. B.C. 1.28. See n. 82.

80. *de Vir. Illust.* 65. Cf. Pareti p.351.

81. *Auct. ad Her.* 4.13.

82. As so often the remarks of Greenidge (1904) p. 171 are perceptive and pertinent. We may, perhaps, add three observations. Asculum could have been one of the places of which Fregellae had expectations. It will also be seen that, in 91, for all the carefully laid conspiracies it was still a spontaneous act of violence which precipitated the rebellion, cf. 3.1. Fregellae's rebellion could be seen as an attempt to invoke pan-Italic sentiment which was not, however, yet sufficiently strong to answer the call.

83. It is a moot point as to how many desired nothing at all.

84. The exact combination of circumstances which led Fregellae to rebel is unknown. For some speculation see Greenidge (1904) p. 170.

85. See below and 2.2.

86. 'On some questions of Roman law', *JRS* 1, 1911 p. 80.

87. The fate of Fregellae may have made people more accommodating. In 2.2. I shall try to demonstrate why I believe the grant of *civitas per magistratum* does not affect the arguments I am making here.

2.2

The Road to the Social War

In the time of C. Gracchus we were permitted to catch a brief glimpse of how the Italians felt about enfranchisement. But, as was stated in the last section, with his death the shutters came down once more and for nigh on thirty years we hear nothing more of the matter. Roman indifference to the Italian question is the prime reason for this state of affairs. Quite simply they were not prepared to give the problem a moment's notice unless their subjects were actively making a nuisance of themselves. The Italians, for their part, lacked, during most of the period, both the will and the means to do just that. One of two conditions would have to be fulfilled before we might see them bestir themselves. They would have to acquire the resolution to make an independent move of their own to get what they wanted or they would have to find another champion like Gracchus who would fight for their cause. But it is not until the 90s that they actually dared to assert themselves with an expression of independent will or that they discovered the man they sought in the younger Drusus. In consequence, since our sources concentrate on what interested and pre-occupied the Romans at this time, they tell us nothing about how the mood of Italy was being shaped or how the citizenship question was developing.

The tribunate of Saturninus which in many ways resembles that of C. Gracchus[1] throws this state of affairs into sharp relief. Contrary to what is sometimes believed he took no interest in the Italian question *per se* since the Italians were unable to force him to do so. As a result, his tribunate, unlike that of Gracchus, sheds no light on the state of affairs in Italy at this time.[2]

When Flaccus made his offer to the Italians they were in a strong position since they could trade land for status. Now, however, they had no such weapon to use against Saturninus. The Gracchan land commission had been wound up soon after the death of Gaius and, unlike Drusus later, Saturninus had no intention of disturbing present arrangements or indeed of interfering in any way with Italian land. All of his settlements were to be overseas. In his first tribunate (103) he established viritane settlements in Africa. In the second (100) he passed a measure to establish Roman colonies over a much wider area. Sicily, Achaia, Macedonia and Cis (or perhaps Trans) Alpine Gaul were all to receive plantations. Thus, it becomes immediately clear that the Italians lacked the means to compel Saturninus to their will. Whatsoever they might receive from his hands would be by his grace and favour alone.[3]

Saturninus did, indeed, have certain plans but I shall now try to demonstrate that they in no way involved the mass enfranchisement Italians sought and they had no immediate relevance to it.[4] His concern, in fact, was not with changing the status of the Italians but with including some of them in his agrarian schemes. What he did do, he did at the behest of Marius for there can be little doubt that the general inspired this particular section of the tribune's land schemes.[5] After the battle of Vercellae, Marius bestowed the citizenship on a thousand men from Camerinum who had conducted themselves with conspicuous gallantry. The act was undoubtedly illegal, not because Marius had violated the *foedus* with Camerinum, but because he had no formal authorisation from Rome. He himself admitted as much when he justified what he had done by saying that the voice of the laws had been drowned out in the din of war. In the event, his grant was allowed to stand and it established a precedent which other commanders were to follow.[6] This tender regard makes it reasonable to suppose that when, a little later, something else was done for the Italians Marius was behind it.

According to Appian, the plebs were so outraged by the favourable treatment being accorded to the Italians that they put up a most violent resistance to Saturninus' laws. He, in turn, was able to call to his aid people whom Appian variously describes as τοῖς οὖσιν ἀνὰ τοὺς ἀγρούς, τοὺς ἀγροίκους, men ἀπὸ τῶν ἀγρῶν.[7] Now, undoubtedly the chief aim of Saturninus' proposals was to provide land for Marius' troops and, as is well attested, he was able to count on their help in removing obstacles from his path.[8] As many of the citizen soldiers were of rustic origin they are to be numbered among those covered by Appian's phrases.[9]

However, Marius' army also contained many Italians[10] so it is natural to ask if Appian could be talking of them too. Scholars divide on this point[11] and, in fact it is impossible to tell from Appian alone.[12] Therefore, in my view, the only way to determine the extent (if any) of Italian participation in these events is to form some idea of what Marius was actually offering them. Once we have done this we should be in a position to estimate what their likely response would be.

All we know of the agrarian legislation, insofar as it affects the Italians, is one clause; Marius had the power to make three people citizens in each of his colonies. There is nothing untoward in this since a like power of enfranchisement had been enjoyed in the past by those who founded colonies.[13] The necessity for enabling legislation is readily explicable. To grant citizenship was the prerogative of the Roman people. Hence, if Marius proposed to create citizens by making foreigners members of his foundations he would have to be given the power to do so by the people. So, the theory advanced by some, that Marius intended to create more citizens, over and above what the law allowed, by simply enrolling more Italians in his colonies, cannot be correct. To do so would be beyond his competence. It could, of course, be argued that Marius intended to resort to fraud but that immediately poses the question of motive. Why should he have recourse to such tactics when it clearly lay within his power to get what he wanted by legitimate means? To put it another way: if a man in his commanding position might have three why should he not have more if he so desired?[14] There is, it is true, one group of Italians for whom no especial legislation was necessary, namely, the Latins. If they were invited to join a colony then all they would have to do was exercise their *jus migrationis*, enrol and become citizens. But it would seem that the Latins were not asked to join *en masse*. One of those who received the citizenship by virtue of Marius' power to enfranchise three individuals was, in fact, a Latin. It would appear to me highly unlikely that the general would squander his gifts in this fashion if another avenue were open to the man he favoured. We are thus driven to the conclusion that if Italians, other than the especial few who were to be enfranchised under the terms of the law, were to be admitted at all to these settlements then it would be as *incolae*.[15]

Assuming that Marius did, in fact, decide to accept Italians as *incolae* in his foundations[16] then the question of land would be an issue for them in this year. Given the validity of this initial premise we would expect that, as in the time of Ti. Gracchus, Italians, hoping to benefit from his schemes, would flock to support Saturninus. They would be drawn from the lower classes or rather, from that part of them who had served with Marius. The upper classes would keep aloof from this particular struggle. They had nothing to gain from such a distribution and nothing to fear either since their lands were not affected. Now, it might very well be argued that the Italian grandees would anyway have marshalled their retainers in support of something which touched them nearly. Modest as Marius' citizenship proposals were they may have been sufficient to win to his side the ruling class. After all, this is the first we hear of any attempt to enfranchise on any scale since the time of C. Gracchus. I am, however, inclined to doubt if this view is correct. As we shall see, in a few years the lex Licinia Mucia was to reveal that what the *principes Italicorum populorum* now wanted was mass enfranchisement. Therefore, in my opinion, Marius' limited measures would be unlikely to have had any widespread appeal and certainly not enough to make people want to hazard life and limb. We may say then that while some lower class Italians may have involved themselves in the events of 100 because of their desire for land, the upper classes did not because the citizenship which was their main concern was not an issue.[17]

And what of the reaction of the plebs? On the surface, at any rate, their violent opposition to the agrarian legislation would seem to suggest that something substantial was being offered to the Italians. Closer examination, however, reveals that this is not necessarily so. Since Saturninus' enemies, the *nobiles*, would naturally muster all possible opposition, it is hardly to be expected that they should neglect to stir up the plebs against him. In the past, people like Fannius had shown a deadly facility for exploiting that extreme sensitivity which the commons had shown with regard to any concessions which might be made to the Italians. It is, therefore, not straining credulity to suggest that they exercised their talents on this occasion as well. Certainly Marius did not propose to give the citizenship to a large number but able propagandists would surely have no difficulty in representing his modest plans as something monstrous and shameful. In any case, if we are right in suggesting that Saturninus' law envisaged land for Italians then the plebs, who were to receive nothing, would not need much additional stimulus to arouse them to a pitch of fury. It would be incorrect, then, I feel to invoke plebian reaction to the *lex agraria* as proof that the law made wide ranging provisions for Italian admission to the citizenship.[18]

Marius is sometimes depicted as a champion of the Italian cause.[19] From the evidence we have just surveyed it is difficult to sustain such a claim. Even on the most generous interpretation he cannot fairly be said to have done much to promote the Italian aim of mass enfranchisement. After the initial dazzling gesture at Vercellae his policy may best be described as narrow and traditional.[20] In enfranchising Italians by admittance to his colonies and in seeking legislative sanctions for it Marius was, as we know, merely following precedent. Further, we have observed that the numbers so involved were quite small and all others would simply have the status of *incolae*. In no way could his colonial programme, insofar as it touched upon the Italians at any rate, be said to set a precedent nor could he be accused of violating the *mos mariorum*. Throughout, his concern appears to have been that of a general anxious to provide for the welfare of his troops. Since the Italians formed part of his army it was but natural that something should be done for them when the Romans were being looked after. We are witnessing a paternalistic attitude which recalls that of Scipio Aemilianus in many ways.[21] Italians must be treated fairly and their merits recognised. Grants of land were, of course, the absolute minimum which might be offered but Marius was prepared to go a little further than that. Unlike Scipio, and unlike most of his contemporaries, he did not see why the bestowal of the citizenship on individuals should not constitute a reward for outstanding merit especially as it was known how highly enfranchisement was prized. Undoubtedly this was a more generous policy than that pursued by most other Romans of the time but it could not be called the policy of a bold reformer. The introduction of these small numbers into the citizen body did not carry with it any of the dangers which Romans feared from mass enfranchisement. In brief, Marius' policy falls far short of the daring radicalism which characterises the measures of Flaccus and Gracchus. Nowhere do we find Marius stating an intention to grant the citizenship to substantial numbers or proposing a bill to that effect. By pursuing limited objectives when he was at the height of his power and influence, Marius showed he had no real interest in changing the established order of things.

This situation is clearly reflected in the fact that only one source, Appian, mentions the Italians in connection with the events of 100 and even then in what is virtually an aside.[22] Had their role been greater than that which I postulated then we might reasonably expect to hear more of them. As it is, the part they play is a subordinate one and they are virtually lost to sight among their Roman allies. And it was land for which they fought, not the citizenship since those who were in a position to make the latter an issue of the day chose not to do so.[23]

But, only a few years later, the Italian question was to force itself on the attention of the Romans for the first time since the death of the younger Gracchus. In 95 the lex Licinia Mucia was passed. It was aimed at Italians who had illegally usurped the citizenship and was intended to force them to revert to their proper status. To carry out the good work a *quaestio* was set up which enquired into men's credentials.[24] By now we should be familiar with the problem of Italian migration and the periodic attempts of the Romans to check it by means of expulsion acts. What we are confronted with here, though, is something of a very different order indeed. As in the past, large numbers are involved but, now, along with men of low standing, there appear the *principes Italicorum populorum*. Since it is in the highest degree unlikely that these people were looking for material gain we have no option but to assume that they sought the citizenship for itself because it would make of them equals of the Romans. Moreover, we may suspect that, as in the past, the Italian commons were acting at the behest of their overlords when they made their usurpation.[25] Furthermore this is not an expulsion act at all. Had the Romans perceived the threat as coming from a large scale influx of Italians into Rome then it would surely have been such. It is not, in fact, concerned with a man's physical location but with his legal status. The danger it is designed to counter is of a different sort from that of the expulsion acts: the deliberate and illegal assumption of the citizenship by a large body of Rome's subjects.[26] The theory that this usurpation was a gradual one over a period of years has been mooted but, in my opinion, it has little to commend it. Plainly those from the lower classes could have crept in now without detection as they had always done if their numbers were not such as to excite undue alarm. However, we do not seem to be dealing with limited numbers but with whole nations and it is straining credulity to believe that even gradual infiltration on such a scale could hope to pass unnoticed,[27] and whatever about the lower classes it is virtually impossible to envisage how the *principes* could hope to slink in unobserved in the years immediately before 95. Since the Romans had a great deal to do with the leading men of Italy[28] they would know them well so that detection would be instantaneous.[29] We may then beg leave to doubt that the indulgence which might be granted to the odd individual like Perperna snr. (2.1) would now be extended to a very large group. To move slowly and cautiously would, therefore, only alert the Romans to what was going on and invite counter measures. The Italians, then, really had no choice but to act openly and swiftly at one decisive moment. Come to that, we may go so far as to claim that they themselves would not have wanted it any other way since their purpose is clear. They were telling the Romans that, because they considered themselves to be citizens, they proposed henceforth to comport themselves as such in full view of the whole world. These considerations seem to me to point fairly decisively towards the census of 96/95 as the moment when the Italians decided to make their move. A census *non jus civitatis confirmat ac tantum modo indicat eum, qui sit census, ita se jam tum gessisse pro cive.*[30] The Italians then simply came forward and declared themselves to be citizens.[31]

For more than a quarter of a century we learn nothing of the citizenship question, but when it does re-emerge now it is abundantly clear that the mood and attitude of Italy is far different from what it had been in the time of Flaccus and Gracchus. Then the Italians had to be educated. They had to be taught that the citizenship was an attainable goal. Now, they had thoroughly absorbed the lesson and were prepared to act on their own initiative. Our sources speak of their anger at the death of Gracchus but that was the anger of impotence for they could do nothing to avenge him or realise his goals.[32] But, for them to have reached the position they had by 97 must mean that this resentment at being denied what they cherished had so grown and so increased that they now felt compelled to act. Since the Romans showed no signs of granting the citizenship the Italians resolved to take it for themselves. Hence their bold gesture. Without any attempt at concealment they came forward and before the censors they openly declared that they considered themselves to be Roman citizens. According to one of our authorities the lex Licinia Mucia was the principal cause of the Social War.[33] I, for one, am prepared to believe this. Plainly the Italian gesture was a direct challenge to the Romans. Would they, or would they not, admit the men of Italy into their body politic? A generous response would compose the quarrel but should the Romans prove obdurate then the Italians would not acquiesce in the rebuff. In the past when their initiative failed the Italians had done nothing but that day was now over. When the Romans showed what they thought of them by passing the lex Licinia Mucia they were greatly angered and that anger led them almost immediately to request the younger Drusus to look for the citizenship for them as a matter of urgency. Behind this request was an implied threat: if he should fail then the Romans could expect trouble.[34]

The connection between the lex Licinia Mucia and the Social War is thus clear. The Italians were now irrevocably committed to obtaining the citizenship and had furnished the Romans with the clearest proofs of their desire. The subsequent chilly response from their masters served only to enrage them.[35] They were willing that Drusus should be given the chance to remedy matters but, if he did not succeed, then their patience was at an end and war would be the inevitable outcome. In other words, the mood of anger engendered by the lex Licinia Mucia was never to be dissipated and at last it brought war to Italy.[36]

Before we proceed to look at what Drusus tried to do for the Italians we must first of all try and form some notion of how it was the Italians had come to assume such an attitude. Why did those who meekly accepted the death of C. Gracchus now show such aggressive determination? As I have already emphasised our sources have nothing to say about this. We have therefore, to examine for ourselves what we do know of conditions in the previous quarter century to see if they could, with any degree of plausibility, be said to have contributed to the great change we have just witnessed.

An obvious starting point is new grievances. If such were to be found then it goes without saying that tempers which were already uncertain were likely to become even more unstable. However, in our natural anxiety to make the most of our somewhat scanty materials we should beware lest we too readily attribute a source of discontent to where none really exists. A case in point is the lex Acilia repetundarum. This granted to all Italians, be they *socii* or Latins, the right to assume Roman citizenship if they wished, should they bring a successful prosecution under the law.[37] On the basis of Cicero *Pro Balb.* 54 it has been generally assumed that subsequent legislation limited this privilege to the Latins alone and there has been debate as to which law wrought this change.[38] If such a change did, indeed, take place then it does not require much imagination to see that the allies would not be exactly happy with it.[39] However, it is extremely unlikely that it ever happened. In *Pro Balb.* 53 Cicero draws attention to the way in which successful prosecutors obtained the citizenship by making reference to the instance of a pair of men from Tibur. They are particularly relevant to his case for two reasons. First of all, the son of one of them was sitting on the jury, while the grandson of the other was well known at Rome. Secondly, the Tiburtines were among the few Latins who could genuinely be called *foederati* and, as is well known, Cicero in this speech is much concerned with what might or might not be done under the terms of a *foedus*. In the opening sentences of the next section he then appears to proceed from this specific example to an enumeration of the general principle that all *foederati* may obtain the citizenship in this way. After that he returns to his exemplar, the Latins and says no law has ever taken from them this privilege. However, keeping in mind the purpose of his speech, he takes care to link the Latins with his general statement and he does this by using the inaccurate words, *id est foederatis*. Thus, he is, in effect, saying that the Latins, whom he has used as an illustration, have never been deprived of what all *foederati* enjoy. All Italians were able to avail themselves of the facility offered by the lex Acilia.[40]

But over and above this shared privilege a far more valuable prize had fallen into the hands of the Latins. To appreciate its importance we need to recall the prominent part played by them in the Gracchan period. Of all the Italians they were the most vociferous in their demand for the citizenship and we may especially remember that one of their number, Fregellae actually revolted.[41] This latter event seems to have thoroughly frightened the Romans and brought it home to them that something would have to be done to quiet the Latins. Hence, in 124 (as is generally believed) they decreed that anybody who held a magistracy in a Latin community would automatically become a Roman citizen.[42] If the dating of this measure is correct then it will be readily seen that its immediate effect was negligible. If it had succeeded in soothing the Latins then we might expect them to abandon C. Gracchus and the elder Drusus would hardly have introduced his own counter-proposal for *provocatio*. We must, I think, assume that in those boisterous days the Latins were not satisfied with something that only a few would enjoy but pressed for concessions which would improve the lot of all.[43] But once the revolutionary excitement had evaporated the passing years brought with them a profound change. There was now a steadily growing band of Roman citizens in every Latin state and it is not difficult to envisage them coming to realise that their true interests and sympathies lay with Rome. After all, their desire for the citizenship had sprung, in the first place, from a wish to be as one with her. And this band comprised the most powerful and influential men in their communities.[44] So, when Italy finally broke with Rome, these same men, heedless of the fact that many of their fellow countrymen had not been permitted to share their good fortune, exerted all their influence to keep their people loyal so that, in the event, only one Latin colony went over to the rebels. If we bear steadily in mind the role the Latins had played when the citizenship question first presented itself we will not find it too difficult to imagine them joining wholeheartedly in the insurrection of 91 if nothing had been done to meet their demands. Politically more mature than the rest of Italy in the 120s how much further would they have advanced by the time even the most backward were clamouring to be admitted to the citizenship? As it is, what we are witnessing here is the moment at which the historical processes which were slowly alienating the allies and the Latins were brought to an end in the case of the latter because the Romans granted to the chief among them all that they wanted. One cannot help but observe that there is a certain irony in the fact that those who once took the lead in agitation were now to become models of fidelity.[45] All unwittingly — and it must have been unwittingly unless they possessed preternatural foresight — the Romans of one generation had staved off disaster in the next. But we may beg leave to doubt if the more immediate consequences of the Romans thus separating the Latins from the rest of Italy were beneficial to them. We hear nothing of allied reaction to the move but we are at liberty to guess and I would suggest that envy and admiration at the good fortune of their brethren were the predominant feelings of the *socii*. But we may go further and add that we will not go far wrong if we also say that a sense of grievance was awakened when it was seen that this new privilege was being applied in such a limited fashion. It would then follow that the allies would resolve that this situation should be remedied. Thus, if the granting of citizenship *per magistratum* to the Latins, ultimately contributed to Roman salvation in the Social War, it may, at the same time, be claimed, with some degree of confidence, that it also helped create that attitude of mind among the allies which led to the conflict in the first place.

Any discussion of allied grievances at this time must also take account of one of the great complaints made on the eve of war: the burden of military service.[46] This may have been a complaint of long standing but the heavy burdens imposed by the Jugurthine and Germanic wars are more than likely to have further exasperated the already disgruntled *socii*. An old grudge was being kept alive.

Yet, as I emphasised at the start of this work, if we are to understand the attitude of mind which informed allied actions, it is not enough merely to dwell on what they thought of as the wrongs done to them by Romans. Along with these injustices (whose importance is not, of course, to be denied) we should weigh all other relevant factors in order to determine how, in sum, they influenced the mood of Italy. We must, therefore, remember that the conditions which I suggested (1.1, 2) led to a desire for the citizenship in the first place still prevailed at this time. It would, then, follow that they would not only keep alive that to which they gave birth but, by their very continuance, would self-evidently, nourish it and help it to grow yet further.[47] Moreover, matters seem eventually to have reached the point where any concession by the Romans would serve only to whet allied appetites and strengthen their desire to have that which they sought. Marius' gifts of citizenship may have been unimportant in themselves and certainly not of such a magnitude as to lead the allies to fight for them. But, however modest they may have been, it seems to me that for such a man to have made such a gesture when he was at the height of his fame and his power cannot but have had repercussions. Italian and Roman had fought together to defend their common homeland from barbarian invasion and the saviour of Rome had acknowledged, both on the battlefield and off it, what he owed to Italy. Was it not proper then that those who had helped shoulder the burden should cease to be inferiors in their own land?[48] I would argue that the allies were mindful of such considerations when, a few short years later, they made their bid for the citizenship.[49]

When we try then to assess the probable reasons for a change in attitudes between 121 and 95 we must give due weight to two things: the persistence, during this period, of the conditions which made the allies discontented in the first place and the appearance of some new factors which had the effect of still further unsettling the minds of Rome's subjects. Important and all as these are it may well be, however, that they are of less moment than something else which we have already remarked upon too. Before the time of Flaccus and C. Gracchus the allies had wanted the citizenship but it was the achievement of these two reformers to show them that their ambitions could actually be realised. After this things could never be quite the same again. Those who desired the citizenship before continued to do so. But enfranchisement was no longer a vague ideal. Rather it was a goal which could be achieved. Moreover, to judge from the numbers involved in 95, they had succeeded in infecting those who had hitherto been lukewarm with their own enthusiasm.[50] Then, as the years passed and the Romans showed no inclination to meet their wishes or acknowledge the justice of their cause, allied anger and frustration mounted until a point was reached where the present state of affairs could not be suffered to continue. Flaccus and Gracchus had channelled allied ambitions in such a direction as to render their continued obstruction eventually intolerable.[51]

Growing allied restiveness therefore formed the background against which the younger Drusus entered on his tribunate in 91.[52] In the ancient and modern tradition he is usually depicted as a champion of the senate. His main aim was to strengthen that body's position by restoring to it the control of the law courts which it had lost to the *equites*.[53] At the same time it is difficult to believe he did not attach almost equal importance to obtaining the citizenship for the Italians. His contacts with them were exceedingly close. Silo, one of the leaders of the agitation for enfranchisement who was destined to be a prominent insurgent, was a guest in his house. Indeed it was said, with some plausibility, that the tribune had actually bound the Italians to himself by means of an oath. At any rate he was well enough informed about what was going on in Italy to be able to warn the consuls of a plot against their lives by extremists.[54] It is hard then to believe that Drusus did not know better than most just how dangerous the mood of Italy had become and that he did not, as a result, regard it as a matter of great importance that he should obtain the citizenship for its inhabitants when he was asked to do so. Therefore, when he proclaimed his intention of enfranchising the Italians at the beginning of his tribunate but left over the fulfilment of his promise to its end, we should not take this as meaning he attached less weight to this aspect of his policy than he did to others but rather we should view the delay as part of the carefully devised strategy.[55]

Potentially Drusus could expect trouble from virtually every quarter in Rome. The *equites*, the senate and the plebs all had their own reasons for resisting his proposals.[56] The opposition of the first mentioned is readily explicable. They could hardly be expected to relish losing control of the courts and they would be further enraged by his intention to make them liable to prosecution in cases of bribery.[57] Although the senate as a whole could be expected to welcome his bills a minority led by the formidable consul L. Philippus and the tribune's personal enemy Servilius Caepio opposed him from the first.[58] In the case of the plebs, they, while largely indifferent to most of his programme, could be expected, as in the past, to set their face against any concessions to the Italians and the fate of C. Gracchus and Saturninus amply demonstrated where that might lead.[59]

Drusus' solution to his dilemma was to so tailor his laws as to make them attractive to the greatest number of people.[60] To compensate the *equites* for the loss of the courts he intended to enrol three hundred of them in the senate.[61] Senators might very well feel some unease at this sudden influx of *equites* into their midst but Drusus seems to have calculated — and his estimate proved correct for a time — that the advantage to be won from regaining control of the courts would be sufficient to win their support notwithstanding.[62] For the plebs Drusus brought forward a *lex frumentaria* and a *lex agraria*. By the terms of the latter there were to be viritane assignments and also colonies which would be planted in Sicily and Italy. These colonies, it is thought, were ones proposed by his father, the tribune of 122, when he was wooing the plebs, but which had never been established.[63] This would ensure not only that the plebs would support his *lex judicaria* but would also make them more kindly disposed towards Italian enfranchisement. Once they were assured the Italians were not being given an unfair advantage then they would be prepared to back Drusus in his efforts to award them the citizenship.[64]

Given then that Drusus recognised that the success of his programmes depended on winning the goodwill of large sections of the population of Rome, it was only to be expected he should leave over until last his citizenship bill. To embark on this enterprise before the plebs had been conciliated would be fatal. Fortunately, the Italians, for their part, were prepared to be patient for a little while and, as it turns out, to put up with a great deal if it meant they would get what they wanted in the end. They appear to have intensely disliked Drusus' agrarian law. Like that of Ti. Gracchus it threatened to deprive them of much of the *ager publicus* which they occupied. Over and above this, it has been suggested it also aimed at seizing those lands made private by the lex Agraria of 111. However, as in the days of Flaccus, most of the allies were willing to sacrifice their land in return for the coveted citizenship.[65]

At first, Drusus' tactics seemed to be succeeding. When the time came to vote on his judicial and agrarian legislation he could count on the support of the plebs to whom the latter was pleasing and on the acquiescence of the majority of the allies who, as we just saw, suppressed their dislike for it with an eye to what Drusus would do for them a little later. Philippus naturally put up a resistance but eventually Drusus' measures passed into law.[66] But the tribune could not command the loyalty of all the allies. According to App. B.C. 1.36 the Etrurians and Umbrians came to Rome, seemingly at the behest of Philippus, to protest against a law of Drusus. I believe that this was the agrarian law.[67] In B.C. 1.35 Appian enumerates what Drusus intended to do for the various interest groups. He tells us of the measures he proposed for the Italians, the plebs, the senate and the *equites*. We next hear of their reactions: neither the senate nor the *equites* were pleased. The plebs are happy but the Italians dislike and fear the agrarian proposals. Now, when Appian goes on to say that the Etrurians and Umbrians ταὐτὰ δειμαίνον τες τοῖς Ἰταλιώταις it must mean that they too were worried about those very same proposals. Care should be taken to note that he does not say the Italians in general or the Etrurians and Umbrians in particular, disliked the *rogatio de sociis*. It would, therefore, follow logically that what the latter were, in fact, protesting about was the land bill. That Appian connects their influx with the death of Drusus, which our other sources say took place while he was trying to obtain the citizenship for the Italians, might, at first sight, lend support to the notion that these men had, in reality, come to fight the *rogatio de sociis*. A consideration of Appian's narrative will demonstrate that this is not necessarily so. In essence it contains but three elements: Drusus' schemes, the hatred they awoke, and his death which came about as a result of this. While this is, broadly speaking, chronologically correct, the narrative, as such, can hardly be said to furnish us with a detailed account in sequence of what happened in this year. For instance, there is no mention of the passing of the laws or of their annulment. Nor do we learn from Appian that the senate for a time actually approved of the tribune's work and only later turned against him. So, if Appian is careless about details and is not over concerned to show the precise stages by which Drusus became widely detested, it is not straining credulity to suggest that with a technique such as his, he has simply shifted the climactic moment of death from the time of the citizenship bill to that of the agrarian.

This reaction of the Etrurians and Umbrians shows clearly that they, unlike the majority of the allies, valued land above citizenship and their attitude is further reflected in their tardy and halfhearted participation in the Social War.[68] Here, yet again, we catch another glimpse of the uneven distribution of the desire for the citizenship throughout Italy. In the time of the Gracchi, it may be remembered, we could detect three levels of development in the political consciousness of the Italians. Now we can still see divisions with some more advanced than others. In contrast with the previous age all want the citizenship. But while most are prepared to sacrifice land and, ultimately, to go to war to obtain it, the Etrurians and Umbrians are still some way behind the others. They refuse to part with their possessions and have to be prodded into joining the insurrection.[69]

Once Drusus had done with the law and the land he turned to the Italian question.[70] But he was not to be allowed to give his undivided attention to this matter. Although unimportant in itself, the opposition of the Etrurians and Umbrians can be seen as an evil omen for Drusus. In trying to please everybody he had pleased nobody or almost nobody. As a direct result resistance to him began to grow. The plebs might be content but the *equites* had not been mollified by his concessions. Most important, the senate had, as we know, from the very start disliked the idea of three hundred *equites* being introduced into its midst. Now that there was actually a law sanctioning such a move mere dislike began to turn into real hatred and opinion started to swing in favour of Philippus. Eventually he was able to command a majority in the house and have Drusus' laws declared invalid on the grounds that they had been passed contrary to the auspices.[71]

How far Drusus' citizenship proposals were also a factor in arousing senatorial wrath is debatable. Although he had never made any secret of his intentions we hear nothing about active resistance even after he had begun to take steps to make them a reality. He does not appear, in fact, to have run into opposition until after his other laws were annulled.[72] This prolonged period of quiescence would seem to admit of only one possible explanation. Since it is highly unlikely that the senators were suddenly and miraculously converted to the idea that Italian enfranchisement was a desirable object in itself we must assume they were prepared to accept it as part of the price they had to pay for supporting Drusus in his efforts to reform the courts. Like the introduction of equestrian senators it was something which would have to be put up with. But once the senate came to the conclusion that the admission of *equites* into its midst was altogether too much to pay for reform then it was inevitable they should lose whatever enthusiasm they had for enfranchisement. If they were to sacrifice the courts to keep the *equites* out then there was no particular reason why they should make concessions to the Italians. In the debate on Drusus' laws it is doubtful if the Italian question arose. After all, what was really at issue — as opposed to the ostensible question of the validity of the legislation — was the admission of the *equites* which was dangerously close to being an accomplished fact while possible Italian enfranchisement was still some way in the future. But from the very moment the senate decided to abandon Drusus and his other schemes, it must also have decided to jettison his Italian policy.[73]

Despite this the tribune did not abandon the cause of the Italians. In truth, he probably had little choice. He had committed himself too far to withdraw and by now the mood of Italy had become very ugly indeed.[74] From the time of the lex Licinia Mucia the allies had been contemplating revolt and it was clear that by the beginning of 91, at the latest, that actual conspiracies were being hatched to that end. The plot against the consuls then had given the Romans a hint of what was likely to happen should Drusus fail.[75] But, if anyone should fail to heed this warning, they were now to be furnished with an unequivocal statement as to what the allies would do if their request was refused. At the behest of Drusus, Silo led a large body of allies in a march on Rome in order to press for the citizenship. They were turned back by the persuasion of a certain Domitius but not before they revealed their intent: to destroy the city if the Romans would not enfranchise them.[76] A situation such as this called for resolute determination and Drusus, it must be said lacked the true killer instinct. His reverence for the authority of the senate prevented him from applying his veto when his other laws were annulled and he now shrank from confrontation by trying to postpone a vote on his enfranchisement bill. On one occasion, in order to buy time, we are told he simulated an epileptic attack and all over Italy prayers were offered for his safety.

The consequences of this indecision are not difficult to imagine. The allies continued to conspire and their resolve hardened. The Romans, of course learned of the plots and inevitably opprobium fell on Drusus. Once before Flaccus and C. Gracchus had been accused of instigating an Italian revolt. Now a like charge was levelled at Drusus and his followers. He had long been suspected of promoting the allied cause in order to further his own political ambitions and achieve a position of dominance in the state. It was easy, therefore, for his enemies to claim that it was he who had brought Italy to the brink of revolt. If he really had tied the allies by an oath it would not take much ingenuity to represent it at this stage as an invitation to rebellion. If he had not, a story that he had was bound to receive wide credence anyway.[77] In this highly charged atmosphere the end came quickly for Drusus. One evening he was stabbed to death in his own house by an unknown assassin.

Notes

1. Cf. Badian (1958) p. 200.
2. Aside from the numismatic arguments *contra* (M. Crawford, 'Saturninus and the Italians', *CP* 64, 1969 pp. 37-8) the thesis of R.J. Rowland, 'Saturn, Saturninus and the socii', *CP* 62, 1967 pp. 185-9 that the head of Saturn on certain coins of this period (including those of Saturninus) is meant to show sympathy with Italian aims is based on the unwarranted assumption that *populares* must necessarily support Italian enfranchisement.
3. Sources: Greenidge and Clay pp. 90-1, 94, 105. Cf. Gabba (1951) pp. 15-16, (1967) pp. 102-3; Badian (1958) pp. 198-9; Greenidge (1904) p. 293; Goehler pp. 202-3; *MRR* 1.565, n. 3, 2.645, Colonies may have been established in Africa by the law of 100 — see Badian (1970/1) pp. 404-5.
4. On the desire for mass enfranchisement see below.
5. I do not, of course, imply that Saturninus was simply Marius' tool, cf. Carney pp. 34-6, 40-4; Badian (1958) pp. 204-5, 208-9. We have no means of telling, in the present instance, whether Saturninus independently agreed with Marius or had perforce to go along with his plans nor, from the point of view of our discussion, does it much matter.
6. Plut. *Mar.* 28. Cic. *Pro Balb.* 46-9 does not mention any formal

proceedings against Marius in connection with this enfranchisement. The only court case he cites is one involving the colonial law (for which see below). He further makes it plain that Marius did not violate the *foedus* of Camerinum. Thus, it seems best to reject Val. Max. 9.2.8 and to take it that those who objected to Marius' grant did so because he had acted without proper authority. Cf. Reid (1878) pp. 11-13, 18-19; Goehler p. 197 and n. 20. below.

7. App. B.C. 1.29, 30, 32. Cf. Gabba (1956) pp. 77-8 and Cuff *passim*.

8. Cic. *Pis.* 20; Liv. ep. 69; Plut. *Mar.* 28; *de Vir. Illust.* 73 with Carney p. 35 n. 176, 41 and Gabba (1951) pp. 15-18. Saturninus, of course, may have had other aims as well, cf. Badian (1958) pp. 204-5.

9. Gabba (1976) p. 24.

10. Gabba (1976) p. 187, n. 61.

11. Contrast, on the one hand, Badian (1958) pp. 207-8 and Carney p. 77 with, on the other, Gabba (1956) p. 77. It may be observed that it would not be physically impossible for Italians to come to Rome now, cf. Nagle (1970) pp. 383-4.

12. Cf. n. 22 below.

13. Cic. *Pro Balb.* 48, *Brut.* 79.

14. Illegality may have been necessary on the battlefield but it was hardly called for now.

15. Willems 2 pp. 681-5; Tibiletti (1950) p. 213, n. 4; Smith (1954) *passim*; Goehler p. 201. The enfranchised Latin is mentioned in Cic. *Pro Balb.* 48. The theory I have tried to refute here will be found in Gabba (1967) p. 105 and Badian (1970/1) p. 404. Last *CAH* 9 p. 169 appears to have recognised that Marius could only enfranchise the number specified in the law but his suggestion that they were destined for Latin colonies does not seem acceptable. For *incolae* in Roman colonies see Salmon (1969) p. 169, n. 29. I do not think viritane allotments for Italians would have been envisaged in 100 although they do appear to have received some in 103 (Badian *loc. cit.*).

Badian (1958) p. 206 suggested that Marius' power to enfranchise was designed to regularise the grants of citizenship he had already made. In view of his defiant attitude (Plut. *Mar.* 28) I consider this unlikely.

16. See further n. 22.

17. See further the pertinent remarks of Goehler p. 202.

18. Cf. Carney p. 43, n. 202.

19. Cf. e.g. Badian (1964) p. 43, 48-9, (1970/1) pp. 402-5.

20. Even Vercellae was not too great a departure from tradition, perhaps, cf. Reid (1878) p. 12. Excuses were certainly found for it. See e.g. Val. Max. 5.2.8.

21. Gabba (1976) p. 187, n. 61.

22. App. B.C. 1.29 may be exaggerated (reflecting contemporary propaganda) but it cannot be entirely discounted. We know enough about Marius' attitude to the allies to make it virtually certain he would include them in his land grants and, as I have suggested above, they would most likely be received as *incolae* in the colonies. See Gabba (1967) p. 105.

23. As the Italians are not mentioned in Cicero's great roll call of those who crushed the *seditio*, Badian (1958) p. 208, n. 1 suggests they

might have remained faithful to Saturninus to the very end. This is possible but I would make two cautionary observations. To judge from App. B.C. 1.32 those collected by Saturninus for the final struggle came from near at hand and are, thus, likely to be citizens. In this context we may recall the harvesters of Plut. *C. Gracch.* 13, cf. Holden *ad loc.* Thus, it could be argued that the Italians had already withdrawn their support from Saturninus without necessarily joining his enemies. Again, although I personally would not accept such a view (see n. 22), it can be inferred from Cicero's silence that, if the Italians were not present at the final calamity it was because they had played no part at all in the events which led up to it, cf. n. 11.

24. Sources: Greenidge and Clay pp. 119-20. See Badian (1958) p. 297, 'Marius' villas: the Testimony of the Slave and the Knave', *JRS* 63, 1973 pp. 127-30.

25. Cf. 1.2 and 2.1. We may note that a little later a *princeps* could marshall a large following to protest at the *lex* (Diod. Sic. 37-13) — see further below.

26. The prosecution in Cic. *Pro Balb.* 48-9 is purely incidental to the main aim of the act.

27. Asc. 67-8C.

28. Cf. e.g. 1.3.

29. Cf. Plut. *C. Gracch.* 12, *Sulla* 8; Cic. *de Orat.* 2.257.

30. Cic. *Pro Arch.* 11. This contradicts Badian's view of the census (1964 p. 48, 1968 p. 53, n. 28), cf. Sherwin-White (1973) p. 140, n. 2, p. 314, n. 4, and must call in question his suggestion that the censors actively encouraged Italians to present themselves for registration. Nor, it may be added, is there any evidence to support the notion that Marius encouraged them to do so. Note here the similarity between Cicero's words and those of Asconius 68C: *pars eorum pro civibus Romanis se gereret.* For some further remarks on the dating see n. 35.

31. It will be seen that my views on this matter are close to those of Badian (1968) p. 53, n. 28. He attacks — in my view rightly — Brunt *JRS* (1965) pp. 106-7 who suggests that Italian usurpation of the citizenship was gradual. This appears to rest solely on a misleading comparison between the events of 187 and those of 95. Bearing in mind the consequences if the Italians were allowed to get away with what they had done, Brunt's description of the lex Licinia Mucia as 'the product of legalistic conservatism' seems inadequate to say the least. I cannot agree with Salmon (1962) p. 113 that Cic. *de Offic.* 3.47 and Asc. 68C show the Italians participating in Roman assemblies.

32. App. B.C. 1.34.

33. Asc. 68C. Cf. Cicero's description of the law (*Pro Corn.* apud Asc. 67C): *non modo inutilem sed perniciosam rei publicae.* For the feelings aroused by the *quaestio,* see Diod. Sic. 37.13 (with n. 76 below) and Cic. *de Offic.* 2.75 with Badian (1958) p. 216, n. 3.

34. App. B.C. 1.35. The well orchestrated response to the failure of Drusus (see below) makes it likely, in my view, that rebellion was being contemplated even earlier. The idea was probably conceived around about now and the groundwork for conspiracies (see below) had doubtless begun to be laid.

35. It may be worth reiterating that if we are right in suggesting that the Italians would choose one particular moment to advertise their claims then a *census* would be their natural choice. The dating of the lex Licinia Mucia would therefore point to that of 97/96 as the one they picked, cf. Badian (1968) p. 53, n. 28. The *lex* was the Romans' unyielding reply to their subjects' pretensions.

36. It will, I trust, be seen that the view I take of the *lex* differs radically from that of Bernardi pp. 78-81.

37. Bruns[7] pp. 72-3 with Sherwin-White (1972) pp. 92-6.

38. Cf. E. Badian, 'Lex Servilia', *CR* 4, 1954 pp. 101-2 and B.M. Levick, 'Acerbissima Lex Servilia', *CR* 17, 1967 pp. 256-8.

39. Though it should be remarked that, if what Cic. *Pro Balb.* 54 says is true, we may wonder how many Italians would actually have wanted to avail themselves of the privilege in practice.

40. See further Sherwin-White (1972) pp. 96-7 who reaches the same conclusion by a slightly different route.

41. See 2.1.

42. Tibiletti (1953) is fundamental for this matter.

43. See further the remarks of Tibiletti (1953) pp. 57-9.

44. See Tibiletti (1953) p. 54.

45. How great a part (if any) they played in the events surrounding the lex Licinia Mucia is a moot point. For convenience I have spoken of 'Italians' when discussing these matters although it should be remembered that the likelihood is that few Latins were participants.

46. Vell. Pat. 2.15.2.

47. Note, for instance, what was said above about military service.

48. Such positive attitudes could, of course, co-exist with the more negative ones concerning the burden of service which we noted earlier. The latter would come to the fore when the allies saw small reward for their labours.

49. See (with caution) Badian (1958) pp. 212-3. Although I disagree with his estimate of Marius' importance (see above and below) it nevertheless seems to me that he is right on one fundamental point: any gesture, however small, on Marius' part towards the allies cannot but have significance. Any historian of the period must, therefore, try and evaluate its probable extent. It is a failure to appreciate this point which vitiates Brunt's discussion (*JRS* 1965 p. 106) of the matter. Something more imaginative than his deliberately reductionist approach seems to be called for if we are to do full justice to this exciting but difficult period.

50. See also 1.2.

51. App. B.C. 1.34.

52. Cf. Sherwin-White (1973) p. 140.

53. Cf. Cic. *Pro Mil.* 16; Thomsen pp. 14-15; *MRR* 2. 21.

54. Silo: Plut. *Cat. Min.* 2; Val. Max. 3.1.2; *de Vir. Illust.* 80; Diod. Sic. 37.13 (see n. 76 below). Oath: Diod. Sic. 37.11. In favour of its authenticity see Pareti p. 527; Bernardi p. 82, n. 4; L.R. Taylor, *Party Politics in the Age of Caesar*, Berkeley, 1949, p. 46; n. 77 below; against: H.J. Rose, 'The Oath of Philippus and the Di Indigetes', *HTR* 30, 1937 pp. 165-81. Plot: *de Vir. Illust.* 66; Flor. 2.6.8., cf. Marcks pp. 226-7.

55. App. B.C. 1.35; Vell. Pat. 2.14.1; Flor. 2.5.9; Liv. ep. 71. Gabba

(1967) p. 117 suggests it remained as a *rogatio*. See further below.
   56. There is no evidence to support the claim of Badian (1964) p. 58 that Marius opposed Drusus.
   57. App. B.C. 1.35; Cic. *Pro Cluent.* 153-4, *Pro Rab. perd.* 16-17.
   58. See the discussion of Thomsen pp. 25-30.
   59. App. B.C. 1.35.
   60. Flor. 2.5.6; App. B.C. 1.35; Liv. ep. 71; Vell. Pat. 2.13.2; *de Vir. Illust.* 66. The picture which emerges from these sources is of a man seeking the broadest possible support and, to that end, prepared to make promises to a wide range of interest groups. As Florus remarks (2.5.2) *alium captat ex alio.* Drusus' famous remark about having left nothing to divide except *caenum aut caelum* is often taken to refer specifically to his agrarian programme, cf. e.g. Bernardi p. 95 and (more hesitantly) Gabba (1976) p. 73. However, to judge from the context in both authors, it would seem to refer to the lavish manner in which Drusus scattered everything, and not just land, which it was in his power to give. In *de Vir. Illust.* it may perhaps, in addition, be applied to his personal extravagance in money matters, cf. Dio fr. 96.2.
   61. App. B.C. 1.35 with Gabba (1967) p. 118. Gruen (1968) pp. 208-9 denies that Drusus wished to conciliate the *equites* but his thesis is contradicted by this passage of Appian and by what we know of the general characteristics of the tribunate (n. 60).
   62. App. B.C. 1.35. See further below.
   63. Sources: Greenidge and Clay p. 131 with Vell. Pat. 2.13.2. See Gabba (1967) pp. 117-18 and Thomsen pp. 17-18.
   64. App. B.C. 1.35. See further n. 68.
   65. App. B.C. 1.36 with Gabba (1967) p. 121. Gabba's view that this passage refers to a period after the passing of the *lex agraria* and the *lex judicaria* is not necessarily correct. The fears it speaks of would surely have been aroused the instant Drusus' intentions were known. See further below.
   66. Liv. ep. 71; Flor. 2.5. 7-9; *de Vir. Illust.* 66; Sen. *de Brev. Vit.* 6.1.
   67. Other theories will be found in Bernardi pp. 94-6; Gabba (1976) pp. 72-3, 168; Badian (1958) pp. 218-19. My position is closest to that of Harris (1971) pp. 212-15 and Strachan-Davidson p. 41.
   68. The theories of Ruoff-Väänänen pp. 73-4 seem to me to be insecurely based. In the time of C. Gracchus colonies were proposed for Etruria, cf. *SRF* I p. 216, 219. With the revival of the schemes of the elder Drusus it is likely the area was threatened again.
   69. The interpretation of the Appian passage presented here renders otiose, in my view, the theory of L. Piatrowicz, 'Quelques remarques sur l'attitude de l'Etrurie pendant les troubles civils a la fin de la Republique romaine', *Klio* 28, 1930 pp. 334-8. He believed the upper classes of Etruria and Umbria opposed enfranchisement because, together with the admission to Roman colonies which would follow from it, it would give the lower orders the political and economic power to overturn their rulers. There is no evidence, now or later, that such tensions as did exist in these societies led to class warfare or the formation of a democratic movement. If a democratic movement did exist then it is strange that its leaders did not support Drusus instead of allowing their people to be led

to Rome to oppose him. See further, Badian (1958) p. 218, 221-2; Harris (1971) pp. 31-40, 114-29, 202-12; H. Rix, 'L'apporto dell' onomastica personale alla conoscenza della storia sociale' in Martelli and Cristofani pp. 64-73.

70. Flor. 2.5.9. This is what we would expect. The allies would now want to be rewarded for their loyalty and patience. The slightest hesitation could only lead to trouble (see below). According to Vell. Pat. 2.14.1 Drusus only began this campaign after his other laws had been annulled. For the reason just stated I consider this unlikely. Velleius also represents his Italian policy as an afterthought. I hope I have been able in this section to show why this, too, is improbable. We may mention that Bernardi pp. 90-1 sees in this passage a reference to the point at which Drusus and the senate parted company on this issue. Cf. n. 72 below.

71. App. B.C. 1.35; *de Vir. Illust.* 66; Cic. *de Orat.* 1.24.3, 3.1-6, *Prov. Cos.* 21; Vell. Pat. 2.13.2-3. Sources for the annullment: Greenidge and Clay pp. 134-5. It has been suggested by Thomsen p. 28 that the creation of new senators was what inspired Philippus' opposition to Drusus from the very beginning. If so, his achievement now was to convert senatorial passive dislike into the kind of active hatred he himself felt. However, there are some reasons for doubting the validity of this hypothesis — see n. 73 below. Vell. Pat. 2.13.2 says the senate disliked Drusus' concessions to the plebs but this can hardly be the reason it turned against him. In the past — witness for instance Drusus' own father — it had been only too willing to buy plebeian support if it were to its own advantage.

72. Only three sources give any clue as to when the Italian proposals first met opposition:
(a) Vell. Pat. 2.14.1 which can be pressed (n. 70) to mean he encountered trouble after his break with the senate.
(b) *de Vir. Illust.* 66 could mean simply that opposition started after his other laws had been passed. But it is at least as likely that it too refers to the time after the break.
(c) Flor. 2.5.9 simply says the allies began to demand *pretium rogationis* immediately after the other laws were passed but that Drusus was unable to redeem his promises. This, of course, does not pinpoint when exactly the tribune met with difficulties.

Our sources, then, do not give a clear cut and unanimous verdict on this question. However, as will appear from my text, I believe there are good reasons for favouring the notion that Drusus' Italian proposals first began to founder after his split with the senate.

73. See further the remarks of Gruen (1968) pp. 211-13 and Thomsen pp. 42-3. Sall. *Ep. Caes.* 6 may be interpreted in two ways. It may simply refer to the time when opposition to the citizenship bill openly manifested itself. On the other hand it could be setting out the real reason why Philippus and his friends opposed Drusus from the very first: their fear of Italian enfranchisement. They knew that if he were allowed to pass his other measures into law he would then be able to grant the citizenship. In favour of this interpretation it may be noted that the remark about men who destroyed themselves in destroying Drusus is very like what we find in Diod. Sic. 37.10.3, a passage which refers to the time the laws were annulled.

74. The sources for what follows are *de Vir. Illust.* 66; Flor. 2.5.9; Diod. Sic. 37.10.3,11,13; Liv. ep. 71; Vell. Pat. 2.14.1; Pliny *NH* 25.52; App. B.C. 1.38. It may be noted that the account of the Livian epitomator seems to be a more careless version of the events narrated in *de Vir. Illust.*

75. See n. 54 above. Dating of plot: Badian (1964) p. 51 and Keaveney *RhM* (1983) pp. 273-4. Commonsense dictates that we date the formation of conspiracies earlier than App. B.C. 1.38 does. This incident supports our view.

76. Diod. Sic. 37.13. Since Brunt *JRS* (1965) p. 93, n. 19 denies a context can be found for this, the following points may be noted:

(a) Despite Brunt's hesitancy the εὐθύνας can hardly be anything else save the investigations being carried out under the lex Licinia Mucia. If large numbers were involved as suggested, then we would expect them to be still in progress.

(b) If Silo is telling the truth about being summoned by the tribunes (cf. n. 54) then we can interpret his remark to mean that Drusus was looking for his help in pushing the bill through i.e. at the very moment he began to actively try to implement his proposal.

(c) Domitius' statement that the senate was willing to grant what the allies wanted may be a piece of mendacity. But, if it is the literal truth, then it would help date the passage to that period before the annulling of Drusus' laws when he could still count on the support of the senate for his citizenship bill.

(d) Pareti p. 527 connects this passage with Flor. 2.5.7 and Sen. *de Brev. Vit.* 6.1 but I doubt this since they appear to me to refer to the passing of the other laws.

77. For Drusus' alleged ambitions see n. 73. I believe the oath to be genuine (at the very least to the extent that contemporaries believed in its existence) since a plausible historical context can be found for it here. It could obviously be used to awake senatorial fears about the large number of clients Drusus hoped to gain by his schemes. Mommsen's suggestion that its title 'The oath of Philippus' derives from the fact that the consul taxed Drusus with it is very attractive.

2.3

Conclusion: Roman Politics and the Italian Question 205-91 BC

War followed almost immediately on the death of Drusus, yet even after the rebellion had started the Romans could have averted disaster had they been prepared to grant the citizenship.[1] Instead they chose to cling to their long standing hostility to such a move and thus rendered the quarrel implacable. On the eve of the Social War then, it is obviously important for us to determine how such an attitude came to be conceived and why it was persisted in even after it had become perfectly clear that it could have only the gravest consequences.

As regards the ruling classes there was what we might call a practical consideration which would make them extremely reluctant to meet the Italians' demands. Collectively the Roman nobility tended to watch with a jealous eye anyone of its members who rose to too great a prominence. It was not held to be desirable that any one man should possess greater political power and influence than his fellows and efforts were made to ensure this did not happen. The lex Villia Annalis which regulated a man's progression in the *cursus honorum* is a typical product of this outlook. It has also been suggested that one of the reasons why colonisation ceased in 177 was the fear that *patroni* would reap a political advantage from the clients thus gained. 'The easiest way to prevent imbalance from developing was to make sure that no colonies at all were founded'. A fear similar to this was what seems to have lain behind the Roman nobility's persistent refusal to grant the citizenship to the Italians. Whoever first moved the motion for enfranchisement would be sure to gain immense power by reason of the votes of the grateful recipients. In addition the assemblies would be swamped by the new voters and the senate too would be imperilled as the notables among the

99

new citizens would now seek to take what they regarded as their rightful places in that body.[2]

Concrete examples of the effects of such anxieties are easy to discover. We may recall that the 'oath of Philippus' was probably paraded before the senators in order to awaken fear of Drusus' possible pre-eminence. Indeed, as I have argued, such fears may have motivated the tribune's opponents from the very start. Again, when the Romans were, at last, forced to concede the citizenship they attempted to minimise the disruptive effect this could have by confining the newly enfranchised to a limited number of tribes. The resistance Sulpicius and Cinna encountered when they tried to alter this arrangement testifies to the importance which was attached to keeping them there.[3]

Motives such as those we have just been describing may, indeed, be selfish but they are, at least, readily explicable and easily understood. They do not, however, in my view provide more than a partial explanation for the Roman nobility's opposition to enfranchisement and none at all for that of the plebs. In order, therefore, not only to complete this partial explanation but also the better to grasp what really underlies it, we must consider something which is less immediately tangible, less easy to describe in a brief compass but which nevertheless played a significant part in determining Roman attitudes towards the Italian question. I speak of the mood of Rome in the second century.

From our point of view, two phenomena which cast a strong light on certain aspects of this mood, seem, at first sight anyway, to be of particular importance. These are the changes in the Roman attitude towards their own citizenship observable at this time and the growth, in certain quarters, of a strong xenophobic sentiment.

The Romans liked to believe that they had been generous in granting their citizenship to others. Cicero, for example, was able to point to large towns and even whole nations which had been, in earlier times, incorporated into the Roman state. Much later the emperor Claudius made appeal to this consistently open handed policy when justifying his own intention to admit provincials to the senate. Cato, too, seems to have recognised that early Rome increased her strength by the admission of outsiders. Foreigners also were struck by the trait. Philip V of Macedon was one. He makes especial mention of the fact that manumitted slaves became citizens and, like Cato, saw in this admissions policy a means whereby the state's resources of manpower might be maintained.[4] A consideration of the various avenues by which the citizenship might be reached[5] will, I think, show that in the second century there was a distinct falling off from the liberal standards of previous ages.

We learn that, in 188, Formiae Fundi and Arpinum, which possessed *civitas sine suffragio*, were admitted to the full citizenship. This is the last such grant we hear of and it is a matter for debate as to whether other communities in a like position received a similar elevation before the Social War. What is certain is that no other communities, which did not already have the citizenship in some form, were now given it.[6] The Romans had been accustomed, as well, to reward individual foreigners who had done the state a signal service with material benefits and the grant of *civitas* (sometimes *sine suffragio*). For instance, in 211, a Spaniard and a Syracusan received land and citizenship in recognition of what they had done for Rome. If we except the grant of the rights of an *ingenua* to Hispala for her part in unmasking the Bacchic conspiracy in 186, we come upon no other such awards until Marius made his controversial gift to the Camertines. It would be unwise, however, to see in this evidence for a change of Roman policy towards individuals like that which had come about for large groups. We should not forget that the lex Acilia and the grant of citizenship *per magistratum* indicate that individuals were still welcome.[7]

That manumission of slaves which so impressed Philip continued now but here there were definite developments. Traditionally freedmen had been confined to the urban tribes. A concession granted, it is thought, by the censors of 179 gave to *libertini*, who had estates valued at over 30,000 sesterces or a child living, the right to be assigned to a rustic tribe. Their immediate successors, in 174, allowed those who had got this privilege through paternity to keep it but did not extend it to those who had achieved parenthood since the last *lustrum*. They did, however, continue to admit to rustic tribes those who fulfilled the property qualification. Although these were not particularly generous concessions they were plainly offensive to some since Ti. Gracchus senior, in 169, wished to disenfranchise freedmen completely. This extreme proposal failed but it was decided that henceforth the freedmen should be confined, as before, to the urban tribes.[8]

From this survey of the evidence the change in Roman

attitudes to the citizenship is tolerably clear. Individuals could still be admitted but it would appear that communities or large numbers could not expect to be made welcome. Where, as in the case of freedmen, it was not felt proper to actually stop them then steps were taken to see that they did not gain an undue influence. Moreover, if the Romans were becoming reluctant to let foreigners obtain the *civitas* they were equally reluctant to part with it themselves. This can be seen particularly in the abandonment of the custom of founding Latin colonies. Despite the undoubted benefits which might be gained in joining such foundations, it was discovered that sufficient numbers of people could not be found who might be willing to give up their citizenship in return.[9] In the second century Roman citizenship had become something prized. It was not easy to gain and it should not be lightly put off.[10]

There is also detectable among certain members of the Roman aristocracy a strong vein of anti-intellectualism combined with a marked xenophobia. In 161, for instance, philosophers and rhetoricians were expelled from Rome. When work was begun on a permanent theatre in 154, Scipio Nasica succeeded in halting the project. That same year some philosophers, who were members of an Athenian delegation, took time off to charm the Romans with their discourses. This so alarmed Cato that he made every effort to have the official business of the embassy completed as quickly as possible in order to get them out of Rome. Natives who attempted to propagate Greek skills in a Latin guise fared no better. In 92 the censors closed down the newly established schools of the *rhetores Latini*. Where stated, the motives for such actions are broadly similar. A theatre was a useless thing and injurious to public morality. A warlike people had no business enjoying Greek pleasures which could only foster *lascivia* and *desidia*. Cato feared this martial race would now value oratory more highly than soldiering. A Roman should have as his inspiration the laws and the magistrates, not speculative philosophy. Sad to say, it was not always possible to tell when a Greek was speaking the truth. Socrates had undermined the customs of his country and inculcated opinions in his fellow countrymen which were contrary to the laws. Roman youth had to be protected from the Latin rhetors who taught them *ut auderent* at their *impudentiae ludus*. Like sentiments were also voiced at the time of the suppression of the Bacchic cult. In a speech which Livy puts into his mouth one of the consuls reminded his listeners that they should venerate only those gods their ancestors had. Alien rites and deities would lead them to crime and lust. Foreign cults were not to be tolerated.[11]

Thus, we can speak of a certain attitude which was prevalent among some members of the Roman nobility during the second century. It regarded foreign ideas and customs as positively harmful and injurious. Were the Romans to adopt them they ran the risk of ceasing to be Romans. Hence they were to be strenuously resisted.

Now, it is easy to draw an equation between these two general phenomena which we have just been considering and the specific refusal of the Romans to admit the Italians to the citizenship: the Romans fearing pollution would not permit an influx of Italians which might destroy their way of life.[12] The temptation to do so should, however, be resisted since, as an explanation, it is not only over-facile but also inaccurate. Exclusiveness and xeno-phobia certainly spring from the same source and can certainly be seen as working together in the way postulated in the case of non-Italians. But, so far as the Italians are concerned, it is the spirit of exclusiveness alone which may be said to have worked against them. This, I hope, will become clear after a consideration of that common fount of both attitudes: Rome's position as the dominant power in the Mediterranean world.

Over a vast tract of territory the Romans were now lords and masters. Having no equals they could impose their will on others as they pleased. Technically, of course, some of those they dominated were allies but, in the final analysis, all who fell under Roman sway were subjects. Rome might, on occasion, defer to their sensibilities but would not tolerate dissent on any matter of consequence. When her public representatives, the magistrates, commanded they expected to be obeyed. The famous anecdote of Popilius and Antiochus IV neatly illustrates the autocratic temper of the Romans. When the king refused to give an immediate answer to a senatorial resolution Popilius drew a circle around him and told him not to leave it until he had made a reply.[13]

A gap thus opens between the Romans and the rest of the world; between the masters and those who obeyed them. To be a Roman meant that one belonged to the race which ruled the earth. Not to be a Roman meant that one was part of a subject people. And this state of affairs was significant not just for the magistrate with *imperium* but for every individual Roman. It is well known that great material benefits accrued to some, at least, of the conquerors but we are not primarily concerned with that here. Rather, what must engage our attention is the power and prestige conferred by the mere fact of being a *civis Romanus*. Within the empire, the citizen, unlike the provincial, was free from arbitrary magisterial violence and enjoyed the right to trial by his peers in Rome. Both within and without the Roman world, the citizen was deferred to and treated with all the courtesy and respect due to one who represented in his own person the leading nation of the day. People knew better than to interfere with somebody who was protected by the majesty of Rome.[14]

This feeling of being set apart, this notion of superiority permeated the plebs as much as it did their rulers. The common people, it is true, did not partake of the riches of empire to anything like the same extent as did the nobles but they nevertheless enjoyed considerable advantages which marked them off from those who were not Romans. The freedom from the arbitrary power of the magistrate which they had abroad was naturally theirs at Rome as well. They no longer paid the *tributum* and they could, if they wished or were persuaded, still assert their authority as the sovereign people. They refused, at first, to sanction the second Macedonian War and were able, on occasions, to extract donatives as a condition for good behaviour in the field. In this connection it is worth mentioning the *de facto* abolition of *verberatio* during campaigns which came about in the second century. Moreover tribunes were prepared to support them when they complained about military service and its conditions. The introduction of lot into the levies and the limitation of service in Spain to six years were the result of such support. Above all, we should remember that if military service gave the Italians a consciousness of their own worth (1.1) it must all the more have enhanced the already high opinion the average Roman had of himself.[15]

In my view, it was this feeling of superiority which bred the spirit of exclusiveness. It does not require much imagination to see how those who held a position of dominance would jealously guard it and hesitate to share it with inferiors who dared to claim they were innately worthy of such an honour.[16]

But, if Rome's position of dominance gave rise to a consciousness of superiority and a swaggering self-confidence for many it also brought with it, for some, fears, doubts and uncertainties. It has been emphasised that the second century was a period of great economic, social and political change.[17] As we shall see in a moment, the Romans do not appear to have fully appreciated what brought about such changes but they could see with their own eyes their consequences and much of what they saw they did not like. In the Bacchic conspiracy, for instance, a decline in sexual morality was revealed and men feared for a time that a revolution was about to take place. Then again, the increasingly outrageous behaviour of some commanders abroad could not but give cause for concern to the more responsible of their peers while the whole sorry mess which was the Spanish Wars seemed to show a decline in Roman military power.[18] As a consequence of this the idea gradually took hold that those same virtues and qualities which had made the Romans great and enabled them to win an empire were now being undermined by the very possession of that empire. With absolute power had come vices which threatened the *mos maiorum*.[19] Therefore, since the problem was viewed largely as a moral one to the almost total exclusion of any other explanation, it was natural that a moral solution should be sought for it.[20] One of the prime corrupting agents, it was felt, was Roman contact with the Greek East. Acquaintance with that part of the world had given Romans a taste for luxury, drink, art and loose women. Strange habits and tastes had been acquired.[21] Thus, while the Romans accepted that there was much in Greek culture which was good and could be easily assimilated to their way of life, it was also felt it could bring with it a lot which was evil and destructive. Hence, in order to preserve the *mos maiorum* it was necessary to keep at a distance all of those things which could be regarded as harmful to it. So, we have that series of actions which we may fairly describe as xenophobic.[22] Rome's position as a world power had made of her a cosmopolitan city and in some that cosmopolitanism had engendered a hatred of things foreign.

Now, as I have stated, the xenophobia and exclusiveness which grew out of Rome's imperial position could often work together. It is not difficult to see why, should the occasion ever have arisen, the Romans might hesitate to admit Greeks, for instance, to their citizenship. Not only were they subjects and inferiors but they were also potential corrupters. But I have claimed also that it is otherwise with the Italians for there is no reason to suppose they were ever regarded as the bearers of a fearful moral contagion. Quite the contrary. They were rather seen as cousins and neighbours, men of the same race and blood.[23] Indeed, throughout the second century, Italians and Romans were gradually tending to draw closer together as we know and men of Italy could expect to share in the Romans' exalted position when abroad.[24] We also discover that not only did the Roman nobility enter into a patron-client relationship with Italians but that some of them actually intermarried with the Italian aristocracy.[25] In his writings Cato showed a just appreciation of Italian virtues and set Rome in an Italian context. It might, of course, be argued that Cato's origin would naturally predispose him to take this view but the same can hardly be said of Scipio Aemilianus. When he scolded those for whom Italy was only a *noverca*, the high value he placed on those he was defending is obvious. Even Fannius did not claim that the Orontes, so to speak, was about to flow into the Tiber but rather, warned of what might result from an influx of like minded people.[26] There is, therefore, no evidence that the Romans regarded the Italians with either fear or suspicion.[27] In fact, it may be remarked that the Romans regarded the Italians with such complacency that they had difficulty even imagining the possibility that they might one day rebel — an attitude which almost brought about their ruin.[28]

It may be fairly said, then, that the Italians, as opposed to other subjects, enjoyed a special relationship with Rome. They were recognised as kinsmen and relatives sprung from the same land. But it has to be clearly understood that this relationship had its strict limits. It simply did not extend to acknowledging even the possibility that the Italians might be the equal of the Romans. They were regarded, certainly, as cousins but country cousins whose position in the world was altogether inferior to that of men who were true *Romani di Roma*. Those who were *domi nobiles* were mere upstarts in the city.[29] However great the degree of social contact, however much fellow feeling might grow, nothing could alter Roman opinion on one fundamental point: the Italians were their inferiors. In short, the men of Rome looked down on the men of Italy.[30] The allies were without doubt acutely aware of this. By the time of the Social War they were imbued with a strong sense of their own worth. Having helped Rome win an empire they saw themselves as the equals of their masters and in no whit their subordinates. As they themselves no longer felt any diffidence towards the Romans or experienced any sense of inferiority in their presence they were not prepared to be despised any longer by them. Those who were of the same race and blood as the Romans should not be treated as foreigners.[31]

It is this spirit of haughtiness which informs Roman rule in Italy and determines its character so that in many respects it resembles Roman rule in the provinces. We have seen that this government had its benign and its malignant aspects.[32] We have alluded to the fact that magistrates could abuse their position of dominance by behaving disgracefully while abroad but it will also be recalled that it was not unknown for them to carry on in precisely the same fashion at home. On the other hand, there were those who did not think it incompatible with the majesty of Rome to govern wisely and well and here we may instance Scaevola's governorship of Asia in the 90s. The Italians, for their part, found in Scipio and Marius men who believed that they must be treated with scrupulous fairness and be given their just deserts. But whether the Romans governed badly or well the same basic principle underlay their actions: they were the masters and all others were their subjects. They commanded, the rest of the world obeyed and this is how things would remain. The special affinity which the Romans felt for many Italians was not sufficiently strong to lead them to make an exception in their favour. They, no less than the provincials, should know their place and should not aspire to leave it. They were not to be permitted to become citizens and share in the ruling of empire.[33]

But, when did the Romans begin to manifest this spirit of exclusiveness towards the Italians? The correct answer, I believe, is that given by Badian:[34] precisely in the time of Flaccus and C. Gracchus. It will be recalled that in 169 certain concessions which had been given to freedmen were withdrawn. The previous arrangements were re-established in the face of opposition from those who wanted to disenfranchise them entirely. Here, as was noted earlier, is a clear indication of the Roman dislike of admitting large numbers of foreigners into the citizenship. Undoubtedly xenophobia was at work. These were lowly strangers for whom Italy was a *noverca*. But over and above this something else was plainly troubling the Romans. If the freedmen should invade the rural tribes in any number then they would acquire a strong voice in the management of affairs. Hence there was a necessity for seeing to it that their influence was limited. To abolish grants of freedom was clearly impossible. Slavery with its concomitant manumission was such an integral part of Roman society that it is difficult to imagine that such a move was even contemplated.[35] But other means of control lay to hand. The extreme proposal of complete disenfranchisement failed but the alternative eventually chosen was just as effective. With the freedmen safely corralled in a small number of tribes their influence would be slight. This episode shows, therefore, that what the Romans feared from numbers was not the numbers themselves but the political consequences they might have and where, as in the present instance, an influx could not be halted measures would be taken to blunt those consequences.[36]

This treatment of the freedmen stands in vivid contrast to that meted out to the Italians in 187, 177 and again in 126. We have reason to suspect that some at least of these had assumed the citizenship (whether fraudulently or otherwise) and the numbers involved were certainly large. Yet, the initiative for expulsion came at first not from the Romans but from the Italians themselves.[37] It may very well be argued that, although the Romans disliked Italian immigration, they suffered it to continue simply because they had no machinery for dealing with it. After all they had no regular immigration service.[38] But this will not do. They were perfectly capable of dealing with the freedmen and, when the need was perceived, with the Italians likewise. The *quaestio* established by the lex Licinia Mucia made the most searching enquiries into men's status and continued with its work for several years.

It would appear then that we have no option but to conclude that the Romans were, for a long time, unconcerned with Italian immigration and assumption of the citizenship and significantly this indifference is to be observed as late as 126. The changes which were to permanently alter Roman attitudes towards the Italians came in the next year. Hitherto, although the numbers involved were fairly large, the Romans do not seem to have regarded them as a corporate body capable of acting in concert but rather as an assortment of disparate individuals who would be comfortably absorbed. Being largely men of lowly origin whose main motive was economic betterment these immigrants had no political ambitions and so posed no real threat. The initiative of Flaccus changed all of that. Instead of a collection of individuals without any leadership there now appeared whole nations demanding the citizenship and they were led by men of quality with manifest and grandiose ambitions.[39] Moreover, it was well known what people like Flaccus stood to gain from championing this particular cause. In other words, the clear politicisation of the Italians brought about an instant and permanent change in Roman attitudes towards them. Individuals the Romans could tolerate but they were not prepared to admit whole nations into their body politic.[40]

Rome's attainment of world domination had, therefore, bred in her people notions of superiority and a consciousness of privilege of which all citizens partook. As a direct result of their unwillingness to share this special position with anyone the Romans resolutely set their face against Italian attempts to acquire the citizenship. But, although high and low at Rome shared a common view of their collective place in the world, nevertheless differences are detectable between the outlook of senate and Subura. We know that into the resistance of the nobility there entered an element of calculation. For them it was not just a question of prestige and self-regard — important and all as these considerations were — but also of the real and immense power they wielded and would not share with any man. They realised only too well the erosion which might follow from the admission of the Italians and hence comes their bitter, constant and unrelenting opposition to enfranchisement. On the other hand, prestige and pride were what largely concerned the plebs since it was only spasmodically that they asserted their power as the sovereign people in the second century. This and the fact that they lacked the tight cohesion of the ruling class which, in contrast, had no difficulty in recognising where its mutual interests lay, goes far to explain the apparent inconsistencies in plebeian behaviour. The Roman people was an instrument waiting for the most skilful performer to play upon it what he would. If Fannius and those who opposed Saturninus, for instance, could appeal to their pride then people like the younger Drusus were able to persuade them to pocket it in return for material gains.[41] Plebeian notions of superiority were real enough, as real as those of the nobles (and, we might add, potentially as dangerous) but since they were not bound up with any other considerations, they were capable of being overcome by the determined.

Viewing the matter in retrospect it is easy to say that the Italians were unwise in choosing the *populares* as the agents whereby the citizenship might be obtained. After all, the record of their achievements in this sphere is hardly an impressive one. But, at the time, it would not necessarily have appeared that things would fall out in the way that they did. At the beginning of his career who could have foretold C. Gracchus' great fall from grace and favour? It may also be remarked that the younger Drusus came very close to succeeding. Most importantly, though, the Italians really had no choice but to have recourse to such people. After all, it was Flaccus and Gracchus who first taught them that theirs was a realisable ambition and, in the face of subsequent unremitting hostility, they had no option but to turn to whoever seemed willing to lend a helping hand. It could also be claimed that, through Italian involvement with the *populares*, the citizenship issue became entangled among other controversial matters and, with prejudice thus aroused, the opportunity to deal with it dispassionately was lost. This is doubtful. From the moment of its politicisation, Roman reaction to the Italian question was one of lordly indifference punctuated by bursts of savage reaction when it was forced upon their attention. There is no indication whatsoever that they were prepared to examine the problem coldly and logically and draw the necessary conclusion. This is amply demonstrated by the lex Licinia Mucia. A harsh law was their reaction when the citizenship question was presented to them unencumbered by any other interests or concerns. Indeed, we may go so far as to claim that, so far from being injurious, the binding of the enfranchisement question with other issues was positively beneficial to the Italians since it enabled them to press their suit. The truth of this has, I think, been sufficiently demonstrated in our survey of the problem this far. So it is legitimate to infer that, since the Roman ruling class would never of its own volition have granted the citizenship, the Italians had nothing to lose by allying themselves with the *populares*.

In essence, then, a refusal to share their power and their privileged position with others was what led the Romans to deny the citizenship to the Italians. In fact, it is hard to avoid the conclusion that towards the end the element of calculation in Roman attitudes took second place to an unreasoning hostility. As pressure increased deep seated irrational prejudice won out over any consideration of what the cost of a refusal might be. It is difficult to believe that men were coldly calculating how best to preserve their power in the state when their actions were now openly inviting the destruction of that very state. The situation was further exacerbated by the fact that those who were lords of the earth and used to obedience for so long found it virtually impossible to conceive how the men of Italy might rebel. The

110

Conclusion

refusal to accommodate those whom they regarded as inferiors led those inferiors to turn on them and, to her surprise, the conqueror of Asia and Europe was attacked from Corfinium.[42]

Notes

1. See 3.1.
2. Hackl pp. 1-5; Badian (1958) p. 179; Salmon (1969) pp. 103-4, 112-13, (1982) p. 121, 128-9; Gabba (1976) pp. 93-4; Earl (1967) p. 29.
3. See 2.2 and 4. 1,2.
4. Cic. *Pro Balb.* 31; Tac. *Ann.* 11.23-4; *SIG* 543; Gell. 18.12.7.
5. On these, in general, see Harris (1971) pp. 192-201.
6. Livy 38.36.7-9, cf. Sherwin-White (1973) pp. 210-4.
7. Hispala: Livy 39.19.5. It is, of course, generally recognised that due weight must be given to the concept of *postliminium* in considering these matters. Thus, it prevents us from drawing any rash conclusions from a comparison of the case of Onesinus (Livy 44.16.7) with those of earlier benefactors (cf. e.g. Livy 26.21.11-13). On the whole question of viritane grants see Sherwin-White (1973) pp. 245-6, 291-311, adding Archelaus (Plut. *Sulla* 23) to his list of Greek examples. Enfranchisement for religious purposes (Cic. *Pro Balb.* 55) is irrelevant to this discussion.
8. On all of this see Treggiari pp. 38-47.
9. Toynbee pp. 142-54; Salmon (1969) p. 96, 99-100, 103.
10. The lex Minicia laid it down that when a Roman and a foreigner without the right of *conubium* married, their offspring should be regarded as foreigners — Greenidge (1901) p. 133. Some scholars, e.g. Salmon (1967) p. 338, n. 4 and Pareti pp. 536-7, would date this law to 91. I am not completely convinced. In that year Roman concern was with large numbers not with some comparatively trifling individual cases. A second century date might be more appropriate. Such a law would, for instance, be in harmony with the spirit which informed the restrictions placed on freedmen. See further the remarks of Galsterer p. 161.
11. Suet. *de Rhet.* 1; Gell. 15.11; Quint. 2.42; Tac. *Dial. de Or.* 35; Liv. ep.48; App. B.C. 1.28 with Gabba (1967) pp. 96-7; Oros. 4.21.4; Val. Max. 2.4.2; Vell. Pat. 1.15.3; Pliny *NH* 7.12; Plut. *Cat. Maior* 22-3; Livy 39.15.2-3, 16.8-10. It has sometimes been argued, cf. e.g. Gabba, 'Politica e cultura in Roma agli inizi del l sec. a.C.', *Athenaeum* 31, 1953, pp. 267-72, that the Latin rhetors were suppressed for political reasons because they were a breeding ground for sedition. However, this notion receives no support from our sources. The explanation they do give is perfectly adequate being in complete accord with the reasons offered for similar earlier acts. See also A.E. Douglas, 'Clausulae in the *Rhetorica ad Herennium* as evidence of its date', *CQ* 10, 1960 pp. 74-7; M. Gelzer, *Kleine Schriften*, Wiesbaden, 1962, vol. 1 pp. 212-15; M.L. Clarke, *Rhetoric at Rome*, London, 1953 pp. 11-13.
12. Salmon (1969) p. 102 appears to hint at such a view.
13. Livy 45.12.4-6. See de Sanctis, *Storia dei Romani*, Florence, 1969, vol. 4.1 pp. 459-60 and Smith (1955) pp. 57-60.

14. Cic. 2 *Verr.* 5.147, 157, 160, 166-7; Plut. *Pomp.* 24. The Italians at Cirta (Sall. *Jug.* 26.1) appear to have been relying on the majesty of Rome for protection. See Keaveney *Crit. Stor.* (1984) pp. 345-57 and n. 16 below.

15. McDonald (1939) p. 125, 129, 136, 142-4; Keaveney *Crit. Stor.* (1984) pp. 357-67, 371-2.

16. We may recall that permitting the Italians to share in the Romans' privileged position abroad eventually led them to seek a like boon in Italy (1.2, 3).

17. So Earl (1967) p. 17. For detailed treatment see McDonald (1939) and (1944).

18. McDonald (1944) pp. 26-33; Hackl pp. 50-118; Toynbee pp. 608-45; Earl (1963) pp. 107-11. In my view, C. Gallini, *Protesta e Integrazione nella Roma antica,* Bari, 1970 pp. 11-96 goes beyond the evidence.

19. See Earl (1967) pp. 17-19, 36 and I. Lana, 'Espansionismo imperiale e teorie suii decadimenti' in *Tra Grecia* pp. 111-19. The Romans themselves were unsure when to date the beginning of the rot, cf. Lintott (1972) pp. 626-38 and Earl, *The Political Thought of Sallust,* Cambridge, 1961 pp. 41-59. For a discussion of the virtues which were allegedly being undermined see L.R. Lind, 'The tradition of Roman moral conservatism' in C. Deroux (ed.), *Studies in Latin Literature and Roman History,* Brussels, 1979 pp. 7-57.

20. Since it is fashionable to deride the Romans for this allegedly simplistic view, it is worth emphasising that the problem did indeed have its moral aspect. Standards were declining.

21. Lintott (1972) pp. 627-8; M. Bonamente, 'Leggi suntuarie e loro motivazioni', in *Tra Grecia* pp. 67-91.

22. Earl (1967) pp. 35-46; McDonald (1939) p. 140.

23. Vell. Pat. 2.15.2.

24. See 1.1, 2.

25. 1.3 and Wiseman (1971) pp. 53-64.

26. Nep. *Cato* 3; Cato frs. 51, 73, 76P; Vell. Pat. 2.4.4; Val. Max. 6.2.3; *ORF*[3] p. 144. Cf. Earl (1967) p. 44.

27. Contra Toynbee pp. 106-15 who suggests that the strain put upon Romano–Italian relations in the Hannibalic War bred a lasting climate of suspicion. I do not think, however, that the evidence will support this view.

28. Cf. 3.2.

29. Cf. Wiseman (1983) p. 299.

30. Harris (1971) pp. 171-2, 187; Salmon (1967) p. 329, n. 3; J.-M. David, 'Les orateurs des municipes à Rome: integration, reticences et snobismes', in *Bourgeoises* pp. 309-23. Wiseman (1971) p. 53 argues that law-court slander about rustic origin should not be taken at its face value. I suggest that it should. As he himself recognises (p. 63) and as I have tried to demonstrate, a degree of social integration is not incompatible with the existence of a deep rooted snobbery. We should recognise that Roman attitudes were complex.

31. Vell. Pat. 2.15.2.

32. See 1.2.

33. Scaevola: Greenidge and Clay pp. 122-3. For Roman worries

about the treatment of allies see Diod. Sic. 34/35.33.3-6; Sall. *Cat.* 10. Note also Lintott (1972) pp. 632-4. Smith (1955) p. 68 suggests that the bestowal of citizenship on all Italy was a concept new to Rome which still had the outlook of a city-state. The earlier more generous enfranchisement policy would seem to tell against this theory.

34. (1970/1) pp. 395-6.

35. Treggiari pp. 11-20; Sherwin-White (1973) pp. 323-7; K. Hopkins, *Conquerors and Slaves*, Cambridge, 1978 p. 117, 127-8, 147.

36. Some scholars, e.g. Reid (1878) p. 12 and Sherwin-White (1973) pp. 322-3, have commented on the fact that while slaves found it easy to become Romans freemen did not. The integral part manumission played in their life and their ability to control it furnishes a reasonable explanation of why the Romans suffered this situation to continue.

37. I am unable to see why Salmon (1969) p. 102 thinks these expulsions might have strengthened Roman convictions of their own superiority.

38. We should bear in mind that they actually professed to dislike expulsions, cf. Cic. *de Offic.* 3.47.

39. App. B.C. 1.34.

40. The confining of the Italians to a certain number of tribes after 89 (4.1) precisely parallels the treatment of freedmen in 169. In both cases the reason is the same: to limit the voting power of the foreign element. The difference is that the threat from the freedmen was perceived much earlier.

41. Cf. Richardson p. 5.

42. Flor. 2.6.7.

Part Three
The Social War

3.1

The Rebellion of Italia

We saw that Drusus and his initiative represented for the Italians[1] the last opportunity for obtaining the citizenship peacefully. If he were to fail then they were determined to go to war (2.2). And, as the tribune's campaign began to falter we noted how, in the closing weeks of his life, conspiracies began to come to a head. Envoys had passed between the various communities, a league was formed and hostages were exchanged as a surety of good faith.[2] The Romans, suspecting something was afoot, sent spies to the affected areas in order to discover more exactly what was happening.[3] They were evidently intended to supply information to the praetors who were already keeping watch in certain parts of the country. The latter would appear to have taken up duty sometime before, perhaps in response to the threat posed by the abortive attempt to assassinate the consuls earlier in the year.[4]

We know who some of these praetors were. Q. Servilius was sent to Asculum together with his legate Fonteius.[5] He is variously described in our sources as praetor, proconsul and legate. This has led to the suggestion that he may have been operating in 90 and not in 91.[6] Servilius, as we shall soon see, was responsible for starting the war and there are good reasons for believing those authorities who place that event firmly in 91.[7] Therefore, we must, with Mommsen, assume that he was a praetor who had been given an *imperium pro consule*. We may suspect that the position of Ser. Sulpicius Galba in Lucania paralleled that of Servilius. He, too, held the rank of praetor and was captured when the rebellion broke out. He managed to escape, however, with the aid of a woman with whom he lodged.[8] Rather more mysterious is the status and identity of that Domitius who persuaded Poppaedius to desist from his march on

117

Rome. If he was an envoy specially despatched by the senate to deal with this situation, then he may, as Walton suggests, be Cn. Domitius Ahenobarbus cos. 96. On the other hand, if we regard him as a praetor having a special responsibility for an area then he might be the Domitius Ahenobarbus who was later killed by Pompey in Africa.[9] As the siege of Aesernia commenced in 91 it seems reasonable to suppose that L. Cornelius Scipio Asiagenus and L. Acilius whose presence is attested there were praetors who had taken refuge in the town.[10] But since the siege of Nola probably did not commence until 90, it is possibly best to assign the praetorship of its commander Postumius to that year.[11]

The Italians were now ripe for revolt and all that was lacking was some stimulus to galvanise them into action. As I have remarked, Servilius obliged. One of the Roman agents in Picenum spotted a hostage leaving and informed the praetor. He immediately went to the town where a festival was being held and so sorely provoked the inhabitants that they murdered him and Fonteius. They then massacred every Roman they could lay their hands on.[12] From this beginning the rebellion spread first to the Marsi and the Paeliginians and then to the other nations which were to make up the Sabellic group of rebels in the north-central area of Italy.[13] Alba Fucens, which like all Latin colonies save Venusia remained loyal to Rome, was soon put under siege.[14] The Picentines lived up to the reputation for fierceness which they had acquired at the outset by torturing and abusing all of their fellow-countrymen who refused to join in the uprising.[15] The Vestini were quick to imitate their example. Pinna had seemingly at first elected to rise and had given children as hostages. When the townsfolk subsequently changed their minds and decided to observe their treaty with Rome they were put under siege and the hostages were paraded before the walls with the threat that they would be killed if their parents would not surrender. When the latter refused the insurgents carried out their threat. The sacrifice was, however, in vain and the town was eventually forced to yield.[16]

In the south, the Lucanians and Samnites, in what was to be the Sabellian area of the rebellion, who were a party to the conspiracy from the start, were not slow to follow their northern allies. We already saw the praetor Galba running for his life from Lucania. Aesernia served as a temporary refuge for those Romans fleeing from Samnium and Apulia before they made their way to Rome. The place was not long destined to play this role however. The Samnites were in hot pursuit and they very soon blockaded the town.[17]

The Social War had begun.[18] As Livy pointed out, people in times of stress readily believed that prodigies could occur. Even though reports of such happenings often rested on the flimsiest authority, they were, nevertheless, prepared to accept them as signs of a great disaster which was about to befall. The period of the Social War was no exception and it will, therefore, not be out of place for us to furnish a representative sample of the kind of omens which awoke fear and foreboding in the minds of men. At Aesernia, which was to figure so prominently in the conflict, a flame shot from the ground. As was fitting for ringleaders of the rebellion, the Marsi saw a woman give birth to a snake, a creature revered by that people. The Vestini endured a rain of stones and sherds while in Cumae a statue was observed to sweat. There were reports, too, of domesticated animals becoming crazy and fleeing from their masters. Such were the kinds of signs which were believed to foretell war.[19]

Not all of Italy rose in revolt, however. Undoubtedly the most important group to remain loyal to Rome were the Latins. With one exception, they followed the example of steadfastness set by Aesernia and Alba. Venusia alone defected and this may possibly be due to a postulated Oscan element in the town. The comparatively generous policy which the Romans had pursued towards the Latins now paid handsome dividends. Those who in the early days had played a prominent part in the agitation for the citizenship now remained quiescent. The granting of citizenship *per magistratum* had given the ruling classes all that they asked for. Thus, seeing no need to have recourse to arms, they held their people fast to their allegiance and dutifully supplied Rome with troops when she called for them.[20] Even where the rebellion did spread, after its beginnings in Asculum and Samnium, not all joined it with equal alacrity. So, in Apulia and Campania men waited until insurgents arrived from elsewhere before joining in. Eventually, however, twelve nations stood out in arms against Rome. They were: the Marsi, the Paeligni, the Vestini, the Marrucini, the Picentes, the Frentani, the Hirpini, the Campani, the Venusini, the Apuli, the Lucani and the Samnites.[21]

A comparison between this list of rebels and the list of places affected by the Gracchan land commission is most instructive. Who the latter were may be deduced from finds of *cippi*, from the evidence of centuriation and from notices in the *Liber Coloniarum*. Naturally, care is necessary in the interpretation of this evidence. For instance, it has been pointed out that the presence of a *cippus* in a particular spot might not necessarily mean the territory in question belongs to a neighbouring community. Nevertheless, making all due allowances for such considerations, it has been plausibly conjectured that the following areas suffered in some degree from the attentions of the triumvirs: Campania, Lucania, Samnium, the Ager Gallicus and Picenum, Apulia, Etruria and the Paeligni. In addition, we saw that the part played by the Latins in the events of the Gracchan age also suggests that they too were hard hit by the resumption of *ager publicus*.[22] The broad similarity between this catalogue and the roll call of rebels have led some scholars to see an element of continuity between the Gracchan age and the outbreak of the Social War.[23] It has been suggested that the binding factor is fear of encroachment (in one form or another) on Italian land.[24] However, the case of the Marsi, if no other, tells against this theory. Their lands appear to have been largely untouched and yet they are among the ringleaders of the rebellion.[25] In fact, although the allies did not particularly like parting with land, they were ready to do so both in the time of Flaccus and again in the time of the younger Drusus if something substantial could be gained in return. Therefore, while I would accept that there is a connection between the Gracchan age and the Social War, I would suggest that it is of a different order from that which has been postulated. Many of those whose property was menaced in 125 were ready to swap land for status. A generation later, the same peoples were ready once more to strike a similar bargain. In other words, the nations whom Flaccus and Gracchus had taught to regard citizenship as an attainable goal were the same nations who revolted some thirty years later in exasperation at the final refusal.[26]

The line from Flaccus and C. Gracchus to the Social War is straight and clear. Many of those for whom they had laboured and died take up arms against Rome in the war. It was the peculiar achievement of the pair to have taught the Italians that they might aspire to the citizenship and it comes as no surprise to discover that their pupils at last became rebels. Once the notion that an Italian could become a citizen took hold those who cherished it never let it go and the continued frustration of the ideal eventually drove Italy to rebel. It is, then, no exaggeration to say that the Social War is the legacy of the Gracchan age.

The pacts which the rebel nations made with each other and secured by the exchange of hostages formed the basis of the great league or confederacy which was to fight Rome. We must now see how this confederacy was organised.[27] Corfinium was chosen as the federal capital. With its name changed to Italica it was to replace Rome as the focus of loyalty for the insurgents and was to be the centre of the new state Italia.[28] As rebel headquarters the town was abundantly stocked with money, food and war materials. Here, too, were installed the organs of Government. The Italians had a senate consisting of five hundred members. How these were chosen we do not know but we must assume that this assembly contained representatives from all the insurgent nations.[29] The senate, in turn, entrusted the direction of the war to a special council drawn from among its own members.[30] We are fortunate in being able to catch some glimpse of this council at work. Upon assuming office it decreed that two consuls and twelve praetors should be chosen annually to prosecute the war and these were to be elected by the full muster of the army.[31] Again, a decree relating to the disposal of war dead, which was designed to boost morale must have emanated from this same source. Although a great deal will have been left to the discretion of the individual commander on the spot, the high degree of co-ordination shown by the allied armies in the first year of the war and the swiftness with which one district brought aid to another argues that the rebel campaign was being directed by one central authority.[32]

It is indisputable that most of what we know of the constitutional arrangements of the allies shows them ordering their affairs with a view to one immediate object; the successful waging of a war. We are singularly ill-informed as to how they proposed to conduct their business in other spheres. For instance, we know they hoped to win but not what they actually proposed to do precisely with their victory. Would Rome be destroyed or would she be incorporated as a member of Italia?[33] And the empire?[34] Was it to be ruled henceforth from Italica? In point of fact, it is doubtful if the confederates devoted much thought to questions such as these. The waging of an all out war must have absorbed most of their energies and largely precluded detailed speculation about a doubtful future. Nevertheless, what we do know of the federal government suggests it would not only be capable of conducting a war but of taking decisions with regard to other matters as well.[35]

I would say that it is most unlikely that the senate, representative as it was of all the nations, should have its functions limited
to delegating its authority over war to a council. Indeed, the very
act of delegation shows it had real powers to hand over and
implies that, in parting with some of them, it retained others. Just
how wide these powers were we cannot say until we have
answered another question: did the confederacy have a primary
assembly as well as a senate? H.D. Meyer answered this question in
the affirmative and pointed to two circumstances which seemed
to support his argument.[36] Firstly, Diodorus tells us that the rebels
built a senate house and a spacious forum in Italica. Since the
confederacy had a short life we may beg leave to doubt if this
ever actually happened. Nevertheless, the mere intent to do such
a thing would, so Meyer suggests, indicate that a primary
assembly would one day fill the forum. Secondly, the method
by which army leaders were chosen would seem to point towards
the existence of just such a body.

I do not find these arguments totally convincing. When the
rebels created Italica they intended it should replace Rome as the
capital of Italy. It was entirely appropriate therefore that this new
capital should equal or surpass the old in splendour and outward
magnificence.[37] Hence, while a great forum might very well be
designed for an assembly it need not necessarily be so. Equally
plausibly it could be said that it was designed to impress. Nor
does the method of choosing the commanders necessarily imply
the existence of a primary assembly either. When the council
took charge of the war, it was empowered to act as it saw fit in any
given situation. Thus, when it was faced with the task of
appointing commanders to what was, after all, a confederate
army made up of men from diverse nations who, though
prepared to co-operate with others, would not normally form
mixed units they adopted a commonsense approach. In the
situation as it stood it was obviously most desirable that the men
of each nation should choose and follow their own generals. It
therefore follows that it is wrong to base any general conclusions
as to the nature of the allied constitution on a single decision
which was made to deal with a specific problem.[38]

It would appear then, that the confederacy had but one
decision-making body, the senate. Further, its unique position
and what we know of its actions renders inescapable the
conclusion that its powers were of the widest.[39] As the body which
alone represented all of the rebel nations it was solely responsible

for deciding all questions which concerned the confederacy as a whole.

One of the distinguishing characteristics of any independent state is that it issues a distinctive coinage of its own and so Italia produced monies bearing legends in either Latin or Oscan.[40] The former were most likely struck in the northern part of the confederacy while the latter came from the south. This, of course, does not imply any kind of disunity. The coinage appears to have circulated as a whole over the entire rebel territory and it reflects the hopes and achievements of the allies.[41] Although the Italians inevitably borrowed many of their types from Roman coins since that was the model with which they were most familiar, they adapted their borrowings to suit their own purposes.[42] Their money, therefore, may be fairly said to proclaim their pretensions, aspirations and successes.

The exact chronology of this coinage is difficult to establish.[43] Fortunately, much of what the coins have to tell us is timeless in that it is a reflection of rebel sentiments which were constant at all periods throughout the Social War. Therefore we do not always need to know exactly when a coin was issued in order to be able to interpret it. In other cases, where it would appear that reference is being made to a specific incident plausible conjectures as to what it might be can sometimes be made.[44]

The commonest figure which occurs on the obverse of the confederate coinage is that of Italia, whether as a head or a bust. In one or two instances we also find her being crowned by a victory.[45] The presence of such a figure requires no gloss. Bacchus also figures on obverses. He is Liber Pater who presides over the fertility of the fields and was the symbol of liberty.[46] His presence on the reverse of one has also been suspected and there he is thought to be accompanied by a panther.[47] Both obverses and reverses feature the Dioscuri. This was especially fitting since they were of a warlike character and greatly revered by the inhabitants of the Italian states. The Dioscuri had once fought for Rome, now it was hoped they would fight for Italy.[48] Finally, it may be noted that the head of Mars has been detected on certain obverses.[49]

Arguably the most interesting of all the scenes depicted on the reverses is that of the oath. With some variations in detail, most notably in the number of participants, all of these coins show warriors with drawn swords sacrificing a pig. What we have here is a graphic pictorial representation of those oaths which the Italians made with each other when they leagued together to fight

Rome. The steel may be held to represent the constancy not only of the god by whom they swore but also of those actually taking the oath. The fate of the pig, an animal much used in Italian sacrifices, would be that of any perjurer.[50] Thus the Italians proclaim their unity and their (so to speak) steely resolve. What these convenanters hoped to achieve is vividly illustrated on another set of reverse scenes which show the bull of Italy (or Samnium) goring the wolf of Rome. This image and the sentiment which informed it endured in Italian consciousness down to the very end of their resistance. In 82, before the walls of Rome, Pontius Telesinus reminded his men that they had come to destroy the wolves who, for so long, had preyed on Italy.[51] As one might expect, scenes depicting victory figure prominently on the Italian coins. Some show Italia seated on a pile of shields while holding a spear and a parazonium. Behind stands a Victory who is crowning her. A triumphal note is struck in another issue which shows Italia riding in a biga. Elsewhere a seated Victory appears carrying a laurel-branch.[52] Other monies have a warrior wearing a helmet and a cloak and carrying a spear. His left foot rests on a Roman standard and by his side is a recumbent bull. Some issues also have a trophy.[53] Undoubtedly some of these coins must advertise the very real and solid achievements of the allies in the early days of the war. Others, however, especially those to which numismatists assign a late date, cannot be anything more than pious expressions of vain hopes.[54]

It is not known exactly when the rebels ceased to mint. Numismatists seem to feel that 87 is the most likely date and one could not quarrel with it on historical grounds. In that year, all Italians became citizens and, although some were still to maintain what was virtually an independent existence, it would appear unlikely that they continued to coin.[55]

I suggested earlier that the rebels probably had made no detailed plans as to what they might do if they should be victorious. Yet it is self-evident they must have had a broad general aim and all the indications are that that aim was independence. Essentially the Italian demand for the citizenship was a demand for equality with the Romans. When it became clear that peaceful agitation had failed they were left with two choices. They might try to wrest the coveted citizenship from the Romans by force of arms or they might recoil entirely and seek to make themselves equals by gaining complete independence from Rome. I would maintain that it was the latter course they embraced. In the first instance, it may be claimed that such a reaction would be entirely natural for aggrieved men who had long had to endure Roman arrogance and intransigence and who had now been goaded beyond endurance. It is not straining credulity to suggest that, believing they would never obtain their rights from Rome, they determined to have no more to do with her and to establish them for themselves. Moreover, if I am right about the implications of their loyalty to Italy and of their pride in their own communities (1.2) then we may go so far as to say that the rebuff suffered in 91 made it inevitable that the Italians should seek independence.

Our ancient evidence strongly suggests that this was, indeed, how things fell out. Sherwin-White emphasises that the more explicit sources speak of the rebellion as a 'breaking away' from Rome. In other words, it was a defection aimed at establishing independence.[56] Further, as we discovered in our examination of the structure of its constitution, the confederacy was equipped for dealing with much more than the simple direction of a war, something which would not have been necessary if the allies merely wished to force the Romans to yield the citizenship. Indeed, the very existence of such a creation as Italia furnishes the strongest argument of all for the view that independence was the allies' goal. All that we know of it suggests it was set up in deliberate opposition to Rome, that it was totally independent of her and that it was intended to be permanent. The actual names Italia and Italica clearly show it was intended to be representative of the peninsula as a whole and as such was a direct challenge to the dominance of the single city of Roma. And that city was to be replaced as the centre of Italian loyalties by the new capital whose forum and senate house showed that the insurgents intended it should endure. The government lodged there certainly bore little resemblance to the Roman model. A senate of five hundred members representative of all the nations, a special war council and commanders who would concern themselves only with military matters have little or nothing in common with the Roman senate, popular assemblies and magistrates who exercise civil and military authority. Finally, we should remember the coinage. The very fact that it was issued at all argues that it emanated from a body which thought of itself as a sovereign state and expected that those who owed it allegiance should use it in place of Roman money. Nor do the symbols that body placed on the coins leave much room for doubt as to its objective. It was nothing less than the defeat of Rome.

We cannot deny, however, that there were those among the rebels who harboured slightly more modest ambitions. After all some sources do speak of citizenship as the allied goal and we have evidence that, during the war, they did indeed try to extract it from the Romans.[57] Sometime after the rebellion had broken out the insurgents sent a delegation to Rome to say that although they had helped build the empire, they had been denied the citizenship. It is, I think, legitimate to infer from this that even now the rebellion could be called off if the Romans would but yield.[58] Likewise we learn of parleys during 90 and 89 at which Romans and Italians discussed the questions of peace and citizenship. It has been plausibly conjectured that a change in Roman attitudes, as indicated by the lex Julia, brought about the last of these discussions. When the insurgents saw the Romans prepared to grant citizenship, they immediately tried to take advantage of the new situation.[59] Thus, it is tolerably clear that some among the rebels were still prepared to toy with the notion of gaining the citizenship.

Indeed, if we look behind the broad banner of independence under which the allies marched to war, we find a familiar phenomenon: a broad range of attitudes among the rebel nations. At one extreme we have a place like Pinna which refused to rise at all. Close to it in outlook are the Etrurians and Umbrians. Only a few of them bestirred themselves tardily late in 90. The rest were content to remain loyal when the lex Julia offered them citizenship. In contrast Apulia and Campania waited but a little while before joining in. Among the ringleaders we find the Marsi prepared to be seduced by the idea of citizenship. Others were made of sterner stuff and actually contemplated the destruction of Rome itself.[60]

Now while it hardly needs to be said that it is important we recognise the existence of these shades of opinion, it is equally important that we form a just appreciation of their significance. In my view, their presence in no way takes from the validity of my thesis that the Social War was a war of independence and, I would further add that, paradoxically, they are yet another indication of Italian unity. If we are right in assuming that the embassy which went to Rome after the rebellion had started had still some hope of gaining the citizenship then yet again we are witnessing something else with which we are well familiar: the allies would go to great lengths in order to obtain the citizenship without bloodshed and only when all hope, however slight, was removed would they have recourse to arms. So, an attempt to make the Romans give way even at this late stage is not surprising. I do not pretend to say who in the confederate senate was behind it but when it inevitably failed it is self evident that they wholeheartedly embraced the ideal of independence and joined in the vigorous prosecution of the war. Subsequent parleys were no more than light flirtations. At no time did any ally break ranks or violate his oath. All remained loyal to the covenant which bound them and fought on until they were crushed in the field. When the citizenship came it was not because the Italians had asked for it but because the Romans chose to give it. In other words, whatever differences of opinion existed among the allies they were not sufficiently strong to lead them to seriously waver from their resolve to remain united and fight for independence.[61]

Notes

1. Although the Latins as a whole did not take part in the revolt we shall continue to speak of 'Italians' when dealing with the rebels. On a pedantic level this is justified by the participation of Venusia in the rebellion. On a broader perspective the rebels claimed themselves to represent all Italy and they certainly had hopes of winning over the Latins to their side (see below).

2. App. B.C. 1.38; Liv. ep.71.

3. App. B.C. 1.38. Because Appian's chronology is wrong (see 4.1) it is difficult to say when exactly these men were sent out but towards the end of Drusus' life seems the most likely occasion. The march on Rome by Poppaedius (2.2) must have warned the Romans that something was afoot.

4. App. B.C. 1.38, cf. 2.2 and 4.1. Self-evidently the praetors were already at work before the spies arrived.

5. Diod. Sic. 37.13.2; Liv. ep.72; Vell. Pat. 2.15.1; Flor. 2.6.9; App. B.C. 1.38; Oros. 5.18.8; Cic. *Font.* 41, 48; Schol. Bob. p. 81 St.

6. *MRR* 2.24, n. 4.

7. Vell. Pat. 2.15.1; Oros. 5.18.1; Eutrop. 5.3; Pliny *NH* 33.55. See 4.1.

8. Liv. ep.72 with *MRR* 2.24, n. 6 and Salmon (1967) p. 337. See also Appendix I.

9. *MRR* 2.69.

10. App. B.C. 1.41 with Gabba (1967) p. 134. See further next note.

11. Liv. ep.73; App. B.C. 1.42. Cf. 3.2. On the status of these three men see further Dom. p. 17; Salmon (1967) p. 337; Haug p. 239.

12. Sources: n. 5 The trouble may have started in the theatre if, as is usually assumed, Diod. Sic. 37.12 refers to this incident. According to

this account there were many Romans (Ῥωμαίων) in the theatre when somebody killed (κατέσφαζαν) an actor who spoke too boldly. The Picentes then resolved to have revenge by killing Saunio, an actor pleasing to the Romans. He, however, escaped by reminding them he was a Latin. For the story to have point the Romans must be the subject of κατέσφαζαν and thus the murderers of the first actor. Thus Ῥωμαίων should actually refer to the Picentes since to take the phrase literally or to emend to Ῥωμαῖον would make nonsense of the passage. What we would seem to have here is an example of the excerptor's clumsiness (Walton). Another example will be found in 37.15.1, cf. Keaveney (1979) pp. 452-3 and 3.2.

I have often wondered if the festival might not have been in honour of Picus, the mythical founder of Asculum (Strabo 5.4.3; Sil. It. 8.440). This might have the effect of heightening nationalist sentiment and murderous passions.

13. Vell. Pat. 2.15.1; Eutrop. 5.3; App. *Mith.* 22. See Letta p. 105 on the prominence of the Marsi.

14. Liv. ep.72; *Auct. ad Herr.* 2.45. Cf. Beloch. p. 450.

15. Dio fr. 98.3.

16. Diod. Sic. 37.19.3-20, cf. Beloch p.598. Walton postulates the existence of pro- and anti-Roman parties in the town while Haug p. 220 points out that the children must be hostages. The town's fall is inferred from Val. Max. 5.47.

17. Sisenna fr. 6P; Liv. ep. 72. Cf. Beloch p. 450.

18. For this and the other names by which the war is known see Dom. pp. 3-5 and Haug pp. 234-9. Further treatment of the chronology of the opening of the war will be found in 4.1.

19. Livy 21.62.1; Obsequens 54; Oros. 5.18.3; Aug. *Civ. Dei* 3.23; Pliny *NH* 2.98-99, 7.34-35, 8.221; Cic. *de Div.* 2.54. See Haug p. 207 and Keaveney apud Deroux p. 52, n. 42.

20. Liv. ep.72.

21. Salmon (1967) p. 316, n. 3, 326-7, 340-4. The Bruttii may have been subsumed in the Lucani (Magaldi p. 171, n. 1) since the view that they did not rebel at all — Salmon (1967) p. 340 — is untenable, cf. 3.3 and 4.2. The Umbrians and Etrurians are a special case and so are not included in the list, see n. 26 and 3.2.

22. Nagle (1970) pp. 385-90; Badian (1971) pp. 397-9; Salmon (1967) pp. 332-3; M. Pani, 'Su un nuovo cippo graccana Dauno', *Ist. Lom.* (*Rend. Lett.*) 111, 1977 pp. 389-400; 2.1.

23. The apparent anomaly of the absence of the Latins from the rebel ranks has already been explained.

24. Nagle (1973); Carcopino (1929).

25. Letta pp. 105-6.

26. It seems reasonable to suppose that some of those whose land was menaced in 125 did not want the citizenship and that they would, therefore, be unwilling to part with it. By 91, the Etrurians and Umbrians alone would appear to have persisted in this attitude, at least to the extent of wanting the citizenship but being unwilling to make sacrifices for it (2.2).

27. The two principal sources are Diod. Sic. 37.2.4-7 and Strabo 5.4.2.

28. 'Federal capital' (Walton) seems preferable to 'capital city' (Salmon 1967 p. 348) as a translation of Diodorus' κοινὴ πόλις, which expression is also found in Strabo. He, together with Vell. Pat. 2.16.4 and Macrob. 1.11.24 calls the city Italica. It would appear from the coinage (see below) that the name Italia which Diod. gives it was, in fact, the name of the league whose capital it was. On the reasons for siting the capital here see Salmon (1967) p. 349.

29. As Meyer pp. 75-6 emphasises. There is no support in our sources for the tentative suggestion of Salmon (1967) p. 350 that a primary assembly chose the senate, cf. below. I would guess that each nation chose a fixed number of representatives to send to the senate.

30. Here see Meyer p. 76 rather than Walton. As he points out (pp. 78-9) this council was exclusively concerned with war.

31. Cf. Meyer pp. 76-7 and further below.

32. See 3.2.

33. The two occasions (Diod. Sic. 37.13; Vell. Pat. 2.27.2) on which the destruction of Rome was proposed do not, I think, necessarily furnish a clue as to what might have happened had the allies achieved total victory.

34. See *Auct. ad Herr.* 4.13.

35. As Salmon (1967) pp. 349-50 points out, Diodorus' statement that the rebels copied the Roman constitution is misleading.

36. pp. 76-9.

37. This is implied particularly by Diodorus but see Strabo also.

38. See also Sherwin-White (1973) p. 147.

39. In my view Meyer pp. 78-9 tends to underestimate the senate's importance. It has been suggested to me that aristocrats might fear an unruly popular assembly. In view of the tight control exercised by the lords of Italy over their followers, this seems to me unlikely.

40. Some bore no legends and one (Sydenham no. 636) is bilingual.

41. Crawford (1964) p. 145. Voirol p. 65 believes that Sydenham no 636 expresses unity but see Crawford (1964) p. 146. For further remarks on rebel unity see below.

42. Crawford (1964) p. 155; Bernareggi pp. 86-9. The inspiration for Sydenham no. 643 is, of course, a coin of Amisus, cf. 3.3.

43. The latest classification is that of Crawford (1964) pp. 145-8.

44. Examples will be found in 3.2 and 3.

45. Sydenham nos. 617-27, 629, 630-2, 634-6, 642. It should be noted that no. 626 may never have existed, cf. Grueber, p. 327, n. 1 and Crawford (1964) p. 155. Sydenham hesitantly identifies the figure on nos. 637-9 as Italia. Grueber p. 332 is confident of this identification in the case of no. 639 (and also no. 640) but believes (p. 331, 35, 36) that Mars is in question in nos. 637-8. See n. 49.

46. Sydenham nos. 628, 641, cf. Grueber p. 327, n. 2. The Bacchus of no. 643 is an altogether different matter, see 3.3.

47. Sydenham no. 631, cf. Crawford (1964) p. 147. Some, however, believe the scene is Hercules with a bull and if this is so, see Grueber p. 339, n. 1 for an explanation of his presence on the coin.

48. Sydenham nos. 617, 625, 633, 635-6, cf. Grueber p. 326, n. 2, p. 338, n. 1 and Mattingly in Sydenham p. 222. Voirol p. 65 believes no. 636

expresses the Italian desire for equality with Rome but this, perhaps, reads too much into the piece.

49. Sydenham no. 640 and see n. 45 above. See Crawford (1964) p. 148 and Voirol p. 66.

50. Sydenham nos. 619-21, 629, 634, 640. See A. Keaveney and J.A. Madden, 'The oath at A.P. V. 245.3', *JHS* 98, 1978 p. 161, n. 9 and Salmon (1967) p. 178. There is no significance in the variations in the number of warriors (Grueber p. 323, n. 1.). Because he attempts to analyse no. 640 without reference to others with a similar scene, it seems to me that Voirol's interpretation of it (p. 66) should not be accepted.

51. Sydenham nos. 628, 641. Telesinus: Vell. Pat. 2.27.2. Voirol pp. 66-7 believes that no. 628 represents a hardening of attitudes among the allies as the war progressed. I, however, have no difficulty in believing they could have harboured such feelings from the beginning, see 1.2 and further below. It may also be noted that Crawford (1964) p. 164 places these issues fairly early in the war.

52. Sydenham nos. 618, 622-4, 633. Sydenham suggests that the figure in no. 633 may be Minerva.

53. Sydenham nos. 627, 630, 638-9, 642, cf. Grueber p. 328, n. 1. For theories as to who the warrior represents see Bernareggi pp. 76-7.

54. Cf. Crawford (1964) pp. 147-8. The occurrence of the word Safinim (= Samnitium) on Sydenham no. 639 probably indicates it was issued when only the Samnites still resisted, cf. Voirol p. 67; Grueber p. 332, n. 1.

55. Crawford (1964) pp. 147-8; Voirol p. 67; 4.2.

56. (1973) pp. 144-6.

57. See Sherwin-White (1973) pp. 144-6 although I feel he may be inclined to underestimate the importance of this phenomenon.

58. App. B.C. 1.39. It is not altogether clear when exactly this delegation was sent but it must have been sometime in the winter of 91/90, cf. 4.1.

59. Diod. Sic. 37.15; Front. *Strat* 1.5.17; Cic. *Phil.* 12.27, cf. 3.2., 3. The negotiations between Metellus and the Samnites, invoked in this context by Sherwin-White (1973) p. 146, n. 3, are not, in my opinion, relevant. See further 4.2.

60. See 3.2, 3 and 4.2.

61. In my opinion the best modern discussion of the aims of the allies in this war will be found in the acute and sensitive treatment of Sherwin-White (1973) pp. 134-49. It seems to me that Brunt *JRS* (1965) pp. 93-7 fails to do justice to the complexity of the contemporary scene.

3.2

The Social War 90 BC

With the coming of spring the allies set in motion the armies they had mobilised. Their object was simple: to break out of their own areas and spread the insurrection in places hitherto untouched. The Romans naturally had as their aim the frustration of such intentions. One of the great obstacles to the advancing Italians was a number of fortified cities which remained loyal to Rome; a good deal of the year's fighting therefore centred on these places as the Italians strove to take them while the Romans tried to beat them back.[1]

However, the first campaign we learn of on the northern front runs clean contrary to this picture of Roman defensiveness. What appears to have been an advance into enemy territory by Pompey Strabo has been attended with a fair deal of scholarly controversy. According to Orosius (5.18.10) he was defeated by the Picentes early in the year. Two other pieces of evidence would seem to indicate he was laying siege to Asculum. A sling bullet with the name T. Lafrenius was found near Asculum. Since this man died before the siege which led to the city's fall the missile must have been used in an earlier assault. Furthermore, a passage of Frontinus has been taken to refer to just such a siege.[2]

Scholars usually try to bring this evidence into harmony with what App. B.C. 1.47 has to tell us. It is often suggested that some of the events narrated there do not belong, as they seem to, to the end of the year but take place earlier, at the time of which Orosius speaks.[3] Alternatively some have argued that Orosius has got things wrong and that the rest of the evidence for an early defeat of Pompey Strabo can also be argued away. It would then follow that his notice should properly refer to what happened later in the year.[4] In my opinion neither of these views should be accepted. I would agree with J. Carcopino[5] that the incidents in

Orosius and Appian are, in fact, completely separate and what both authors have to tell us is fully worthy of credence.[6]

U. Laffi has convincingly demonstrated that Asculum was not besieged early in the year. As he points out, the sling bullet was not found before the town but about 20 kilometres away. This effectively disposes of the evidence for Lafrenius' presence at a siege there. I am not as sure as Laffi seems to be that the Frontinus passage actually has to refer to the siege at the year's end. I would prefer to say that such is its brevity and its vagueness that it is impossible to assign it with confidence to any date and it should not, therefore, be invoked to support any particular theory.[7] Furthermore, I shall try to demonstrate at the appropriate point in this chapter that events later in the year fell out exactly as App. B.C. 1.47 says they did and that nothing in his narrative can be assigned to a putative earlier siege. Thus we are left with Oros. 5.18.10. It should be carefully noted that he does not speak of a siege but only of a defeat. Moreover, we may point out that he clearly differentiates between the earlier action of Strabo's and the later one which is also described by Appian.[8] This strongly suggests that no confusion exists in his narrative and it would therefore follow that his evidence could only be overthrown if it were to be demonstrated that a defeat for Pompey Strabo could not have taken place at the time he says it did. Laffi, indeed, attempts to do this but his argument is not particularly strong.[9] He rightly points out that Roman strategy in the earlier part of 90 was largely defensive. He then goes on to claim that Pompey in consequence would not have gone over to the attack. This is an overly schematic view. As our story unfolds we shall see that Roman commanders did take the offensive when the occasion was right. And I would suggest that a man like Pompey Strabo would not be slow to seize such an opportunity if one presented itself.

We may therefore postulate that Pompey Strabo was operating out of the Latin colony of Firmum. From here he advanced against Asculum only to meet with and be defeated by a force of Picentes. He was then forced to retreat to his base.[10]

This was not the only reverse the Romans suffered at this time on the northern front. The legate Perperna made a bid to raise the siege of Alba Fucens but was overwhelmed by the Italian commander Praesenteius. So great was the disaster that Rutilius deprived Perperna of his command and gave the remnant of his army to Marius.[11]

Nor did any more cheerful news come from the southern front for the Romans. There the consul L. Julius Caesar was to spend almost the entire year combatting the rebel threat to Aesernia in Samnium and Acerrae in Campania. It was Aesernia which first received his attention. On his way to relieve the town he fell in with a mixed force of Marsians and Samnites possibly near Atina. These were commanded by Vettius Scato and were apparently coming to reinforce the besiegers. The result was a defeat for the consul. With two thousand of his men dead on the field he pulled back to Teanum Sidicinum and left Scato free to proceed on his way to Aesernia.[12] Roman attempts to bring aid to the town were now made even more difficult by the fall of Venafrum to the enemy. Aided by treachery within Marius Egnatius and his Samnites captured it at about this time.[13]

Elsewhere in the south, at the time of Caesar's defeat, the picture was one of a steady and relentless rebel advance. In Lucania, P. Licinius Crassus the legate was attacked by Lamponius the local praetor. Lamponius firmly believed that if the Italian aristocracy claimed the right to lead their peoples wherever they wished then they should give concrete demonstrations of their fitness for that role. In pursuance of this principle he himself rushed headlong at Crassus during the battle. The Roman's discomfiture was completed with the destruction of his camp. Lamponius had fired some woodland nearby and the flames had engulfed the camp so that Crassus, thoroughly routed, was obliged to take refuge in the nearby Roman colony of Grumentum.[14]

This account must now be brought into harmony with some other ancient notices which speak of a Roman capture of Grumentum and of the destruction of the town.[15] There are a number of possibilities. If, on the basis of Liv. ep.72, we assume the Italians had already captured Grumentum in 91 then we may take it that Crassus had besieged and retaken it before his defeat at the hands of the Lucanians.[16] However, since Grumentum is not specifically mentioned by the epitomator, it is equally plausible to postulate that it only fell into rebel hands after a siege by Lamponius which followed on the defeat of Crassus. Indeed, the general pattern of warfare in this year strongly suggests that the latter was bringing relief to the beleaguered town when he met with his reverse. In support of this view, it may further be pointed out that the place must have been still intact when Crassus chose it as a bolt-hole.[17] Thus its destruction (whether by

Romans or Italians) almost certainly took place at a date subsequent to this defeat of the legate. It would then follow from this that a Roman siege could be as easily numbered among the events of 89 as those of 90.[18]

In Campania, too, the rebels had been scoring striking successes. Aided by treachery, presumably on the part of townsfolk who were sympathetic to his cause, the insurgent consul Papius took Nola. He gave the Roman garrison the option of joining his own army. The common soldiers accepted the offer but their officers refused and were starved to death. Among those who perished in this way was the praetor L. Postumius who held the command here. It has been suggested that this incident shows Papius trying to demonstrate that the blame for the war rested with the Roman upper classes. While this is clearly not impossible it seems to me that more practical considerations will have governed Papius' action. The allies did not have the resources of manpower which were available to the Romans and were therefore obliged to seek recruits wherever they might be found — the employment of a scoundrel like Agamemnon neatly illustrates this point. The desire to augment his army, rather than to make a striking gesture was, I would suggest, Papius' principal motive here. After this he continued his advance to the coast and captured, in succession, Stabiae, Surrentum and Salernum. Here again, he added to his army by impressing slaves and prisoners. Nuceria willingly joined the ranks of the rebels but it was necessary to apply pressure to Pompeii and Herculaneum. Papius was obliged to ravage their territories before they too yielded and furnished him with foot and horse.[19]

Having thus got a grip on port towns the allies were now in a position to launch a naval offensive against the Romans. Details are, unfortunately, scant but it would appear that apart from military targets they attacked in particular vessels bringing corn supplies from Sicily. Roman counter-operations were in the charge of a legate called Otacilius. The insurgents also made raids on the coasts of Latium and that part of Campania which was still in Roman hands. These become so severe that, towards the end of the year, the senate was obliged to enlist freedmen and used them to garrison the coast between the city and Cumae.[20]

Papius' augmented army was at this point joined by the Lucanians who had succeeded in taking Grumentum by now. With these combined forces he advanced on Acerrae. This place was to prove to be the furthest northern point reached by the

Italian drive through Campania for, when Papius laid siege to the town, the consul Caesar hastened (from either Teanum or Capua) to its rescue. At first fortune favoured the allies. Caesar had in his army a number of Numidian and Mauretanian auxiliaries, doubtless supplied by the faithful client King Bocchus. Papius, however, paraded before them in royal garb a man called Oxynta who was a son of Jugurtha and had been set free from captivity in Venusia. Many of the Africans, acknowledging this man as their king, promptly deserted and Caesar was obliged to dismiss the rest as untrustworthy. Papius then attacked and made a breach in the consul's camp. The latter, however, issued from another gate with his cavalry and inflicted a sharp defeat on the rebels. He then withdrew. Since the pressure on Acerrae had been eased he seems to have judged it best to turn his attention to Aesernia once more. But his victory had awoken great enthusiasm among the Romans. The gloom engendered by a long series of defeats which was soon to culminate in a great disaster on the northern front was temporarily lifted. Caesar's success was hailed as a major achievement. In the field the commander was hailed as *imperator* by his troops and at Rome *saga* were now put aside.[21]

The list of allied advances in the south is completed with Apulia. Here the Picentine praetor Vidacilius arrived to stir up the rebellion and the near contemporary pattern of events in Campania was duplicated. Pro- and anti-Roman factions struggled to gain the upper hand. Canusium and Venusia, along with some other towns, voluntarily went over to the rebel side. Others which would not submit were put under siege. Captured Roman citizens were put to death while slaves and others were enrolled in Vidacilius' army.[22]

We may now return to the northern front where Rutilius and his legate Marius had concentrated their forces near each other on the river Tolenus, possibly near Carseoli. When we encounter them they had built bridges across the river and this strongly suggests they were intending to advance along the Via Valeria in another bid to relieve Alba Fucens. They were opposed, however, by the Marsi. Scato who had returned from Atina pitched his camp on the opposite bank closer to Marius than to Rutilius. The widespread belief that Drusus and his supporters had encouraged the Italians to revolt had led to a witch-hunt in Rome after his death and ill-feeling now surfaced in the camp. When it was discovered that intelligence was being leaked to the enemy,

Lupus suspected the patricians in his ranks and laid information against them at Rome only to discover that Marsian spies were responsible. Bad feeling arose too between the consul and Marius who was his kinsman. Rutilius wished to attack but his legate advised delay pointing out that the Roman army was largely composed of raw recruits and that the enemy anyway would soon have to withdraw for lack of provisions. Although the sequel was to show that the experienced soldier had gauged the situation accurately, the consul viewed his advice with suspicion. It was well known that Marius was seeking military *gloria* in order to recover the position of pre-eminence he had once held and Rutilius believed he was merely offering this counsel in order the better to garner for himself the credit which could be gained from the eventual combat.

So the consul persisted with his plan. Even though the liver at the preliminary sacrifice had no head, he launched an attack on the morning of 11 June. Scato who, as we saw, was well informed about what went on in the Roman camp, allowed him to cross the bridge and then sprang his trap. Men whom he had positioned in ambush in some ravines nearby the night before fell upon the Roman army. Many Romans were killed on the spot and others were driven into the river. Rutilius himself was hit on the head by a missile and died soon afterwards. Marius learned of the disaster when he saw the bodies of the dead floating downstream. He instantly crossed the river, routed the enemy who faced him and captured Scato's camp. The Marsi were thus forced to spend the night on the battlefield and, on the next day, retreated because of the failure of food-supplies.[23]

Some consolation for the Romans could be found in the fact that the Paeligni, who were probably advancing at the same time as the Marsi to press upon Roman positions, suffered a severe reverse at the hands of Ser. Sulpicius Galba. Nevertheless the funeral of Rutilius at Rome was the occasion for extravagant displays of grief and mourning. The senate, alarmed at the deteriorating morale thus revealed, decreed that henceforth bodies should be buried where they fell. Apparently similar fears exercised the allied war-council for they soon issued a like proclamation for their own side.[24]

With his hands full, Caesar, the surviving consul, was unable to return to Rome to hold the *comitia* and so nobody was selected in place of Rutilius. Nevertheless a replacement would have to be found for him on the northern front. Marius was the obvious choice but this presented the senate with a dilemma. While wishing to make the fullest possible use of his talents, the fathers did not want to give him the slightest opportunity to further his ambitions. His scope for independent action was therefore to be limited. So they instructed the urban praetor to send somebody with *imperium* to the area. Marius, naturally, was picked but he was regarded as the praetor's delegate and the *imperium* he exercised was the praetor's, not his own. A second rebuff soon followed. When Caepio, who also seems to have been operating in this area, scored a minor success by making a sally against the enemy who besieged him, the senate, ever anxious to keep Marius within bounds, promptly granted him a command on the same terms as the other commander so that the two were now equal in status.

This elevation, however, soon proved to be a mistake for Caepio was unequal to the responsibilities which now rested upon him. Somewhere on the river Tolenus he found himself facing an army of Marsians and Vestinians commanded by Poppaedius the allied supreme commander in the north. Poppaedius made his way to Caepio feigning to be a deserter. As pledges of his good faith he brought with him two slave babes clad in purple whom he said were his own sons and — revealing an intimate knowledge of the Roman character — a mass of base metal plated with gold and silver. Caepio took the Italian and his bullion at their face value and followed him when he offered to bring the Romans to the now leaderless allied army. In reality they were being led into a trap. When they reached the appointed place Poppaedius gave a signal, his men sprang from hiding and slew the greater part of the enemy army together with its commander. After this debacle the senate had no choice but to join the remnant of Caepio's forces with those of Marius.[25]

He seems to have been still uneasy about the quality of his troops but to have decided, nevertheless, to go over to the offensive in order to do something to repair the damage caused by two successive defeats. This view rests on the assumption that here is the most logical point in our narrative sequence for the events narrated in Diod. Sic. 37.15.[26] So the Romans advanced against the victorious Poppaedius. Whether Marius foresaw the result we do not know. What is beyond dispute is that soldiers on both sides recognised friends and relatives and called out friendly greetings to each other. This eventually led to a mass fraternisation. The two commanders, yielding to the spirit of the occasion, came together to discuss the prospects for peace and the citizenship. It also seems reasonable to suppose we can assign to this campaign two incidents narrated by Plut. Mar. 33 although it is somewhat difficult to establish with certainty where they ought to be placed in relation to the story in Diodorus. On one occasion, when an opportunity for attack presented itself, the Romans would not fight and both sides eventually pulled back. Marius, then exclaimed that his men were frightened of the enemy's back while the enemy were scared of their necks. This is probably separate to the incident in Diodorus although it may possibly have been a preliminary to it. Again, we are told that Marius was once surrounded by enemy entrenchments but refused to budge. Poppaedius taunted him by saying if he were a great general he would come out and fight. Marius replied that if Poppaedius was a great commander he would make him. This probably occurred after the incident in Diodorus and most likely refers to a further deterioration in the Roman position which we shall have to consider in due course.[27] First, however, we must briefly return to the southern theatre.

When we left Caesar his victory over Papius had temporarily eased the pressure on Acerrae and this, in turn, had enabled him to withdraw with a view to bringing a like relief to Aesernia. His efforts which were probably contemporaneous with those of Marius against the Marsi, were not, however, crowned with success. Somewhere in Samnium he was ambushed in a rocky defile by Marius Egnatius. He struggled back to a river (possibly the Volturnus) only to lose the greater part of his army as he crossed the only bridge over it. He then made his way back to Teanum where he regrouped and received reinforcements. He did not, however, make another attempt to relieve Aesernia. Leaving that task to a subordinate he made once more for Acerrae where Papius had tightened the siege. No battle ensued though and both sides settled down to keep a wary eye on each other. As there appeared to be no immediate danger, Caesar felt free as the year drew on to a close, to return to Rome. There he passed the lex Julia de civitate and presided over the consular elections.[28]

I argued above that Marius' campaign against the Marsi may have, at best, been inconclusive but, at worst, may have resulted in the Romans being pinned down. Confirmation of this may be found in Serv. ad *Aen.* 9.587 which speaks of rebel activity in the Liris valley which would be the natural line of advance for them if conditions on the northern front were favourable.[29] Servius mentions the presence at Sora of a force of Picentes under T. Herennius. Salmon (1967) p. 356 believes these could either be from Campania or from Asculum and appears to favour the former notion. In either case, he claims that they had managed to evade Sulla who spent most of the year in the Samnite region protecting his commander's flank while he operated against Aesernia and Acerrae.

I find this implausible. While it is obviously not impossible that a force from Campania could have evaded Sulla or, for that matter, Caesar, what we know of the conditions on both fronts strongly suggests that the situation on the northern front was more likely to give rise to an allied advance than that on the southern. And, still keeping that situation in mind, I cannot agree with Salmon that, 'it is not easy to see what a Picentine would be doing in the Liris valley'. It is in fact, far easier to visualise than a Campanian there. As exemplified by Vidacilius,[30] the Picentes showed a marked tendency to wander far afield. Finally, when Eutropius (5.3.2) calls Herennius a Picentine we have no real reason to suppose that anything other than an Asculan Picentine is meant.[31]

Rejecting Salmon's hypothesis, I would offer the following reconstruction of events. Marius' lack of success had allowed a rebel incursion into the Liris valley and thus the Roman position in the north had deteriorated. However, with Caesar's second march on Aesernia now under way, it appears to have been judged safe to send reinforcements to Marius under the command of Sulla. The latter defeated the enemy in the valley of the Liris and then went on to join Marius probably somewhere near the Fucine Lake. The Marsi and the Marrucini attacked Marius but were heavily defeated and the Marrucinian praetor Asinius was killed. The Roman commander pursued the enemy to some vineyards and then called off the pursuit, allowing them to make their way out on the other side. There they found Sulla waiting for them. He attacked them once more and inflicted further heavy casualties. After this, the allies received reinforcements but mounted no further offensive. Winter was approaching and, as with the armies at Acerrae, both sides were content to simply watch each other.[32]

Sulla seems to have returned to his own theatre of operations almost immediately after this victory. Since Caesar was still at Acerrae, the task of making another attempt to relieve Aesernia now fell on him. In this he was spectacularly, albeit temporarily, successful. On his march he, like Caesar before him, was trapped in a defile by the Samnites under a legate called Duilius. Forced to negotiate, he slipped away leaving a trumpeter to sound the watches and give the impression he was still in position. He then proceeded to lift the siege of the town. Eventually, however, he was forced to fall back, probably because of the difficulty of obtaining provisions in the hill country in winter. As the two Roman commanders originally in charge of the town, L. Acilius and L. Scipio, had sometime previously escaped in the guise of slaves M. Claudius Marcellus was now put in command and it was he who presided over its surrender later that winter. Famine at last compelled the defenders to give in. They had driven all the slaves from the city in order to reduce the number of worthless mouths and had dined off dogs before finally yielding.[33]

About the time Marius and Sulla won their victory over the Marsi, two other campaigns began on the northern front. The first of these requires but a brief mention. A rebellion of the Saluvii broke out in Cis-Alpine Gaul and was crushed by a certain Caelius (or Coelius).[34] The second fought in Picenum, calls for a far more elaborate treatment.

In order to deal with it adequately it is necessary for us to decide what value we should assign to one of the main sources, App. B.C. 1.47. On the surface this appears to deal with events in the area towards the close of 90. Pompey Strabo is defeated near Mount Falernus and shut up at Firmum. He overcomes the besieging army and makes his way to Asculum which he then places under siege. As I remarked earlier in this chapter a number of scholars have expressed doubts about this sequence. They have suggested that the battle near Mount Falernus took place earlier in the year or alternatively have distributed all the events of the passage over the whole year.[35] The inducement to make these rearrangements appears to be the seeming difficulties posed by the movements of Vidacilius. In B.C. 1.42 he is in Apulia but in B.C. 1.47 he turns up in Picenum. This, so the argument seems to run, is unlikely so it makes more sense, and presents a neater picture if we assume Vidacilius first defeated Pompey at Mount Falernus early in the year and then went south. Such a reconstruction is unnecessary since the account in our sources is perfectly plausible as it stands. In the first instance it may be noted that Oros. 5.18.10 does not mention Vidacilius in connection with the earlier battle. He could, therefore, have left

Picenum before Pompey's defeat. But, even if we did assume a clash with Pompey, there is still ample time for him to have operated in Apulia and returned in time to fight the battle of Mount Falernus later in the year since the two bouts of conflict are obviously months apart.[36] Nor, it may be added, is there anything untoward in armies going their separate ways after winning a victory. We have already seen examples of this in both the allied and Roman spheres of action. Thus, I believe that the battle of Mount Falernus should not be conflated with the earlier defeat of Pompey Strabo and that there is no reason for doubting what Appian tells us.

So, proceeding from the premise that Appian's evidence must be accepted exactly as it stands, we may offer the following reconstruction of the war in Picenum. After his defeat early in the year Pompey, as we saw, took refuge in Firmum and there he remained for several months.[37] What induced him to stir abroad once more was the news that a new Roman army was marching towards Picenum. At its head was Sextus Julius Caesar the consul of 91. He seems to have departed for his province early in that year and to have just come back to Italy now. Upon his return he was invested with proconsular *imperium* and succeeded to the position of supreme commander once held by Rutilius.[38] Strabo, therefore, advanced on Asculum only to be met at Mount Falernus by a combined army under the command of Vidacilius, Lafrenius and Ventidius.[39] Heavily defeated he was forced to retreat back to Firmum. After this Vidacilius and Ventidius went their separate ways leaving Lafrenius to besiege Pompey. Upon hearing that the relief army was now close, Pompey sallied forth while at the same time, another legate P. Sulpicius attacked the enemy rear. For a time the issue was doubtful until he succeeded in firing the enemy camp. The allies then retreated to Asculum in disorder leaving Lafrenius dead on the field. The victorious Romans pressed on in their wake and laid siege to the town. When the news of this success was brought to Rome magistrates once more assumed their purple bordered togas and other insignia of office.[40]

After defeating an enemy force, possibly composed of Paeligni, on the road, Caesar himself now arrived to take charge of operations. Shortly afterwards, however, he died leaving Baebius in charge as *legatus pro-praetore* and this man continued to command until the new year when Strabo, freshly elected consul, took over.[41] We may at this point leave Picenum in order to turn our attention to a new rebellion which had just broken out. Etruria and Umbria had at last decided to throw in their lot with the rebels.[42]

The revolt was a partial and hesitant affair and the Roman response to it was twofold. They sent agents around the disaffected areas to announce that the lex Julia had been passed granting citizenship to all allies who had remained loyal. This had the desired effect of confirming the faithful in their resolve and strengthening the wavering. As a result the propraetor Cato easily subdued the Etruscans while Plotius dealt with the Umbrians. Details of the campaigns are sparse. Faesulae and Ocriculum were almost certainly destroyed in the fighting. Iguvium and Perusia are also mentioned in our sources but whether in the context of the diplomatic or the military effort is unclear. There was, too, a grim coda to the whole affair. After the rebellion had been crushed, a force of allies, in ignorance of the changed situation, arrived from Asculum to bring aid to the insurgents. Pompey Strabo, who was now consul, fell upon them and killed a large number. The rest struggled home through a trackless region. In the severe winter weather, about half of them perished.[43]

It is fair to say that Roman morale was low for the greater part of this year. The alarm felt at the extravagant displays of grief at the funeral of Rutilius furnishes a dramatic illustration of this. The senate, it will be recalled, decreed that henceforth the fallen should be buried where they died. In this we may detect a concern both for the spirits of those who remained at home and of those who were to take the field. The populace was already badly unsettled by the political quarrels of the day and it would be dangerous to allow them to become further disturbed. Likewise, those who were about to serve should not be allowed to know of the slaughter on the battlefield. Reluctance to undertake military service had been a feature of the second century and now the problem presented itself once more. A certain C. Vettienus cut off his fingers in order to avoid conscription. We may suspect that others shared his feelings if they did not imitate his example. At any rate, the senate moved swiftly and ruthlessly to discourage those who might be of a like mind. Vettienus' goods were sold by public auction and he himself was condemned to perpetual imprisonment.[44] In this sort of atmosphere it is hardly surprising the Romans should want to make the most of whatever successes came their way. Hence the excessive rejoicing at the news of Caesar's victory at Acerrae and the joy with which Pompey

Strabo's victory in Picenum was greeted. Equally unsurprising, too was the desire to placate the gods and make amends for any neglect of ritual which could have angered them and led them to visit mankind with the scourge of war. Caecilia Metella, daughter of Metellus Balearicus announced that she had seen Juno Sospita fleeing from her temple because of the filth which had accumulated there. In her dream Metella had barely been able to induce the goddess to return by her prayers. The consul Caesar therefore had the temple cleaned up and a ceremony of prayer was held there when it had been restored to its former state. This repaired past neglect but measures had still to be taken to secure the future well being of the state. So it was decreed that games should be celebrated in honour of Juppiter Optimus Maximus once the republic was whole again.[45]

Any sketch of the Roman mood at this time must, of course, recognise that not everybody shared in the general gloom. For the profiteer it was a time to wax fat. A man could lay the foundations for a fortune with his munitions manufacturing and prisoners of war provided an abundant supply of slaves.[46] It must be recognised too that however low morale was it did not prevent the Romans from filling the ranks of their army. The mixture of severity and cajolery we have described above proved to be effective. Unfortunately the quality of some of these armies often left much to be desired. We have seen, for instance, the kind of quarrels which convulsed Rutilius' staff. It will also be recalled that Marius had well founded doubts about his own troops and Cato, in the next year, commanded soldiers, many of whom were said to be too old for military service. Fraternisation, inexperience and unfitness for service were not the only problems; mutiny was also a hazard faced by some commanders and in our next chapter we shall meet one, Albinus, who fell a victim. That same year, 89, the consul Cato was attacked by his men when he spoke harshly to them. Fortunately for him, clods of earth rather than stones were the only weapons available and he survived. The ring-leader of the mutiny, a man called Titinius, was sent to Rome but escaped punishment through the intervention of a tribune.[47]

The panic and fear which gripped the Romans is, I believe, directly attributable to the immense shock of finding their Italian allies in arms against them. They had for so long been used to lording it over those same Italians and generally bullying them that now, when the oppressed finally turned against them they were taken completely by surprise and totally demoralised. As

Florus (2.6.7) says: *cum regum et gentium arbiter populus ipsum se regere non posset, et victrix Asiae et Europae a Corfinio Roma adpeteretur.* In other words, from being masters of the world, the Romans found themselves threatened with total destruction. The fear of annihilation hung over them and they were obliged to fight for their very existence.[48] Two incidents from the war serve to throw into relief how great the Romans felt the danger to be. At the outset they donned *saga* and did not put them off until Caesar's success showed them that victory was possible. And, even as late as 88, when the allies were everywhere in retreat, it was still considered more important for Sulla to reduce Nola rather than fight Mithridates.[49]

We are less well informed about the mood of the allies. However, it is surely not without significance that they saw fit to copy the Roman decree about the disposal of war dead. The measure may, indeed, have been purely prophylactic but we cannot totally rule out the possibility that war casualties were already having an unsettling effect. What is certain is that the Italian leaders took particular pains to see that their men were keen to fight. Their natural loyalty to their lords was to be reinforced by the prospect of material gain. So, especial care was taken over the distribution of the booty in the well founded belief that tangible rewards would enhance the attractiveness of the more abstract delights of liberty.[50] Any attempt to assess Italian feelings must of course recognise that the diversity of the peoples involved meant they could not be uniform. That fanatical cruelty, manifested by such as the Picentes, which visited stern retribution on all dissenters must be set against those instances where allies were prepared to fraternise with the enemy. In general, however, it seems safe to say that morale was high among the insurgents at the end of 90 for they had scored a number of notable successes. They had firmly established their own state and had made it work. They had won several important victories and killed a consul in the process. Finally, they had succeeded in spreading their rebellion far afield.

Yet, a dispassionate observer might have noted that their position was not, in truth, strong.[51] Many of their troops having served in the Roman army, were of good quality and they certainly contrasted favourably with Marius' raw recruits and Cato's geriatrics.[52] Unfortunately there were not enough of them. Even after the rebellion started the Romans still controlled the most populous regions of Italy and they naturally drew heavily

144

upon them to make up their armies. The failure of the Latins to rise was a particularly bitter blow to the allies for it left intact one of the principal sources of Roman manpower.[53] Likewise, the Romans could summon aid from overseas. The Numidians we saw in Caesar's army had many (and more reliable) counterparts elsewhere.[54] Thus, we should probably not see in the use of freedmen and middle-aged men evidence of a shortage of manpower. Rather it seems to indicate that the Romans were throwing every possible man into the fray in order to overwhelm the enemy by sheer force of numbers.[55]

With the loss of much territory the Romans were now heavily dependent on Sicily and Campania for money, munitions and food. Inevitably the calls made on such resources could not always be answered and we hear of Roman and allied troops fighting over the crops in the fields.[56] Strains appeared in other areas too. The vast expenditure of money from depleted reserves brought on a financial crisis and the weight and value of the currency had to be reduced. The loss of income to both state and individual as a result of the war in Italy was further compounded when Mithridates overran the rich province of Asia. The result was a debt problem both private and public. When the praetor Asellio tried to do something for debtors he was lynched by creditors. A little later when Sulla set off to fight Mithridates the state could only give him 9,000 *librae* of gold.[57]

We may sum up by saying that it was, we know, vital for the allies to spread their revolt far and wide in order to recruit the largest possible numbers and have access to sources of supply. In pursuing this aim they had achieved some notable successes but, by the end of the year, there were two ominous developments. The swift reduction of Etruria and Umbria showed clearly what would happen to those peoples who rose without the aid of their brethren, and it was becoming increasingly obvious that such help would not be forthcoming in the future. The Italian advance had reached its furthest point and was now firmly blocked by the enemy on all fronts. The allies had lost the initiative which was now to pass to the Romans.

Notes

1. Mommsen p. 240; Salmon (1967) p. 352.
2. *ILLR* 1089; Front. *Strat.* 3.17.8. See Laffi (1975) p. XXIV.
3. See e.g. Gabba (1967) pp. 142-3; Salmon (1967) p. 353; Dom. pp.

23-4; Marcks p. 50, 73, 91; Laffi (1975) p. XXIII.

4. Laffi (1975) pp. XXIV-XXV.

5. pp. 375-6.

6. It may be stated at this point that my approach to Appian is fundamentally different from that of Marcks pp. 39ff who believes he does not furnish us with a chronological narrative. I hold exactly the opposite to be true and have tried to demonstrate this in *RhM* (1983) passim.

7. Laffi (1975) pp. XXIV-XXV, XXXVIII. Since Frontinus is speaking of a sally by the Asculani it is worth noting that the mood of the town, during the great siege, was not always in favour of such a move (App. B.C. 1.48).

8. Oros. 5.18.17. See further below.

9. (1975) p. XXV

10. See further below.

11. App. B.C. 1.41 with Carcopino p. 388; de Sanctis p. 53.

12. App. B.C. 1.41; Liv. ep.72 with Keaveney *RhM* (1983) p. 278; Salmon (1967) p. 354; Pareti p. 544.

13. App. B.C. 1.41 with Gabba (1967) p. 134. If, as is possible, Venafrum fell before the battle near Atina then the Samnites who fought under Scato will have come from here.

14. App. B.C. 1.41; Diod. Sic. 37.23; Front. *Strat.* 2.4. 15-16, 4.7. 40-1.

15. Macrob. 1.11.23; Sen. *de ben.* 3.23.2 (= Quadrigarius fr. 80P); Flor. 2.6.11.

16. So Gabba (1967) p. 135 and Dom. p. 24.

17. This, of course, assumes that Florus is not exaggerating. The rest of our evidence suggests he is not. The views of Beloch p. 494 are to be preferred to those of Taylor (1960) p. 94, n. 45, since she does not give due weight to App. B.C. 1.41.

18. So Peter on Quadrigarius fr. 80. In view of the state of our evidence the dismissal of this suggestion by Gabba (1967) p. 135 ('errato il comm.') is unjustified.

19. Sources: App. B.C. 1.42; Liv. ep.73; Sisenna fr. 62P, cf. Gabba (1967) pp. 135-6. Here, as elsewhere in my narrative, I have only used such fragments of Sisenna as can, with some certainty, be applied to a particular event. For some speculation as to what the others may refer to, see P. Frassinetti, 'Sisenna e la guerra sociale', *Athenaeum* 50, 1972 pp. 78-113.

On the divided counsels in Campania see Onorato (1951) p. 126. The scholarly dispute over the attitude of Nuceria to which he refers may be settled by reference to Cic. *Pro Sulla* 58. Although some, e.g. Salmon (1967) p. 344, interpret this to mean the town was pro-Roman, it was pointed out long ago by Reid *ad loc.* that it means precisely the opposite. Its destruction (Flor. 2.6.11) will then have been at the hands of the Romans, probably in 89. As Florus here also seems to mention Picentia, Salmon (1967) p. 358, n. 2 suggests that, after the fall of Nuceria, the nearby Picentes joined the rebellion. There is no evidence for the theory of Dom. p. 18 that it was Pontius Telesinus who brought Pompeii over to the rebel side.

20. Otacilius *legatus*: Sisenna fr. 38P. *MRR* 2.37 assigns him to 89 but I think the previous year more likely. Attacks on both military and

civilian shipping may be seen in Sisenna fr. 39P. The other fragments relating to these operations (9, 104-7) are uninformative. Corn supply: Cic. 2 *Verr.* 2.5. For some of the personnel of the Roman fleet see n. 54. Freedmen coast guards: App. B.C. 1.49; Liv. ep.74; Macrob. 1.11.32, cf. Gabba (1967) pp. 146-7. Dating: see below.

21. App. B.C. 1.42; Liv. ep.73; Oros. 5.18.14-15; Cic. *Leg. Ag.* 2.90. From the presence of the Lucanians here (Oros.) I infer the fall of Grumentum. In my opinion de Sanctis p. 62 underestimates the importance of this victory. The view that this battle took place after Caesar's second attempt to relieve Aesernia and that the *comitia* were held after it is without foundation, cf. Keaveney *RhM* (1983) pp. 278-9. Sydenham no. 640 bears the inscription *Mutil Embratur* (= *Mutilius imperator*) and probably imitates Caesar's title of *imperator*. It most likely commemorates his victory in 90.

22. App. B.C. 1.42 with Gabba (1976) p. 222; Carcopino pp. 377-8; Keaveney *RhM* (1983) p. 277, n. 11. For a further discussion of the dating see below. Since Oxynta had been released from Venusia, Vidacilius' campaign must have begun before Papius advanced on Acerrae (see n. 21). It is reasonable to suggest that both campaigns, in their respective areas, began about the same time and, as both had to subdue opposition, that they extended over a period.

23. App. B.C. 1.43; Oros. 5.18. 11-13; Dio fr. 98, 1—2; Liv. ep.73; Eutrop. 5.3.2; Flor. 2.6.12; Ovid *Fasti* 5.563-566 with Gabba (1967) pp. 138-9; Carcopino p. 376; Salmon (1967) p. 354; de Sanctis p. 54; Marcks p. 50, n. 1. It should be noted that the reverse of Sydenham no. 628 may be a punning reference to the defeat and death of Rutilius, cf. Grueber p. 327, n. 2.

This is one of the few incidents in the war which can be dated with certainty. Our sources do not usually allow us to do more than establish the chronological sequence of events. See further Marcks pp. 77-82 on these matters. It is difficult to say when Carseoli was destroyed. Three possibilities present themselves: (a) it had been taken by the rebels after the defeat of Perperna and before Marius and Rutilius came on the scene to recapture it; (b) it fell later when Marius had to retreat; (c) or when Caepio was defeated (see below). On Marius' ambitions see Keaveney (1983) pp. 42-4. This emphasises his hopes of *gloria* in the East but it is obvious the Social War would serve his turn just as well.

24. Liv. ep.73; App. B.C. 1.43; Flor. 2.6.12 (wrong consul).

25. App. B.C. 1.44; Liv. ep. 73; Oros.5.18.14; Eutrop. 5.3.2; *ILS* 29, cf. Keaveney *RhM* (1983) pp. 275-6. Since Marius took over Caepio's forces the latter must have been operating on the Tolenus. For another view of Caepio's position which I do not think acceptable see de Sanctis p. 57. I would not agree with Haug p. 250 that Front. *Strat.* 4.2.2 refers to the Social War. It surely belongs in the Cimbric Wars.

26. For the excerptor's error see Walton *ad loc.*

27. On this interpretation of the evidence see further below.

28. App. B.C. 1.45 with Keaveney *RhM* (1983) p. 279; Pareti p. 544. *RE* 'Egnatius' no. 10 suggests the river was the Savo but it is doubtful if the rebels advanced this far north. Haug's treatment (p. 228) seems arbitrary to me.

29. This was pointed out by Dom. p. 25 although this theory that the Paeligni would make this advance is not acceptable — see text.

30. On whom see below.

31. See Appendix II.

32. App. B.C. 1.46; Oros. 5.18.15; Serv. ad *Aen.* 9.587; Eutrop. 5.3.3; Liv. ep.73-4; Sisenna fr. 60P. In general see Keaveney (1983) pp. 48-50. The following specific points may be noted:

(a) The battle at the vineyards took place before Sulla's attempt to relieve Aesernia, cf. Keaveney *RhM* (1983) p. 281, n. 3. Thus, I postulate that an offensive by Caesar would leave Sulla free to advance northwards.

(b) Servius mentions a battle near Sora and it is thus likely that Sulla, on his way to Marius, fought it.

(c) Both Appian and the Livian epitomator speak of two battles. I equate Appian's first with that in which Asinius was killed but it is just possible the epitomator is referring to some earlier combat.

(d) The solution to the problem of Sulla's appearing in two places at the one time here adopted will be found in Keaveney, 'Four puzzling passages in Appian', *GIF* 12, 1981 pp. 247-8.

(e) The *dubio eventu* of Liv. ep.74 probably refers to the position of stalemate described by Appian. Like me Gabba (1967) p. 142 does not accept Haug's contention (p. 220) that it is impossible to locate the incidents in Diod. Sic. 37.15.1-3 and Plut. *Mar.* 33. He would place them after the vineyard battle but I have already indicated I do not believe this to be correct. An attack, such as that in Diodorus, accords ill with Marius' quiescence immediately before and after that battle. Likewise, fraternisation is less likely after the vineyard battle than before — I agree with Marcks p. 63 on this point although I do not accept his other arguments. Nor does it seem likely to me that, after such a victory, soldiers should be reluctant to engage an enemy they had defeated once before. Finally, the picture of Marius encircled accords ill with what we find in Appian who implies the armies faced each other.

33. Oros. 5.18.16; Strabo 5.4.11; Front. *Strat.* 1.5.17; App. B.C. 1.41; Liv. ep.73; Sisenna fr. 16P; Diod. Sic. 37.19 with Keaveney (1983) p. 50. Dating: Keaveney *RhM* (1983) p. 281, n. 3; Dom. p. 27. Against Salmon (1967) p. 359 see Haug p. 208, n. 2. Marcks' view (p. 69) that Front. *Strat.* 1.5.17 could be a doublet of *Strat.* 1.5.18 seems to me as unlikely as the theory of Th. Reinach, *Mithridate Eupator*, Paris, 1890 p. 167, n. 4 that the latter belongs to the first Mithridatic War, cf. Keaveney *LEC* (1980) p. 155, n. 34.

Appian puts the escape of Scipio and Acilius after Caesar's first relief attempt but before the fall of the town. It should, therefore, have taken place before the next Roman relieving army, that of Sulla, reached the place. From this it would follow that Marcellus had come with Sulla.

34. Liv. ep.73. Cf. Appendix I.

35. See n. 3 and 4. It will be remembered that some identify the battle at Mount Falernus with the defeat in Oros. 5.18.10.

36. See further Carcopino pp. 375-6 and Keaveney *RhM* (1983) p. 274, n. 5.

37. Laffi (1975) p. XXIII.

38. Keaveney *RhM* (1983) pp. 273-6. The theory of Dom. pp. 25-6,

taken over and elaborated by Salmon (1967) p. 354, that Caesar replaced Messalla is groundless, cf. Keaveney *RhM* (1983) p. 277, n. 12. Equally baseless is Salmon's further contention — (1967) p. 357 — that, 'Vidacilius must have operated against the forces of Sex. Julius Caesar at Picentine Asculum not against those of L. Julius Caesar at Apulian Ausculum' in mid-year, cf. Keaveney *RhM* (1983) p. 274, n. 5 and the discussion of the war in Apulia above.

39. The emendation Οὐέττιος made by Schweighauser and accepted by Dom. p. 24 is based on a misdating of the incident recorded by Cic. *Phil.* 12.27. See 3.3.

40. App. B.C. 1.47; Liv. ep.74; Oros. 5.18.17 with Laffi (1975) pp. XXVI-XXVII.

41. App. B.C. 1.48. Cf. Keaveney *RhM* (1983) pp. 276-8 and (with caution) Gabba (1967) p. 145. Marcks pp. 51-2 makes unnecessary difficulties because of a failure to examine Sextus' career.

42. The following points enable us to establish the outline chronology of the revolt:

(a) App. B.C. 1.49 says events on the Adriatic coast excited these peoples to revolt. Obviously we have here a reference to a time before the siege of Asculum since that could hardly be said to offer encouragement. I would guess that our author has the battle of Mount Falernus in mind. Appian also says the rebellion began before the passing of the lex Julia.

(b) Liv. ep. 74 and Oros. 5.18.17 put the defeat of the rebels after the start of the siege of Asculum.

(c) Since Cato as propraetor subdued the Etruscans (see below) this must have occurred before he returned to Rome to the elected consul.

(d) The relief force found the rebellion over while it was still winter (see n. 43).

43. App. B.C. 1.49-50; Liv. ep.74; Oros. 5.18.17; Flor. 2.6.11, 13; Sisenna frs. 94, 95P with Ruoff-Väänänen pp. 55-7, 75-6 and Gabba (1967) p. 148. In view of what Appian tells us of the effect of the lex Julia and of the chronology (n. 42) we may reject Orosius' description of the Roman campaign as being attempted with *plurimo sanguine inpenso et difficillimo labore.* The notion that the allied defeat in App. B.C. 1. 50 is to be equated with that in Oros. 5.18.18-21 has found a number of adherents, e.g. Gabba (1967) p. 149; Dom. p. 28; Marcks pp. 75-6 but, in my view, de Sanctis p. 77 is right to differentiate between the two. The one feature both accounts have in common is the death of soldiers in inclement weather in the mountains and this is hardly sufficient grounds for conflating the two since one source speaks of a battle on the road to Etruria while the other mentions one before Asculum. Given the nature of the terrain and the state of the weather it is not straining credulity to believe that both sets of survivors met a like fate — see 3.3.

44. Val. Max. 6.3.3. Cf. Keaveney *Crit. Stor.* (1984) pp. 371-2.

45. Obsequens 55; Cic. *de Div.* 1.4, 99; Suet. *Aug.* 23.

46. Cic. *In Pis.* 87, *Pro Cluent.* 21.

47. Dio fr. 100; Sisenna fr. 52P. It is doubtful if Cato sent the culprit to the tribunes as Dio says. The senate would be more likely to be the recipient of this particular gift, cf. e.g. Livy 29.9.8-10. However the mention of tribunes leads me to suspect that it was they who, in this

instance, fulfilled their normal function of intervening on his behalf. See Keaveney, *Crit. Stor.* (1984) p. 354, 359, n. 68, 371, n. 124. On the possible political significance of this incident see 4.1.

48. Cf. Diod. Sic. 37.22.

49. Keaveney (1983) pp. 59-60.

50. Diod. Sic. 37.14 with Haug p. 219.

51. On this see, in particular, Salmon (1967) pp. 345-6.

52. *Auct. ad Herr.* 4.13.

53. Liv. ep.72; App. B.C. 1.39; *Auct. ad Herr.* 4.13.

54. There were Mauretanians in Sulla's army: App. B.C. 1.50. Sertorius recruited men in Cis-Alpine Gaul and also gathered arms there: Plut. *Sert.* 4, cf. Sall. *Hist.* 1.88M; Sisenna frs. 29, 71P. Gabba (1967) p. 130 believes Sertorius may have been recruiting citizens. The Gauls in Cluentius' army (App. B.C. 1.50) may have been deserters, cf. Gabba (1967) p. 151. Spaniards as well as Gauls are found with Pompey Strabo: *ILS* 8888; *ILLR* 1095. There was a Cretan in Caesar's army: Diod. Sic. 37.18.

Seamen come from Heraclea Pontica, Miletus, Clazomenae, Carystus: Memnon 21(Jacoby 3B p. 351); Sherk no. 22.

The Romans also employed loyalists among the rebel nations (Vell. Pat. 2.16.2-3). Salmon (1967) p. 352, n. 2 says Cic. 2 *Verr.* 1.38 and Ps. Asc. p. 234 St. are to be taken as evidence for the attitude of Beneventum in this war. In fact, they refer to the first Civil War.

55. Cf. Pareti p. 537.

56. Cic. *Leg. Ag.* 2.80, 90, 2 *Verr.* 2.5, 5.8; Diod. Sic. 37.24. I do not know why Dom. p. 26 and Salmon (1967) p. 355 take the last source as evidence for a truce.

57. Keaveney (1983) p. 68, 85.

3.3

The Social War 89-88 BC

Throughout the winter of 90/89 the siege of Asculum continued without a let-up. The first allied attempt to break it came late in 90 and was not a success. Vidacilius, fearing for the safety of his native town, hastened to its rescue. He sent on word beforehand that the townsfolk should make a sally to coincide with his attack. This they failed to do but he was able, nonetheless, to burst through the besiegers and gain the town in safety.[1]

Early in the new year another allied army, composed of Marsi under the command of Vettius Scato, arrived to bring further aid. Here again, there occurred one of those parleys to which the Marsi seem to have been so given. Cicero, who was serving in the Roman army, witnessed friendly discussions between Strabo's brother Sextus and Scato.[2] As on the previous occasion these ultimately came to nothing and the Marsi launched an attack while the Picentes made a simultaneous sally. The result was a crushing defeat for the Italians in which one of their legates Fraucus lost his life. The sequel was gruesome. A large number of Italians fled from the battle to the mountains and there perished in the snow.[3] In Asculum itself Vidacilius held a magnificent banquet and then took poison before flinging himself on a funeral pyre.[4]

Although we do not know as much as we would like concerning the circumstances surrounding Vidacilius' death, nevertheless we can give the outlines of the story. Those who refused to sally may very well have been induced to believe that by the passing of the lex Julia, some kind of deal was possible with the Romans and so could see little point in such an adventure.[5] If that is so, the failure of the talks between Sextus Pompey and Scato, if nothing else, must have made them change their minds fairly quickly for they went on to sally soon after and then grimly endured almost another year of siege. On the other hand, it is equally possible strategic considerations lay behind the decision. What was possible with Scato's army might have been difficult with Vidacilius'. Now we cannot be sure — the sources are silent on such matters — if considerations like these actually did weigh with those who favoured inaction. But if, as appears reasonable to conjecture, they did in fact do so then they were fully in harmony with what the ancients actually say was the main motive inspiring those who refused to aid Vidacilius; a malignant desire to thwart him at all costs. He had enemies of long standing in the town and they did not hesitate to seize this opportunity to strike a blow against him. He, for his part, took his revenge on them just before dying. His suicide came about because he clearly recognised that the position of Asculum, after the defeat of Scato, was now hopeless. It might hold out for some time — as indeed it did — but its fall to the Romans had by this time become inevitable.[6]

In the meantime the other consul Porcius Cato had been campaigning vigorously against the Marsi, having taken the place of Marius who had retired disgruntled at his failure to receive the supreme command. Although Cato, like his predecessor had disciplinary problems with his troops, he was able to win a number of victories and may even have managed to relieve Alba Fucens. Eventually, however, in the early spring he was defeated and killed while storming a Marsic camp near the Fucine lake. According to one story he was murdered in the battle by the younger Marius because he had boasted that the elder Marius had not done better than he. Bearing in mind the unruly nature of the consul's troops it is certainly not impossible that he had been killed by one of his own men. Whether the younger Marius was actually the assassin will always, no doubt, be a subject for debate but, in that debate, prominence should be given to the fact that he was of a savage disposition and the family itself was notoriously touchy when they thought they had been robbed of what they believed to be rightly theirs.[7] The allies celebrated their victory with a coin, the reverse of which, in derision, copies a denarius of M. Cato issued that same year.[8]

Contemporaneously with these campaigns of Pompey and Cato the Roman advance in the south began, directed in Campania by Sulla and in Samnium by Cosconius.[9] The campaign in Campania opened with a siege of Pompeii by land and sea. Sulla commanded the land forces, while the fleet was in the charge of another legate Albinus and they were aided by a legion drawn from among those of the Hirpini who had remained loyal to Rome. Albinus was unpopular with his troops, either because he was a harsh disciplinarian or because they suspected him of some kind of treachery. Eventually they mutinied and stoned him to death. Sulla was able to quell the disturbance only by appealing to the troops' sense of honour. He told them he would expect them to redeem themselves by their valour on the field of battle.

A Samnite legate, Cluentius, now appeared on the scene. He camped a little distance from Sulla who was positioned close to the foothills of Vesuvius which extend towards the section of city walls contained between the Vesuvian and Herculanean Gates. Stung by this boldness, Sulla attacked without waiting for his foragers to come in and suffered a reverse. But when the foragers did join him, he was able to halt his flight and inflict a defeat on the Italians. Cluentius now pulled back but, after receiving reinforcements, he once more went over to the attack. In the ensuing battle he was thoroughly routed and fled to Nola with the Romans in hot pursuit. Great slaughter of the defeated took place during the pursuit and before the walls and Cluentius himself was among the slain. Sulla, who had been voted a grass crown for having saved his men from a great danger, now put Nola under siege but it was not destined to fall for many years to come.

But if Nola eluded the Romans other Campanian towns did not. Pompeii fell soon after. Stabiae was taken on 29 April. The Hirpini captured Compsa and aided another legate, Didius in subduing Herculaneum. Such, however, is the state of our sources that we cannot establish the relative chronology of these events.[10]

Contemporary with these events we hear of a great battle won by Cosconius and Lucceius (Lucanius?) over the Samnites in which Marius Egnatius perished. The pair then went on to conquer a number of towns in northern Samnium. Although some scholars have tried to conflate the two, this campaign is to be strictly differentiated from the one which Cosconius later conducted in Apulia. The interval of time in our sources is sufficient to allow him to carry out both comfortably and an advance from northern Samnium to Apulia by way of the territory of the Frentani is perfectly feasible. Moreover, it should be noted that the names of the commanders he defeated in the two separate theatres are wholly different.[11] What is not altogether clear is who Cosconius was serving under at this juncture. If he was a legate of the consul Cato then it is possible his brief was similar to that of Sulla the previous year. He was to protect the Roman flank during operations in Campania.[12] Others believe he was a legate of Pompey Strabo's who had been despatched south along the coast from Asculum. Then, his battle with the Samnites could, as Dom. p. 30 suggested, have taken place in the territory of the Frentani. The difficulty with this theory, however, is that it is by no means certain that the nations between Asculum and the Frentani had yet been subdued so as to allow passage to Cosconius at this time.[13]

We may now return to the northern front to consider the problems presented by Pompey Strabo's campaign against the Vestini and the Marsi. According to Liv. ep.75 he received the surrender of the Vestini about this time but in ep.76 we learn that he was proconsul when they and the Paeligni yielded to him. Appian (B.C. 1.52) places the surrender of the Marsi, Marrucini and Vestini to him about the same time. In ep.76, however, we are told that Sulpicius overthrew the Marrucini while Cinna and Caecilius Cornutus beat the Marsi in several battles. According to Oros. 5.18.25 it was Sulpicius who defeated the Marrucini and the Vestini. How may these notices be reconciled? Discrepancies over the names of the conquering commanders are not difficult to resolve. Formal surrender would naturally be made to the commander-in-chief although some of the actual fighting will obviously have been done by his legates. In these circumstances, it need not occasion surprise that abbreviated sources should directly attribute to Pompey campaigns which had been carried out by others under his general supervision. It also seems safe to assume that the surrenders took place in 88. We know of no reason why the campaigns should not have dragged on and the agreement of Liv. ep.76 and App. B.C. 1.52 on this point is a strong argument in favour of this view.[14] The notice in ep.75 is most likely to be an error or a garbled reference to the beginning of the campaign.[15]

We may now delineate the campaigns fought on the northern front from about the beginning of spring until the end of the year. Once Pompey Strabo was satisfied that the siege of Asculum could not be broken then it was obvious he would give some attention to subduing other rebels. Therefore, it is not unreasonable to suppose, as we have done, that Liv. ep.75 refers to the start of a campaign against the Vestini. When exactly it began we cannot say but if, as some have thought, it started while Cato was still alive then the two may be regarded as mounting a kind of joint operation. Pompey seems, eventually, to have handed over the direction of this campaign to his legate P. Sulpicius.[16] The latter also waged war on the Marrucini. Orosius 5.18.25 tells us of a great battle won by Sulpicius in this campaign. It was, he says, fought at the Teanum river and in it there perished the Italian commanders Poppaedius and Obsidius.[17] However, there does not appear to be any river called Teanum and Poppaedius almost certainly survived into 88. Carcopino p. 397 thought the river Trinius was meant but it is unlikely Sulpicius penetrated this far south; he would surely have had more than enough to do dealing with the Vestini and the Marrucini and it is only of these nations that our sources speak in his regard. Two other suggestions are more attractive. Marcks pp. 88-9 thought the river Aternus was in question while Salmon (1967) p. 365 n. 3 located the battle at Teate the Marrucinian capital.[18] Either of these suggestions has the merit, over that of Carcopino, of locating this important battle where we would expect to find it; in the heart of the territory of the Marrucini. Although Poppaedius did not die in the action it is perfectly possible that he was present. If the war situation in this area was deteriorating then we should expect the commander-in-chief to try to do something about it.[19]

With the death of Cato, operations against the Marsi were then taken over by two legates, Cinna and Cornutus. Details of their campaign are scant but a mention of several battles leads us to conclude that the Marsi put up the stout resistance we would expect of them before succumbing.[20]

By the end of the year the Social War was virtually at an end on the northern front. To all intents and purposes the Marsi and the Vestini were now crushed and it simply remained to receive in the next year their surrender together with that of the Paeligni.[21] Asculum itself surrendered in November. Pompey Strabo executed the ring leaders of the rebellion, sold all the slaves and booty and then released the common people after having despoiled them. He somewhat besmirched his reputation by hanging on to the proceeds of the booty and, in so doing, laid up trouble for his son a few years later. For the moment, however, the prevailing Roman mood of self-congratulation allowed this to pass and on 17 November Pompey was proclaimed *imperator* and granted the citizenship to some Spanish cavalry who were serving as auxiliaries in his army. He then went on to Rome to celebrate a triumph over Asculum.[22]

These campaigns naturally threatened the Italian capital at Corfinium. The rebel government, however, appears to have remained until the very last moment. Diodorus tells us that it was not until after Cosconius' victories in Apulia (see below) and the surrender of the Marsi that they decided to move. So it was that early in 88 Aesernia became the new seat of government.[23] Because App. B.C. 1.55, in a passage which clearly refers to 89, speaks of Bovianum Undecimanorum as a rebel headquarters it is often assumed that this town was the rebel capital for a time before it was transferred to Aesernia. However, this is not necessarily so. As Marcks p. 88 pointed out, Appian is probably referring to a purely Samnite assembly place.[24]

We may now turn to the southern front to look at those campaigns which took place about the time of the ones we have just been considering. With Nola under siege and with the rest of Campania in a satisfactory state,[25] Sulla was now free to turn his attention elsewhere and so he began a drive into the territory of the Hirpini. Arriving before the town of Aeclanum he demanded its surrender. The inhabitants who were expecting aid from Lucania asked for time to consider and were granted an hour. When it was up Sulla fired their wooden walls and in terror they yielded. However, by a strict application of the rules of war, they were deemed to have been stormed and so the town was given up to the sack. Sulla then continued his progress through the Hirpinian land but spared all towns which surrendered voluntarily.

Sulla's next target was the Samnites. Their commander Papius Mutilus seems to have believed Sulla would make directly for the Caudini. Instead he returned to the region of Capua-Teanum and from there advanced into northern Samnium. Taking Mutilus unawares he defeated him and destroyed his camp somewhere between Aesernia and Bovianum Undecimanorum. He then laid siege to the latter town which boasted of three citadels. The Romans tied down the main defending force in one of these while they captured another. When a signal proclaimed its fall a general assault was launched and the town fell within three hours.[26]

The subjugation of Campania left the way open for the Romans to advance into Lucania. Aulus Gabinius stormed many towns — including, possibly, Heraclea and Grumentum — before falling in an attack on an enemy camp. His place in the command was probably taken by Papirius Carbo.[27]

Like Sulla, Cosconius continued to fight successfully for the rest of the year. Overrunning the territory of Larinum he passed from Samnium into Apulia where he ravaged the territory of Ausculum and then burned Salapia to the ground. He next received the surrender of Cannae before launching an attack on Canusium. There he received a check. A force of Samnites under Trebatius defeated him and he was forced to retreat to Cannae with the enemy in pursuit. The river Aufidius separated the two sides and Trebatius sent word to the Roman either to come over and fight or withdraw and let him cross. Cosconius pulled back and then routed Trebatius as he crossed. The defeated Samnites then withdrew to Canusium. Cosconius, however, marched south to ravage the territory of Venusia before going on to subdue the Poediculi in two days.[28]

The year 88 found Sulla once more before the walls of Nola. Although he had been designated to take charge of the war against Mithridates it was felt he should first reduce this rebel stronghold before going to the East. During his absence, occasioned by the disturbances in Rome, the siege was carried on by subordinates but to no purpose for Nola still held out.[29]

Elsewhere the picture is far less static. At their new capital of Aesernia the remaining rebels regrouped their forces and appointed Poppaedius Silo as supreme commander with four praetors under him. They then cast around desperately for allies and lighted upon Mithridates the king of Pontus whose armies even now were sweeping through Asia. That they should choose the man who had just massacred so many of their cousins in the East may seem strange but the plain fact is that they had little choice in the matter. In the past they had not been over particular about whose aid they invoked and now, in their desperate plight, they were willing to accept help from any quarter. Coinage was issued to mark the occasion of these overtures to the king. A unique gold piece bears the name of the otherwise unknown Minius Ieius who may just have been part of an embassy to the king. On the obverse is a head of Bacchus with a wreath of ivy tied with a fillet. The reverse has a thyrsus tied with a fillet which rests against a *cista mystica* and on this is the skin of a fawn. The type is borrowed from a bronze of Amisus and is obviously intended to pay a compliment to Mithridates. This is not the symbol of liberty but the new Dionysus with whom Mithridates wished to be identified.

Another coin has on its obverse two figures in military dress, one holding a spear, the other a round object. The figures grasp each others' right hands. On the right is a vessel on the forefront of which appears a sceptre bound with a fillet and two spears with shields. Some scholars believe this was issued to welcome Marius back to Italy in 87. However it is also possible that it could have been issued at the time the Italians were negotiating with Mithridates. One of the figures will then be an Italian ambassador bearing a gift to the king or it may be the regal ambassador arriving in Italy. Indeed, it could even be a depiction of the anticipated arrival of the king himself, according to yet another interpretation.

In any event, the negotiations bore little fruit in the end. Mithridates, indeed, expressed a willingness to come to Italy but said it would have to wait until he was finished with Asia.[30]

This, of course, was of no real use to the Italians who had to contend with a determined Roman assault. Mam. Aemilius Lepidus, legate to the propraetor Metellus Pius, inflicted a defeat on the Samnites under the command of Poppaedius. The latter, however, did something to retrieve the situation by recapturing Bovianum Undecimanorum. Determined to boost morale by making the most of this signal success he had himself brought in triumph into the city. But he forgot that a triumph enters the conquering city not the conquered and the evil omen was soon fulfilled. Metellus had been operating in Apulia in succession to Cosconius where he beat the enemy in battle and captured Venusia. He now marched into the Samnite country to join his legate. Their combined forces overwhelmed those of Poppaedius and the Italian commander lost his life in the battle.[31]

Thus, by the end of 88, the Italians were in a sorry plight indeed. The Samnites still held Nola, a mixed force of Samnites and Marsians occupied Aesernia and the Lucanians continued to resist in Bruttium. But that was all.[32] With the rebels everywhere in retreat we may, for the moment, leave the Social War. The insurgent cause was soon to undergo a revival but that revival came about largely because of Rome's own internal disputes. Henceforth Italian fortunes were to be intimately bound up with the fortunes of those who were even now quarrelling in Rome. So it is most appropriate that the later history of the confederate rump should be narrated as part of the story of those quarrels.

Notes

1. App. B.C. 1.48 with Laffi (1975) p. XXVIII and Gabba (1967) p. 145. This must not, of course, be conflated with the notice in Oros. 5.18. 18-21 as it is by Gabba (1967) p. 149. The detail of the sally and the commander's name clearly mark them off as separate.

2. Cic. *Phil.* 12.27; Macrob. 1.11.24. Despite the misgivings of Badian (1969) pp. 454-5 I find the reconstruction of Cicero's movements in this year by Cichorius pp. 81-4 perfectly satisfactory. It is certainly a good deal more convincing than that of Onorato (1949/50) pp. 420-1 or of Dom. p. 9 (accepted by Haug p. 254) which tries to cram too much into too short a time span. I myself would add the following observation: for much of 89 Pompey campaigned elsewhere (see below) and he would hardly have done this if he had had to beat off attacks at Asculum at the same time. Accepting, therefore, that Cicero must have been at Asculum early in 89, it follows that Scato was also and that he must be connected with what follows.

3. Oros. 5.18.18-21 with de Sanctis p. 77-8 who suggests that failure of provisions may have forced the Italians to give battle and Marcks pp. 75-6 who rightly points out that Vell. Pat. 2.21.1 also refers to this battle. Liv. ep.74 (second mention of Pompey) also notes it, as was pointed out by Gabba (1967) p. 149 (although I do not accept the rest of his thesis). The Loeb edition of Appian (p. 92, n. 4) connects it with B.C. 1.52 but that is probably to be equated with the evidence of Liv. ep.75. The suggestion of Gabba (1967) p. 149 that Scato fell in this battle is not necessarily correct. There are other equally plausible occasions (see below) and we should certainly consider the possibility that it was he who led the force to Etruria. See 3.2. I accepted there the attractive suggestion of Gabba (1967) p. 148 that it came from Asculum. Pompey will then have pursued and defeated it after his victory. The suggestion of Marcks p. 76 that this force was coming to aid Asculum is without foundation.

4. Mommsen p. 521; Gabba (1967) p. 145 and Keaveney *RhM* (1983) p. 277, n. 12 all believe that the notice of Vidacilius' death in App. B.C. 1.48 is an anticipation of Oros. 5.18.21 but this is not necessarily so. Rather, it would appear that Appian, having omitted the battle in Oros. 5.18.18-20, has made the death the consequence of the wrong action. It will be remembered that something similar is to be found in B.C. 1.36, cf. 2.2. See also Haug p. 229 and Dom. p. 29 — Gabba (1956) p. 30, n. 4 is not totally convincing. We may further note that both Appian and Orosius put the death in roughly the same place in the chronological sequence of events and thus Gabba's suggestion — (1967) p. 145 — that it occurred late in 89 seems unlikely.

5. See Salmon (1967) p. 361.

6. For some further remarks on this matter see Laffi (1975) pp. XXVIII-XXIX. In passing note that some Samnites also came to aid (Cic. *Pro Cluent.* 21).

7. App. B.C. 1.50; Liv. ep.75; Oros. 5.18.24; Dio fr. 100; Sisenna fr. 52P; Vell. Pat. 2.16.4; Eutrop. 5.32 with Dom. pp. 29-30; Haug p. 251; Keaveney *RhM* (1983) p. 276 and Carcopino pp. 383-4 who suggests Cato may actually have raised the siege of Alba. It will be seen that I take more

seriously than Haug p. 210 the story that Marius junior murdered Cato.
For the chronology see n. 9 below.

8. Sydenham no. 618 and Crawford no. 343. See Grueber p. 325, n.
1 and Crawford (1964) pp. 141-2. *ILLR* 146 probably does not refer to
this campaign, see Gabba (1976) p. 202, n. 185.

9. The relative chronology of the campaigns of Pompey, Cato and
Sulla is established from the following data:
(a) Pompey obviously fought at Asculum in the winter.
(b) Cato fell that same winter (App. B.C. 1.50). His campaigns must have
taken some time and Appian's remark can be taken to mean he died just
as spring was beginning, cf. Haug p. 251.
(c) Sulla captured Stabiae in spring, on 29 April (Pliny *NH* 3.70).
Narrating southern events before northern, Liv. ep.75 and Oros 5. 18.22-
23 describe Sulla's campaigns up to the assault on Nola before narrating
the death of Cato. Appian, narrating northern before southern, reverses
the order, cf. Keaveney *RhM* (1983) p. 280 n. 2.
(d) Cicero's presence at Nola (*de Div.* 1.72.2.65) indicates that by then
Pompey Strabo had the situation at Asculum so well in hand that he
could afford to transfer men elsewhere, cf. n. 2.

10. On all of this see Keaveney (1983) pp. 50-1 There I neglected to
take account of Front. *Strat.* 1.9.2 (cf. Marcks p. 69) which shows how
serious the mutiny was which Sulla quelled by his timely display of
moderation. Herculaneum and Compsa: Vell. Pat. 2.16.2; Sisenna frs.
53, 54P with Haug p. 216. Nuceria also appears to have been attacked
about the same time; Sisenna frs. 55, 56P with Haug p. 216. There is no
basis to the theory of Onorato (1949/50) p. 425 that the sacrifice in Cic. *de
Div.* 1.72, 2.65 was offered at Pompeii as a propitiation for the death of
Albinus. The location is Nola and it is a sacrifice before battle.

11. Liv. ep.75. I prefer to follow Gabba (1967) p. 155 rather than
MRR 2.36 or de Sanctis pp. 84-6.

12. His failure to attack Aesernia need not militate against this theory.
Cosconius, like other commanders, was not afraid to leave some towns
unsubdued in his wake. There can be little doubt that northern
Samnium was his theatre of operations. The Samnite towns mentioned
by the epitomator can only have been there since Sulla later subdued
southern Samnium.

13. See further Appendix I and below.

14. Haug pp. 203-4 argues very strongly for the view that the notice in
ep.76 is not on interpolation. Accepting this, we may, perhaps, suggest
that it has become misplaced within the epitome itself. It may have been
originally between *captum est* and *Caesis et.* This would make more sense
and give a better chronological sequence since what then follows took
place in 88. The narrative of 89 would end with the capture of Asculum
and that of 88 begin with northern rather than southern events.

App. B.C. 1.52 does not contradict the sequence in the Livian
tradition. After narrating in B.C. 1.50-1, the greater part of the year's
events in the south, he now briefly summarises the contemporary events
in the north before returning yet again to the south.

15. For another explanation see Laffi (1975) p. XXXIII, n. 98.

16. de Sanctis p. 78; Dom. pp. 29-30.

17. I assume that the whole of this section of Orosius refers to the same campaign. For another view see n. 19. The Roman capture of Pinna (Val. Max. 5.4.7) must have taken place during this campaign, cf. Laffi (1975) p. XXXI1 n. 95.

18. At least I assume this is what he means although he talks of, 'Teanum, the principal settlement of the Marrucini'.

19. de Sanctis p. 99 n. 54 would see in this mention of Poppaedius a reference to the separate battle in which he perished in 88. This, however, upsets Orosius' chronology without good reason and, as will become clear, would introduce unnecessary confusion into the account of what happened then. Further, if Sulpicius is the trib. pleb. of 88 (Appendix I) then he could not have taken part in the battle.

20. Liv. ep.76.

21. It is not clear who subdued the Paeligni but they were probably dealt with after the other two. The sources (Macrob. *Sat.* 1.11.24; Sen. *de ben.* 3.23.5) which speak of the death of Scato do not say when it occurred. The detail that his men were about to hand him over to Pompey does suggest, however, that it was about the time of the final surrender of the Marsi.

22. See Laffi (1975) pp. XXXIV-XXXVI.

23. Diod. Sic. 37.8-9. This must call in question the chronology proposed by Gabba (1967) pp. 153-4. See further below.

24. See also Pareti p. 547, n. 2.

25. The record of Roman successes was not, however, an unbroken one. On 11 June Didius was defeated and slain — Ovid *Fast.* 6.568 with Haug p. 208, 224.

26. Keaveney (1983) pp. 51-2.

27. Liv. ep. 76; Oros. 5.18.25. Grumentum: see 3.2. Heraclea: Cic. *Pro Arch.* 8; Schol. Bob. p. 175, 177 St. Flor. 2.6.13 reads: *Gabinius Marsos Carbo Lucanos.* The first notice is wrong. The second might be right.

28. App. B.C. 1.52; Diod. Sic. 37.2.8. Although I have found his discussion helpful it will be clear that I differ on some points from the conclusions of Marcks pp. 87-8.

29. Keaveney (1983) pp. 56-76.

30. Literary sources: Diod. Sic. 37.2.9-11; Athenaeus 5.213c. Dating derives from Diod. Coin of Ieius: Sydenham no. 643 with Grueber p. 334, n. 1 and Bernareggi pp. 62-4 (not satisfactory on Bacchus). On 'ambassador' coin: Sydenham no. 632 with Grueber p. 337, n. 1. Salmon (1967) p. 370 may be right in suggesting that the *fugitivi* of Front. *Strat.* 2.3.17 were Italians who had taken refuge with Mithridates but I am less convinced by his other suggestion that the Italians did not expect much from Mithridates. The arrival of his armies in Greece showed that he might be a real ally indeed. Poppaedius, of course, continued to fight after his nation had surrendered, cf. de Sanctis p. 98.

31. Liv. ep.76; Diod. Sic 37.2.10; App. B.C. 1.53; *de Vir. Illust.* 63; Obsequens 56 with Keaveney *Klio* (1984) p. 138 and Marcks p. 89. I see no reason to accept Dom's suggestion (p. 31) that Liv. ep.76 is to be taken to mean Lepidus captured Ausculum.

32. Keaveney *Crit. Stor.* (1981) p. 501.

Part Four
From Confrontation to Integration

4.1

Roman Politics and the Italian Question
91-88 BC

It will not have been forgotten that Drusus had, at the end of his life, incurred hatred and suspicion because it was believed he had been a party to the conspiracies being hatched at that time in Italy. With the outbreak of war, after his death, it was natural that this hatred and suspicion should continue to be directed against his friends and supporters. Capitalising on the prevailing mood, one of the tribunes of 90, Q. Varius, set up a *quaestio* to try those who had encouraged or aided the allies in their revolt from Rome.[1]

Cicero says that when, as a young man, he first entered the Forum he found *judicia intermissa bello*. The only court active in that year was that set up by the lex Varia. Asconius tells us that when many men were being unjustly condemned by this commission and when the rebellion of many Italian nations was being announced, the senate lit upon this as an occasion for a *justitium*. It was decreed that, while there was a *tumultus Italicus*, *judicia* should be suspended.[2] This seeming contradiction in our sources can be removed if we accept that Cicero is speaking of a *de facto* cessation of all court proceedings (except, of course, the Varian) which came about as the inevitable consequence of war. Though no formal suspension had been made those who normally presided over the courts were now away on campaign. Only the new *quaestio* continued to function doubtless because it was held, by some at any rate, to be actually contributing to the war effort by rooting out traitors at home.[3] Asconius, on the other hand, is describing the moment when a decree officially closed all the courts.[4] But, though all were affected, the real target was plainly the Varian *quaestio*. The number being unjustly condemned there is given as one of the main motives for the senate's

165

action.[5] The debate which the measure provoked in *contiones* can only be explained if a controversial *judicium* i.e. the Varian commission was in question.[6]

Thus, as a result of the press of war, all Roman courts, except that established by Varius, ceased to function *de facto* soon after the beginning of 90. Some time later, in order to muzzle the Varian commission, the senate promulgated a measure which made official the cessation of all judicial business.[7]

There is no reason to doubt that Varius was a *popularis*. Seizing on the widespread belief that Drusus and his friends had somehow encouraged the allies to revolt he persuaded the people to establish a *quaestio* to punish the guilty. As might be expected from a body set up at such a time and with such a brief, a disinterested search after the truth did not always characterise its proceedings. The *equites* who manned it were only too delighted to have an opportunity to be revenged on those who had attempted to deprive them of their judicial powers, nor does it come as a great surprise to discover that Philippus and Caepio continued their assault on Drusus' supporters through this new medium. In the end, however, this vindictiveness proved to be the undoing of both the tribunal and its author. Like many another *popularis* Varius soon discovered the plebs could be a fickle friend. Their initial enthusiasm for the tribune soon turned to revulsion at seeing so many distinguished men being put on trial. In other words, the people of Rome soon deserted their erstwhile champion and gave their allegiance once more to those whom they customarily regarded as their rightful leaders. It was this change of heart that the senate capitalised on when it proposed that the Varian court be suspended. It is, I think, fair to say that the majority of senators had, from the outset, small enthusiasm for prosecuting Drusus' followers. They are hardly likely to have viewed with equanimity such an assault on their order. But there was yet another pressing consideration. The decision to kill the commission was taken at a time when the full magnitude of the revolt was being revealed. In such circumstances the need for unity in the face of the foe was clear and with a witch hunt in progress at Rome that was hardly likely to be achieved. The dangers attendant on such divisions spilling over into the camp were only too well illustrated, for instance, in the quarrel between Rutilius and the patricians.[8]

It is, therefore, correct to speak of a reaction among the plebs but not in the senate where there never had been anything but hostility to the court from the first.[9] Then, with morale improving at Rome as the war situation got better in 89, the senate felt strong enough to move decisively against Varius. When the *justitium* came to an end, the Varian court resumed its activities but with a change of personnel. The lex Plautia judicaria had been passed and juries were now to be composed of senators, *equites* and even, it is said, some plebians.[10] As two of these groups were hostile to Varius it comes as no surprise to learn that he was hauled before his own tribunal and condemned.[11]

What we are witnessing here is a further shift in public opinion. From a disgust with Varius' prosecutions people had moved to an active hatred of the man himself. In the highly volatile atmosphere of contemporary Rome pity for Varius' victims very quickly led to the belief that they were innocent and that the real culprit was the tribune. This notion that the activities of the court had led to the revolt of the allies is, in fact, found in our sources and it must be said that there is some justification for it.

The vast majority of sources are agreed on the chronology and the sequence of those events which constitute the outbreak of the Social War. In late 91, with the death of Drusus the revolt began. It started with the massacre at Asculum and then spread rapidly to other areas.[12] App. B.C. 1. 37-39 gives a different order. He says the Varian commission was set up on Drusus' death and condemned a number of distinguished men. This upset the people. More important it also angered the allies. The activities of the court and the death of Drusus showed them there was no hope of obtaining the citizenship. They, therefore, began to form conspiracies. For a long time the Romans, distracted by the trials in the city, knew nothing of these plots. At last, when they did realise what was going on they sent out praetors to investigate and one of them provoked the revolt at Asculum. The rebellion then spread. Next the allies sent ambassadors to complain that they had helped build the empire but had been denied the citizenship. The senate said if they repented of what they had done they could send ambassadors, otherwise not. The war then began in earnest.

This account is to be rejected for the simple reason that the Varian commission was not set up until 90. It therefore follows that Appian is self-evidently wrong in seeing certain consequences as flowing from it in 91. Nor could they have come from it in 90 either since there would simply not be enough time for them before the beginning of campaigning. Thus, while Appian, in agreement with our other sources, rightly puts the sending of praetors, the massacre at Asculum and the spread of the revolt in 91 he is in error when he connects them with the Varian *quaestio*.[13]

This does not mean, however, that we should entirely reject the idea — found also in Val. Max. 8.6.4 — that the activities of the Varian court led, in some way, to the rebellion of the allies. While the court could not have had the effect Appian says it had in the context in which he places it, it could, indeed, have had such an effect at the beginning of 90. It will be remembered he tells us that, after a large part of Italy took up arms, the insurgents paused and sent an embassy. This is not improbable in itself and it receives a certain amount of corroboration from Vell. Pat. 2.15.2., whose description of allied grievances closely resembles those which Appian represents his embassy as articulating. As this embassy is placed after the initial furious outbreak of rebellion and the beginning of what some of the ancients saw as the first year of the war[14] we can assume the allies took advantage of the lull occasioned by the winter season of 91/90 to make one last attempt to reach an accommodation with Rome. When the ambassadors arrived we cannot say but early 90 is at least as likely as late 91. And we know that the court was active at precisely that time. It is, therefore, not straining credulity to suggest that the Italians would have learned of its work and drawn the appropriate conclusions. These prosecutions, together with the senate's reply, were convincing proofs that a compromise was now impossible. In this sense then the Varian commission can be described as one of the proximate causes of the Social War. To postulate, therefore, as some have done, that Varius was accused of provoking or prolonging the war with his tribunal would appear to be correct.[15]

Although I have claimed that the Varian court was often used as a means to pursue political quarrels, it is obviously of some importance to determine if any of those who were hauled before it could be said to have been, in any way, legitimately charged and to have had some kind of case to answer. We may, I think, assume that none of those accused actually incited the allies to revolt but were there any among them whose support for Drusus' enfranchisement proposals was so wholehearted and enthusiastic as to leave them open to the accusation that they, in fact, did so? This question can be put in another way: were there among the supporters of Drusus prominent aristocrats who, abandoning the traditional hostility of their class, urged him on in his efforts?[16]

Of those condemned there can be little doubt that C. Aurelius Cotta wholeheartedly supported Drusus' Italian policy since he was one of those designated to carry on the tribune's work. Likewise the subsequent career of another heir, P. Sulpicius, shows clearly where his sympathies lay. He is generally believed to have escaped prosecution because he was away on military service.[17] Pompeius Rufus, the consul of 88, was also obliged to defend himself before the tribunal. Since he *conjunctissime et amantissime vixerat* with Sulpicius it is likely he agreed with him on the Italian question. It is difficult to imagine their friendship surviving a disagreement over this issue. Indeed, the subsequent breach between the two seems to have come about precisely because Pompeius changed his mind on the matter.[18] If the position of these men is tolerably clear the same can hardly be said of the other defendants or potential defendants. What Scribonius Curio's connection if any, with Drusus was, for instance we do not know.[19] Among those who advised Drusus was Aemilius Scaurus. He had, in the past, shown hostility to the Italians as had that other prominent Drusan supporter L. Crassus, co-author of the lex Licinia Mucia and now deceased. Whether the backing of this latter pair for Drusus meant that they had had a genuine conversion to the Italian cause is open to question. The only motive we hear attributed to Scaurus is that he wished to reform the courts. Thus, while it would be safe to say that the pair, like another adviser L. Memmius, had, at the very least, accepted that enfranchisement was a price which might have to be paid for judicial reform, it would be hazardous, in the absence of any firm evidence, to suggest more.[20] Much the same may be said of Antonius. He was an intimate of Crassus and is described as his *consiliorum in republica socius.* Such credentials make it likely he offered some support to Drusus and it was because of this he was accused. We are not told however where he stood on the Italian issue.[21]

It would appear therefore that Drusus' most fervent supporters on the Italian issue were mainly the promising young or the merely obscure. Of those who could claim to be elder statesmen, it can only be said that there is not sufficient evidence to allow us to divine their attitudes, so we must conclude that it would be dangerous to speak of a major shift in attitude by significant members of the Roman ruling class.

But whatever their views before, as the war progressed the Romans conceded that citizenship would, after all, have to be granted to the Italians. We will, therefore, proceed to an examination of the contents of the enabling legislation in order to evaluate its significance. We may begin with a notice of a lex Calpurnia which tells us that, under this law, a commander might reward valour with the gift of citizenship.[22] We are not told when this law was passed but two considerations point to a date early in 90. In the first instance, the Romans, in their present plight would surely want to encourage foreigners to fight and so enabling legislation would be a priority.[23] Secondly, we know that the lex Julia de civitate contained a like clause but that this law was not passed until late in the year.[24] Thus, it must have been by virtue of the powers conferred by the lex Calpurnia that Caesar himself was able to offer citizenship to a Cretan in the course of the year.[25] It therefore follows that the lex Calpurnia preceded the Julian law and that the latter was intended, in this respect anyway to supersede it.[26]

But, as is well known, the lex Julia de civitate was far wider in scope than the lex Calpurnia. It, in fact, granted the citizenship to all those allies and Latins who had not joined the uprising. It made no provision, however, for those who having rebelled, might subsequently surrender.[27] The citizens thus created were to be enrolled, not in the existing tribes, but in a number of new creations which finally seem to have totalled eight.[28] These new tribes do not appear to have been created altogether but piecemeal over a period of time as new accessions required it. This we may infer from a fragment of Sisenna (17P) which reads, *Lucius Calpurnius Piso ex senati consulto duas novas tribus.* I do not believe this notice refers to the Calpurnian law we discussed earlier. We may beg leave to doubt that battlefield enfranchisements were so numerous as to require two new tribes to accommodate them. Moreover, given what we know of the scope of the lex Julia it also appears unlikely that any law passed previous to it could have dealt with the enfranchisement of the Italian communities. We can, therefore, say with reasonable confidence that we have caught here a glimpse of the implementation of the lex Julia. Two new tribes are being created and others no doubt followed especially as the number of citizens was to be further swollen by the lex Plautia Papiria.[29]

This law was passed in the next year (89). As the war turned against the allies it became necessary to make arrangements for those who had yielded. The provisions of the lex Julia were to be extended to *dediticii*. Those who surrendered within a specified time were to be admitted to the citizenship on the same terms as those who had not rebelled.[30] The procedure followed for admittance seems to have been the same under both acts. The senate decided that a particular people was eligible and the people then passed a law admitting it to the citizenship. The Italians were thus incorporated as communities, not as individuals. Ceasing to be sovereign states they now became *municipia*.[31]

One might have expected that this recognition, however belated, by the Romans of Italian claims should have put an end, once and for all, to the citizenship question. The new policy ought to have ended the problem but, instead, the mean spirited and ungenerous manner in which it was implemented was destined ere long to create fresh turmoil and trouble. Earlier in this chapter we delineated a shift in mood at Rome and it is important now that we remind ourselves precisely what this entailed. It means that the blame for inciting the allies was shifted from Drusus' followers to Varius and his friends and that is all. There is nowhere any evidence that the Romans had now acquired a tender regard for the Italians themselves. For them the admission of the Italians still represented a threat to their position which had to be countered. What they had done, they had done from necessity but, having been forced to grant now what they had earlier refused, they intended to see to it that the minimum of upset to existing arrangements should follow. In 90 the war had not gone well for the Romans and towards the end of that year they were faced with the horrid prospect of further serious defections from among the ranks of those who up until now had remained loyal. To confirm the waverers the lex Julia was passed and great care was taken to broadcast its provisions as widely as possible.[32] From this it was but a short step to the lex Plautia Papiria since it was obvious to everybody that Italy would never be at peace until all were enfranchised. At the same time, the Romans had no intention of sharing actual power with the newcomers if they could help it. Hence those enfranchised under the two laws were carefully segregated into eight tribes where their votes would be of little use. But when the Italians realised how they had been duped they were furious and their efforts to seek redress with the aid of Roman allies plunged Rome into a fresh crisis. As their hopes of independence faded, the problems of the Italians once more became bound up with the politics of Rome.

It is true that discord appears to raise its head first because of a separate issue, the recall of the Varian exiles but, as we shall see in due course, this was, in fact, intimately connected with the Italian question. A move was made, either late in 89 or early in 88, to recall the Varian exiles. It was, however, vetoed by the tribune P. Sulpicius.[33] Nor was this the only way in which he may have manifested hostility to the exiles' return. The orator Caesar Strabo had made an illegal bid for the consulship of 88 and it would appear he intended to bring back the victims of the Varian commission. He was immediately opposed by Sulpicius and matters went so far that their respective supporters fought each other on the streets of Rome.[34]

This behaviour of Sulpicius is distinctly odd. Some of the exiles, like himself, had been keen supporters of Drusus and yet we now find him opposing their return to Rome. Why he should have behaved in this way is a matter for conjecture but such conjecture must begin from one unalterable fact: by his subsequent behaviour, Sulpicius showed, beyond a shadow of doubt, that he still saw himself as Drusus' successor and intended to complete his work by bringing about the redistribution of the Italians among all of the tribes. Bearing this in mind, I would deduce that he turned against his old friends purely as a matter of policy. In opposing Caesar's candidature and the recall of the exiles he must have been acting in accordance with someone else's wishes and I would guess that this someone was, in fact, the senate. The most influential man of the day, Sulla, had little reason to love either Caesar Strabo or the exiles, nor would the majority of senators approve of an illegal candidature or an attempt to disturb *concordia* by bringing back those who had been expelled. If I am right in suggesting that Sulpicius had thus closely identified himself with senatorial interests then we may further assume he intended to seek the support of those same interests in his efforts to effect the redistribution of the Italians and that he had some expectation of getting it. In the event, his calculations proved to be ill-founded and he was thus obliged to look for backing elsewhere.[35]

In view of what we know of the usual senatorial attitude towards the Italians it is easy to accuse Sulpicius of naivety in expecting the fathers to give their blessing to his schemes. But a man of his background would probably not have acted otherwise. He had, as it were, two models whom he might follow, C. Gracchus or Drusus. All of his instincts and experience must have impelled him to follow in the footsteps of the latter. A trial would have to be made of the attitude of the senate and Sulpicius, like Drusus, would have to try and sway it before he would consider embracing *popularis* methods.

Now, rebuffed he turned to Marius for help. As we know, the old general had, in the past, showed a certain generosity towards the Italians but could, by no means, be described as their passionate and committed champion. At this point all that changed and he flung himself wholeheartedly behind Sulpicius' comprehensive schemes. This change of face may be directly attributed to motives of self-interest. He had long cherished the ambition of obtaining another great military command which would allow him to restore some of his dimming prestige. Recent events had shown, however, that he could not expect such a boon from his enemies in the senate. They had carefully circumscribed him in the late war and had appointed his arch-foe, Sulla to be general in the coming conflict with Mithridates. He was therefore prepared to lend his support to the schemes of Sulpicius on the understanding that the tribune would then bring it about that the Eastern command would be transferred to him.

Thus, in forming this alliance, Sulpicius, like other Romans before him who had made the Italian cause their own, bound the problem of Italy to contemporary Roman political issues. And, as in the past, this union was to prove fatal to its author in the end. What is surprising is that Sulpicius took so few measures to minimise the risks attendant on the course upon which he was now embarked. It is true that when he unveiled his *popularis* programme he was prudent enough to say nothing about the proposed change in the Mithridatic command. But he made no secret of what his principal objective was: the distribution of the new citizens and the freedmen among the thirty-five tribes and he made no effort to forestall the plebian ire this would provoke. To propose such a scheme, without giving the commons something substantial at the same time, would now be especially dangerous. Their natural hatred of concessions to Italy must have been considerably sharpened by their sufferings in the late war. Yet Sulpicius seems to have chosen to ignore this elementary fact of political life. He was either unable or unwilling to offer the plebs anything. It may very well be that, having his following swollen by enthusiastic Italians, he calculated that he could trample down all opposition from the people of Rome and hence there was no need to offer them any accommodation.

If that is so, then Sulpicius was, for a time, proved correct. Rioting broke out almost immediately after the proposal for redistribution was published and intensified as the day for voting on the measure drew nearer. In this crisis the consul Sulla was recalled from Nola and he, together with his colleague Pompeius Rufus, proclaimed *Feriae*, i.e. a cessation of public business. Sulpicius, however, confident of the strength of his following, was not to be balked. Arming his followers he attacked the consuls as they were holding a *contio* and forced them to call off the moratorium. When the day for voting then arrived he was able by sheer force to intimidate the assembly and have his bill passed into law.

At this point it must have seemed that the Italians had secured their objective: the citizenship in a full and meaningful form. Unfortunately the fragility of Sulpicius' position and the weakness of his power base were now to be revealed although it should, in fairness, be stated that the revelation was as great a surprise to his enemies as it was to him since his destruction came from so unexpected a quarter. With redistribution out of the way Sulpicius now had to redeem his secret promise to Marius. Sulla, however, while perforce having to accept concessions to the Italians was not prepared, under any circumstances, to tolerate the loss of the Mithridatic command. After his recent humiliation he had withdrawn to Nola once more and now, putting himself at the head of his troops, he marched on Rome. In this instant the world was drastically changed. Hitherto, when Roman political quarrels had proceeded to violence, it had been confined to fighting between rival mobs. Now, for the first time, the army took a hand in the business and Sulla's success soon emboldened others to do likewise. The army was to become a factor in political disputes in the years immediately after 88. This was a circumstance which, as we shall soon see, the Italians were able to turn to their own advantage. For the moment, however, Sulla's intervention was to prove catastrophic both for them and their ally. Sulpicius' mob showed itself to be no match for the soldiers and after a brief struggle its resistance caved in. The tribune and some of his leading supporters were then made public enemies. He alone was captured and killed and with him there perished his schemes for the Italians since Sulla had all his laws declared null and void.

Two factors, however, ensured that the matter was not destined to end there. In the first place, the Italians were not to be cowed. Their role in the events which now followed makes it quite plain they were determined to seize the next available opportunity to get what they wanted. For them the destruction of Sulpicius was no more than a temporary setback. They would find another champion and the second factor, namely the peculiarity of Sulla's position at this time, ensured he would not fear to come forward. Sulla had claimed to have done what he had done in order to free Rome from tyrants. If he were not to make a mockery of this claim then he would have to allow free elections and acquiesce in the election of men who were hostile to himself. Moreover, the threatening situation on the war front meant he must soon depart for Greece. So, anybody who wished to bring up the Italian question again would have to wait but a little while until he was gone.

In this situation the man who emerged as the new champion of the Italians was the consul of 87, Cinna. What is beyond dispute is that he was some little while into his consulship before he made his move. What is less easy to determine — since he is a shadowy and enigmatic figure — is whether this represents a late conversion to the cause or whether it simply shows that Cinna was a long committed partisan who prudently kept quiet until Sulla was safely out of the way.

It may very well be of course, that Cinna's intentions, if he had any, were known long before he actually attempted to introduce his bill since there is no doubt that Sulla had his own suspicions of him. Fearing that Cinna would upset the present arrangements he made him swear on oath to be faithful to his policies. Logically this could mean that, along with other schemes, Cinna was known to be contemplating a change in the way the Italians voted since, although the present system had not originated with Sulla, it had been dramatically reaffirmed by him and formed an integral part of his recent hasty remodelling of the state. One consideration must, however, give us pause. Sulpicius had amply demonstrated that high and low alike were not prepared to countenance Italian redistribution. I consider it unlikely, therefore, that Cinna would choose such a platform when he went to face the electorate. Rather, it would appear that he capitalised on the widespread hatred felt for Sulla because of his march on Rome. There were many who, while brooking no interference with those of Sulla's laws which profited themselves, were prepared to make consul someone who intended to have him punished for what he had done. Certainly, when Cinna assumed office, his first overt move was to try with the aid of a friendly tribune, to have Sulla stripped of his *imperium* and forced to return to Rome to stand trial.[36]

Thus, we must confess that the timing of Cinna's conversion to the Italian cause is as dark as the motives which impelled him to such a course.[37] What we should have no difficulty in appreciating, however, are the consequences which were to flow from his espousal.

Notes

1. Sources: Greenidge and Clay pp. 136-7. On the nature of Varius' law and his *quaestio* see Badian (1969) pp. 447-52 and Seager pp. 37-40. Dating: Gruen (1965) p. 159; Badian (1969) pp. 459-60.

2. Cic. *Brut.* 303-4; Asc. 73-4C. On the date Cicero entered public life see Badian (1969) p. 457, n. 28.

3. This view takes full cognisance of the fact that Cicero's account of his early career in the *Brutus* can be misleading — on which see Badian (1969) pp. 453-8. It also meets, I think, Badian's point — (1969) p. 460 — that *judicia* must surely have been suspended once war began, see further n. 4. We may further observe that, since Cicero's main interest is in telling us of the orators he heard, there is no compelling reason why he should actually mention the suspension of the Varian *quaestio*.

4. As was rightly stressed by Badian (1969) p. 452 the piecemeal manner in which the rebellion spread (3.2) means that Asconius' mention of *crebraeque defectiones Italicorum* can be taken to refer to a point some little time into the year 90. We are at the stage when the gravity of the situation is being fully realised.

5. For the full significance of the senate's motives see below.

6. So Badian (1969) p. 452 after Bauman. It may also be remarked that it is difficult to see what court Curio feared and escaped save that of Varius.

7. This reconstruction does not involve us, as does that of Badian (1969) pp. 453-4, 460 in rejecting sections of Asconius' evidence. In particular it can be noted that, while Asconius' remarks on Curio may, as Badian says, be only a guess, they are, I feel, a better guess than Badian's own.

8. Varius *popularis*: Cic. *Sest.* 101. *Equites*: App. B.C. 1.37. Philippus and Caepio: Cic. *Brut.* 304; Asc. 22C. Popular revulsion: App. B.C. 1.38 with Badian (1969) pp. 466-7, 475-81. Circumstances of the *justitium*: Asc. 73-4C. Rutilius: 3.2. The man who engineered trouble in Cato's army (3.2) probably got off because the senate did not want to antagonise the plebs. On all of this see further the pertinent remarks of Seager pp. 41-3.

9. See also the remarks of Badian (1969) pp. 467-8.

10. Asc. 79C, cf. Badian (1969) p. 470, n. 66.

11. Sources: Greenidge and Clay p. 151. Varius, it would appear,

went into exile and the story of his execution must therefore refer to some other time (Seager p. 41). I find very attractive the suggestion of Strachan-Davidson that he perished in the Sullan proscriptions. That was notoriously a period when old scores were paid off and old injuries avenged, cf. Keaveney (1983) p. 153.

12. Vell. Pat. 2.15.1; Flor. 2.6.4,9-10; Liv. ep.72; Oros. 5.18.1-8; Diod. Sic. 37.2.2. Cf. Gabba (1967) p. 126.

13. It is also improbable that the Italians waited until after the death of Drusus to form conspiracies. So, we must accept the testimony of those sources which, unlike Appian, place their formation before. On the nature of Appian's mistake see Gabba (1967) p. 126; Haug p. 226; Marcks p. 46.

14. Asc. 79C.

15. Cf. Badian (1969) p. 462.

16. The cases are fully discussed by Gruen (1965) pp. 61-7 but not all of his conclusions seem acceptable. I have taken my cue from the more cautious approach of Seager pp. 42-3 although I am not as conservative as he.

17. Cotta: Gruen (1965) p. 64. Sulpicius: Cic. *de Orat.* 3.11, *Brut.* 304.

18. Cic. *Brut.* 304, *de Amic.* 2, cf. Keaveney (1979) pp. 454-5.

19. Asc. 74C. But see n. 20.

20. Scaurus: Cic. *de Orat.* 2.257; Asc. 21-22C, cf. Gruen (1965) pp. 62-3. Memmius: Cic. *Brut.* 304 with Sumner pp 85-90. He was the father-in-law of Scribonius Curio. He should probably not be conflated with the Mummius of App. B.C. 1.37, cf. Badian (1969) p. 469, n. 65. The motives of L. Calpurnius Bestia (App. B.C. 1.37) are dark, see Gruen (1965) pp. 64-5.

21. Cic. *de Orat.* 1.24, *Tusc. Disp.* 2.57. As Badian (1969) pp. 456-8 points out, Cic. *Brut.* 304 causes problems since it describes Antonius as absent. He therefore tentatively suggested that Antonius was prosecuted not in the first phase of the court but in the second when the jury panel had been reformed. This seems to me unlikely. Since we have evidence to connect Antonius with the Drusan group it would appear reasonable to suppose he was prosecuted when they were. It is, I feel, less probable that he should be accused when the court was turning its attention to opponents of the group. His trial would therefore belong to the period before Cicero entered the Forum. Likewise I do not believe, as I did once (Keaveney 1979 pp. 458-9), that Pomponius' career would make of him the defendant of Asc. 79C.

22. Sisenna fr. 120P.

23. On the necessity for such legislation see Luraschi pp. 326-30.

24. Sources: Greenidge and Clay p. 142. Niccolini pp. 110-11 tries to put it early in the year but his arguments are not convincing, cf. e.g. Luraschi p. 323, n. 5. *ILS* 8888 shows the citizenship being conferred on soldiers by the terms of this law. The idea that Pompey Strabo might have gone beyond the strict letter of the law — discussed by Criniti pp. 43-5 — seems unnecessary. After Marius and the Camertines the senate might be expected to assert its authority over such grants by legislation, cf. n. 23. Luraschi pp. 330-4 suggests that the lex Julia under which Strabo operated is different from the lex Julia de civitate. This seems to

me no more than a vain attempt to bolster the unlikely hypothesis that the lex Calpurnia was posterior to the latter act (see next note). Certainly, the argument that our literary sources for the lex Julia do not mention viritane grants can hardly carry much weight in view of the fragmentary nature of the evidence.

25. Diod. Sic. 37.18.

26. For a refutation of Niccolini's argument (pp. 119-21) that the lex Calpurnia was posterior to the lex Julia and intended to modify and supplement it see Gabba (1976) pp. 90-1. His case is not demolished by Luraschi pp. 326-7 who forgets that a Roman law often takes over provisions from previous legislation it is intended to supersede and that the lex Julia could have been intended to act as an enabling law for the duration of the war. The enfranchisement of Minatius Magius(Vell. Pat. 2.16.3) was probably sanctioned by the lex Julia.

27. Cf. Gabba (1976) pp. 91-2; Keaveney *Crit. Stor.* (1982) pp. 502-4.

28. This is the figure given by Vell. Pat. 2.20.2 in a passage which is to be dated after the lex Plautia Papiria, cf. n. 30. App. B.C. 1.49 also mentions the creation of new tribes but what he means by δεκατεύοντες is not clear. The two most recent attempts to explain it are not entirely convincing. One, Lewis pp. 273-91, seems somewhat strained while the other, M.W. Seston, 'La lex Julia de 90 av. J.-C. et l'integration des Italiens dans la citoyenneté Romaine', *Comptes Rendus de l'Academie des inscriptions et belles lettres*, 1978, pp. 529-42 proposes what appears to be an unduly complicated solution.

29. See further Lewis pp. 275-83 and Gabba (1976) p. 91.

30. Sources: Greenidge and Clay pp. 151-2 with Sherwin-White (1973) pp. 151-3; Keaveney *Crit. Stor.* (1982) pp. 503-5; Luraschi pp. 340-60.

31. Sherwin-White (1973) pp. 150-1, 153, 159-65; Luraschi pp. 360-9; Laffi (1973).

32. App. B.C. 1.49 with Gabba (1976) pp. 91-4.

33. *Auct. ad Herr.* 2.45, cf. Keaveney (1979) pp. 455-6. It may be noted that Cicero himself uses non-technical language in speaking of the Varian exile Cotta: *est expulsus* (*Brut.* 305), *ejectus est e civitate* (*de Orat.* 3.11). This furnishes a further argument against the view that the *Auctor* is to be taken literally when he uses such expressions as *vi ejectos*. Cicero also says (*de Orat.* 3.11) that Sulpicius as tribune started to deprive his friends *omni dignitate*. This may be a reference to his supposed attempt to strip Pompeius of his consulship — for which see Keaveney *Eirene* (1983) pp. 60-2 — but to judge from the context, it is more likely to refer to action taken against the Drusan group. If that is so, then Cicero must be referring to the situation described by the *Auctor*.

34. Cic. *de har. Resp.* 43, *Brut.* 226, *Phil.* 11.11; Asc. 25C; Quint. 6.75 with Keaveney (1979) pp. 451-4, 457 although I do not now believe that Caesar was allowed to proceed with his candidature. In considering Caesar's aims I rejected the evidence of Diod. Sic. 37.2.12 and we may add that this kind of error is found elsewhere in Diodorus, cf. e.g. 37.11.12 with Walton *ad loc.* For a different view of Caesar's motives see Levick pp. 507-8.

35. See Keaveney (1979) pp. 457-60.

36. Sources and discussion in Keaveney *Eirene* (1983) and (1983) pp. 56-76. To the bibliography there add now Levick. I am not so sure as I then was that Cinna would campaign for the return of the exiles. That, too, might be a dangerously controversial issue for a consular candidate to raise.

37. The story that Cinna received a present of 300 talents from the Italians (App. B.C. 1.64) might be true. He could have been affected by the debt crisis like so many other Romans (3.2) and he would, of course, have had electoral expenses. I doubt, however, if bribery was the only reason for Cinna acting as he did.

4.2

Roman Politics and the Italian Question
87-81 BC

Once Sulla was safely out of the way, early in 87, Cinna was able to get to work without further waste of time. Then, we are told, he encouraged the friends of Marius and Sulpicius to stir up the new citizens to revive once more the demand that they be distributed among the thirty-five tribes. I take this to mean that while the consul was the moving spirit behind and lent the weight of his authority to a bill embodying this proposed change, he was not its actual author who was most likely one of the tribunes. The measure was no more palatable to senate and people now than it had been a year or so before and, as the new citizens flocked to Rome to press their suit, the Romans made ready to resist it. The inevitable riot rapidly developed into a pitched battle. Cinna was worsted in the fray and obliged to flee from Rome.[1]

But he did not go far.[2] He had suffered much on behalf of the Italians and he could, in consequence, count on their aid. So he made a progress through the towns of Latium gathering men and money. He then proceeded into Campania and continued on his way until he came to Nola. There an army under Appius Claudius Pulcher was still prosecuting the siege of the town. Although the commander remained loyal the troops went over to Cinna's side. Meantime, those who had fled from Rome with the consul had been busy in like enterprises, visiting Italian cities and winning support for the cause. The campaign was a great success and Cinna soon found himself at the head of thirty legions or at least that is what the ancients say. With this army he made ready to assault Rome.[3] Cinna was not, however, the only man at this time who presumed on the goodwill of the Italians. After being chased from Italy, Marius had taken refuge in Africa. On hearing of this new turn of events, he set out for home and landed at

Telamon in Etruria. Since Cinna and his friends had not come this way Marius appears to have calculated that the area would provide him with an ideal recruiting ground. He certainly neglected no means by which he might increase his following. Capitalising on the glamour of his name he reminded the inhabitants of the services he had rendered the state in order to induce them to serve under him. He also recruited widely among the slave population and even went so far as to break open *ergastula* in his search for bodies. One might have thought this would have alienated the local upper classes since it raised the spectre of upheaval and revolution but, in fact, it appears that it did not. Possibly Marius' recruiting among such people was on a comparatively modest scale but more important was his pledge to back Etrurian interests in the matter of the vote. It was this, above all, which won their hearts. The Etruscans had never been opposed to the acquisition of the citizenship, merely to the surrender of land for it. Now, angered like the other Italians by the treatment meted out to Sulpicius and Cinna, they made ready to support Marius who had himself also given the most signal proofs of his devotion to their cause. Thus it was with forces collected in Etruria that Marius now marched to join Cinna.[4]

We see, then, where imitation of Sulla's example could lead. Those who wished to crush their foes by means of an army would have to recruit many Italians to its ranks. We shall soon discover that the implications of this state of affairs was not to be lost on either party to the transaction.

For the moment we may go on to observe that Cinna and his allies were now blockading Rome.[5] Cinna's enemy, the other consul Octavius, had deposed him from his consulship and put one Merula in his place. He had then made ready the city's defences and summoned the proconsul Pompey Strabo to his aid. The government's war effort was not helped by the latter's tendency to intrigue with both sides and very gradually Octavius' position worsened.[6] Then two events brought home to him the necessity for seeking further help. Marius captured Ostia which meant food supplies were now jeopardised. At about the same time, reinforcements from Cis-Alpine Gaul were intercepted by the Cinnans and, after a brief struggle, they threw in their lot with their opponents.[7]

Somewhat surprisingly, perhaps, in view of what it was had brought him to this pass, Octavius, like Cinna before him, turned to the Italians for help. The lex Plautia, it will be remembered, had granted the citizenship to those rebels who had laid down their arms by a certain date. In its hour of need the senate jettisoned this last proviso and gave the citizenship to all *dediticii* irrespective of when they made their submission. Whatever hopes there may have been that this move would significantly augment the government forces proved abortive, however, when only about sixteen cohorts put in an appearance.[8] The allies could have no reason to feel friendly to Octavius and his followers and there was no compelling necessity to oblige them either since it was beginning to look as if Octavius would lose this war.

This meant that recourse would have to be had instead to the other proconsul still in the field, Metellus Pius. His position was a difficult one. The civil war at Rome had presented the Italian rebel remnant with an opportunity to repair their fortunes and they had not been slow to avail of it. In Bruttium the Lucanians were sweeping all before them in a drive on Sicily. Further north Cinna's removal of the besieging forces from Nola left the Samnites in that city free to sally forth. They ravaged Campania and beyond, burning Abella in the process. Metellus was campaigning against them when a senatorial delegation arrived and instructed him to try and come to terms with the enemy in order to be free to bring his army to the defence of Rome. When approached the Samnites demanded citizenship for themselves and all deserters to their side. They further demanded that all deserters from their own ranks, together with all capitives, be restored to them. Finally, they were to retain all their booty. These were severe terms and Metellus, who had a proper regard for the majesty of Rome, refused to accept them. Others were not so scrupulous. Through the agency of Fimbria, Marius and Cinna granted the Samnites all that they asked. The upshot was that Metellus could only bring a part of his army to Rome and the remainder, under the command of the legate Plautius, was soon overwhelmed by these new allies of Cinna.[9]

In the event, the arrival of Metellus' forces did the government no good. The siege and its attendant battles continued until, at last, the senate was forced to yield and the victorious Cinna entered the city.[10]

Thus, Cinna became master of Rome and was to remain such for the next three years. A good deal has been written about his period of dominance and some have found things to praise in the system of government which he established. I do not intend, at this point, to enter into the debate on the quality of Cinna's rule since it is not germane to my purpose.[11] We are here primarily concerned with the position of the Italians under his regime. We have just seen how they played a large part in bringing Cinna to power since his armies were largely composed of them. Thus, in a short time, the Italians had gone from being defeated *dediticii* to being one of the decisive forces in contemporary Roman politics. In order therefore to delineate Cinna's relations with them after his victory we do not have to decide whether he was a good ruler or not but rather to ask how he tried to retain the power he had now seized.

Although it might, at first, appear that Cinna had swept all before him, in truth his position was not strong. Master of Italy he might be (although even here there was, as we shall see, cause for disquiet) together with Sicily and Sardinia but beyond all was uncertain or openly hostile. Valerius Flaccus with his army in Spain and Gaul was an unknown quantity who would require careful handling and Africa for much of the period was to remain out of Cinna's control. Worst of all, the East was totally lost as a result of the Mithridatic War and there also was Cinna's greatest enemy, Sulla, at the head of an army. It is true that, at this particular moment, the proconsul was experiencing considerable difficulties but Cinna could by no means count on his inevitable destruction, and, if Sulla should, in fact, emerge triumphant then it was certain he would come looking for revenge, aided and abetted by other dissidents like Metellus who had fled before Rome fell.[12]

Thus, if Cinna were ever to be secure Sulla would have to be neutralised or destroyed. To accomplish such an aim it was obvious he would need the whole-hearted support of that part of the Roman world which he ruled over. If he were to deal with Sulla he would need to have both old and new citizens behind him. Unfortunately their backing would not necessarily be automatic. We know of course that it was largely with Italian support that Cinna had become master of Rome but he could not rely upon their unquestioning obedience should he call upon them simply to maintain him in position regardless of what he might do. They had not fought for him but rather for his policies. He could count on them only for as long as they believed him to be the man best fitted to serve their interests. He was certainly in no position to coerce those who had put him where he was. While this is true of all Italians it was especially so in the case of the Lucanians and Samnites. Although they had been foiled in their bid to attack Sicily, the Lucanians still held Bruttium while the Samnites yet retained their hold on Nola and Aesernia. Moreover, both had wrested from Cinna terms which rendered them virtually independent.[13] Equally problematical was the attitude of the old citizens. Upon his entry to Rome Cinna had wreaked vengeance on his leading opponents by killing or exiling them. This can hardly have made him many friends in the senate.[14]

It is clear then that Cinna would have to woo those over whom he ruled. His energies appear to have been in the main directed towards the senate. Once he had actually disposed of his most important enemies Cinna called a halt to the killings and the policy of restraint was further aided by the death of Marius who, far more than Cinna, had been motivated by thoughts of revenge. During the struggle to regain the city, Cinna had shown a willingness to treat with those he did not regard as irreconcilables. Now he set out to win those who had not compromised themselves too far. Clearly differentiating, by his studied moderation, between those who had committed what he regarded as criminal acts against himself and the great majority who could be held to be blameless, he set about conciliating the latter and associating them in his rule.[15]

The fruits of this policy are to be seen in the events of the next few years which clearly show Cinna having to defer to the wishes of those in the senate who wanted to compose the quarrel between him and Sulla. While the Mithridatic war was still in progress, an army was despatched to replace that of Sulla. Its commander was ordered, however, to try and make terms with Sulla before bringing him to battle. It is not, I think, unreasonable to suggest that the inspiration for this conciliatory gesture came from the senate and its *princeps* Valerius Flaccus and that Cinna had, perforce, to acquiesce in it.[16] Again, when the war was over, Cinna seems to have been unable or unwilling to prevent the senate from entering into full scale negotiations with Sulla in an effort to try and avert the coming civil war.[17]

Towards the Italians Cinna showed himself far less accommodating. We saw that all of them had been admitted to the citizenship by 87 but their redistribution was not carried out until 84 after Cinna's death even though this was one of the issues which had caused him to go to war in the first place.[18] This will admit of two possible explanations. If we accept the view that Cinna had never been wholly sincere in his championship of the Italian cause then it is not difficult to see why he would not regard this work as a matter requiring urgent attention. Having got what he wanted from them, he was prepared to let the Italians wait. On the other hand, it is equally probable that Cinna was sacrificing what was for him a real point of principle in order to secure his own position. In the conditions which prevailed between 87 and 85 it is quite possible he felt the support of the senate to be more important than that of the Italians. Being ready to defer to that body in so many other matters it is also likely he would try to accomodate them on the enfranchisement question. In other words he was prepared to yield to a senate which still opposed any further concessions to the Italians.[19] But whatever Cinna's motivation, it is clear that by 85 he stood in great need of Italian support once more.

Now that Sulla had done with Mithridates he made it plain he would soon be returning home. To meet this threat it was necessary for Cinna to have an army ready. So he and his consular colleague Carbo turned once more to their old friends the Italians and began to recruit among them. They said they were in mortal peril precisely because of their efforts on behalf of these same Italians. The protestation must have rung hollow in the ears of many of their listeners. Up until this Cinna had not redeemed his promise to redistribute and now, continuing to try and conciliate the senate, he still persisted in this attitude. In consequence many Italians appear to have decided there was no particular reason why they should involve themselves in this quarrel. Thus, when, early in 84, Cinna tried to lead an army against Sulla in Greece it mutinied and he was murdered. Carbo then concluded that the temper of Italy was now so uncertain that drastic measures would be necessary to ensure its loyalty. He therefore proposed to extract hostages from all the towns and colonies as a pledge of their good behaviour. In this he was foiled by the senate and instead a more emollient policy was applied. Recognising the vital necessity of conciliating Italy, the Cinnans at last implemented the long awaited redistribution.[20]

But, for the Cinnans, the damage had already been done. Cinna had failed to identify where his true interests lay and this was to have the gravest consequences for his followers. Wooing the senate proved, in the end, to be a very bad mistake indeed because, when war came, most of that body simply chose the other side. And sacrificing the Italians for the sake of this misguided policy did not just mean that they viewed the Cinnans with a jaundiced eye but opened the way for somebody else to offer to act as guarantor of their rights.

About the time Cinna and Carbo began their recruiting drive a letter from Sulla arrived at Rome.[21] Characteristically it vowed vengeance on his enemies but it also made plain that Sulla had no quarrel with the vast majority of Romans, be they old or new citizens. Whether we have regard to its immediate, medium or long term effects, it is impossible to over-emphasise the importance of this letter. First of all, it cannot but have contributed to that Italian reluctance to fight which Cinna and Carbo had come upon to their cost. From the start, some Italians obviously wondered why they should support a man who had so far refused to fulfil his promise. Now they must have put themselves a further question: why should they fight against someone who said he would do them no harm?

But this is not all. Sulla's profession helped determine the Italian attitude (or rather attitudes) in the Civil War which was soon to begin. For the Romans the main issue in this war was a fairly simple one: was it Sulla or was it his opponents who represented legitimate authority? The Italians, however, were concerned with something rather different: obtaining and keeping the full rights of citizenship. Further, it was precisely because their numbers could be decisive in any conflict that both sides were prepared to listen to their demands. The Italians had become a force in Roman politics once more. And it was the Cinnans who by their bad faith and hesitancy ensured that men would listen when Sulla made his bid. Abandoning his earlier obduracy he, in effect, told the Italians that they might keep whatever rights they had gained.

This letter, therefore, gave the Italians a clear choice: they might choose the Cinnans as their champion or they might choose Sulla. Neither of these paladins could be described as being disinterested. The Cinnans had delayed granting redistribution until the threatening military situation made it a necessity. On the other hand, Sulla's previous record was not such as to inspire total confidence in either his sincerity or the purity of his motives. Therefore, the Italians would have to decide who was most likely to win the war and who, when he did, would then keep his word. In the event there was not to be unanimity in Italy on these questions.

We have just seen how, at first, things seemed to be going Sulla's way. His own opportunism seems to have weighed less heavily with the Italians than did Cinna's cynicism. The Italians would not fight and Carbo conceived grave doubts about their loyalty. What appears to have wrought a great change in this situation was the arrival of Sulla himself in Italy. I would guess that abhorrence of the notion that Italia should be invaded in this fashion was a potent factor in helping many, who had hitherto wavered, to declare for the Cinnans. Whatever the truth of this explanation, it is known that while Sulla could count on Calabria, Apulia and most of Picenum, he discovered the Samnites and Lucanians to be hostile along with a large part of Campania, Etruria and Umbria. But even after the war started neither side despaired of wooing further Italians to their side or detaching them from their enemies. Throughout the winter of 83 both Cinnans and Sullans furiously lobbied the Italians. Sulla himself signed a treaty with certain nations whereby he guaranteed them the rights they had recently won. At no time are the divided counsels then prevailing in Italy brought into sharper relief. A place which had declared for Sulla might yet harbour Cinnans or vice-versa. In contrast with the days of the Social War, the Italians no longer spoke with one voice. Individuals, groups, towns and nations had to decide for themselves whom they would support.

As is well known Sulla ultimately emerged as victor in this war. His triumph meant two things for the Italians. For those on the losing side it meant confiscation of land and in some cases, death or banishment. But, more important, for all Italians, winners or losers, save for the sons of the proscribed, it brought with it the achievement of the goal they had long set themselves. Sulla's victory set the seal on their work for he kept his word. Redeeming the promise made in his letter, he suffered them to maintain the position they had won for themselves. He acknowledged that henceforth their rights and privileges should be the same as those of other Romans.[22]

Both the Social War and the Civil War cost the Italians dear in terms of lives lost and material destruction. Yet, in one sense, they could be called the winners in both. In the Social War they had wrested the citizenship from the Romans; in the Civil War they had successfully ensured they should retain it and that in a form which made it worth retaining.

Notes

1. Principal sources: Greenidge and Clay pp. 171-2. All of these speak of Cinna as being the prime mover but App. B.C. 1.64 can, I think,

be taken to reflect a situation such as I describe in my text. This same passage offers some support also for those who think Cinna's conversion to the Italian cause was tardy, cf. Bennett p. 6. Some sources give the impression that Cinna first tried to recall the exiles. On this see Bulst pp. 308-9.

2. Exup. 4 is wrong (Bennett p. 9,n. 40).

3. App. B.C. 1.65-66; Vell. Pat. 2.20.3-4; Liv. ep.79; Sall. *Hist.* 1.27M. Appian specifically mentions Praeneste and Tibur among the towns Cinna visited in Latium. He also says Cinna seduced the army at Capua. This is probably a reference to its staff quarters, see Gabba (1967) p. 185. For those who fled with Cinna see Bennett p. 9. I take it they must have shared in his recruiting otherwise the army would hardly have grown so quickly.

4. Sources: Greenidge and Clay pp. 172-4, cf. Bennett pp. 11-12. Although I would not accept all the details it seems to me that the general thrust of Ruoff-Väänänen's argument (pp. 78-9) is correct. Marius, like Cinna, was capitalising on his past services to the Italians. See also E. Rawson, 'Caesar, Etruria and the *Disciplina Etrusca*', *JRS* 68, 1978 pp. 133-4; F. Sartori, 'Cinna e gli Schiavi' *Actes du Colloque 1971 sur l'esclavage: Centre de recherches d'histoire ancienne VI*, Paris, 1973, vol. 6 pp. 151-69.

5. App. B.C. 1.67; Oros. 5.19.9; Lic. 17F, Flor. 2.19.3; Liv., ep.79; Plut.*Sert.* 5, cf. Bennett p. 13.

6. App. B.C. 1.65-67; Vell. Pat. 2.20.3; Liv. ep.79; Lic. 18F; Oros. 5.19.10; Plut. *Mar.* 41, cf. Gabba (1967) p. 184 and Keaveney *CQ* (1978) pp. 240-1, *AC* (1982) pp. 111-13.

7. App. B.C. 1.67; Oros. 5.19.10-13; Lic. 18, 20F, cf. Bennett pp. 15-16.

8. Liv. ep.80; Lic. 21F. Cf. Keaveney *Crit. Stor.* (1982) pp. 502-5.

9. Dio fr. 102.7; Lic. 20-21F; Diod. Sic. 37.2.13-14; Sall. *Hist.* 1.28M; Liv. ep.80; App. B.C. 1.68. See Keaveney *Crit. Stor.* (1982) pp. 500-2.

10. Sources: Greenidge and Clay pp. 172-7.

11. My position on this question will be clear from Keaveney (1983).

12. Keaveney (1983) p. 84, *Klio* (1984) pp. 133-4.

13. Keaveney *Crit. Stor.* (1982) pp. 501-2. I infer present Italian attitudes from their behaviour a little later. See further below.

14. See Bennett pp. 24-35 and Keaveney *Klio* (1984) pp. 115-17.

15. On this see Gruen (1968) pp. 239-47.

16. Cinna's understanding with the *princeps* must have contributed towards the quiescence of the latter's cousin in Spain and Gaul.

17. See Keaveney (1983) pp. 117-24, *Klio* (1984) pp. 131-41.

18. Keaveney *Crit. Stor.* (1982) pp. 499-507. See further below.

19. Cf. Badian (1958) pp. 240-1.

20. App. B.C. 1.76-78; Liv. ep.83-84, cf. Keaveney *Crit. Stor.* (1982) pp. 505-7. For convenience I continue to call Sulla's opponents Cinnans.

21. App. B.C. 1.77 with Keaveney *Klio* (1984) pp. 134-5.

22. See Keaveney (1983) pp. 117-202 for a fuller discussion and bibliography.

4.3

Conclusion: Tota Italia

Sulla's victory brought to an end ten years of warfare, uncertainty and political strife in Italy. It remains for us to ask in what state they had left the Italians.

The Italians, as we know, were incorporated into the Roman state not as individuals but as whole communities. Thus the erst-while independent states of Italy became self-governing *municipia* with an *ordo* and magistrates. In the case of those areas which already had an urban structure the existing towns were given municipal status. In places which lacked such structures the tribal areas became the basis for the new arrangement. Thus a man had obligations to the *municipium* to which he belonged while, at the same time, owing allegiance to Rome whose citizen he was. He had two *patriae* of which Cicero speaks and the loyalty he gave to his native place was not in any way inconsistent or incompatible with his loyalty to the state to which he now belonged.[1] Local patriotism survived but it was never again destined to inspire centrifugal tendencies for it was now definitely subsumed in a wider loyalty.[2]

Once incorporated the Italians immediately began to play a part in public life. With the ending of the Social War and the consequent dashing of their hopes of independence it was natural they should embrace once more their long cherished ideal of the *civitas* with the equality it would bring. The citizenship they had obtained by 89, but only in an imperfect form. If full equality were to be achieved then the disabilities they laboured under would have to be removed. Hence, with this aim in view, they took a prominent role in the political life of Rome in the years 88-82. In the end, they prevailed for they were able to wring from the victorious Sulla all that they desired.[3] The fact that some Italians had, in their native places, a distinctly inferior position vis-à-vis the Sullan settlers[4] and that others, who were the sons of proscribed men, were forbidden to enter public life does not, in my opinion, alter the picture of an Italy now, on the political level, at one with Rome.[5] In any consideration of the position of Italians as a whole we should consider these people as marginal. If the descendants of the proscribed had to wait for Caesar to remove their disabilities, there were many others who were well able to play their part in the transaction of public business.[6] Having obtained full rights they went on to exercise them. The census of 70-69 ensured that the politically aware *principes* of Italy took their places in the centuriate assembly and henceforth the Italian vote was a force to be reckoned with.[7] Moreover, when Sulla, a few years earlier, set about filling his enlarged senate he included a number of Italians in the new intake and after this there is observable a gradual increase in the number of municipal men in that body.[8]

This picture of an Italy now firmly united with Rome holds good not only in the political but also in the social sphere. In a sense the Social War was both an interruption and a catalyst in the history of ancient Italy. We have seen how, before the war, the natural tendency of the Italians was towards Rome although there were factors which naturally tended to retard that movement and, indeed, to alienate them from her. The war, for a moment, gave those very factors pre-eminence and the Italians turned their backs on Rome. The ties which bound both sides together snapped. But once the rebellion was over they were swiftly renewed. The patron-client relationship which linked Rome and Italy was once more resumed,[9] and within its framework, the gravitation of the Italian towards the Roman which, for a little while, had ceased, resumed what we may call, without too much exaggeration, its inevitable course. In other words, the process of Romanisation continued on its inexorable way. We can point, for example, to how local languages continued to give ground before Latin and to the widespread urbanisation observable in Italy in the first century.[10] It is not, I think, unfair to say that, in 81, the history of Italy began again where it left off in 91.[11] But with this important difference: the forces for change were now working in a unitary state and were, in consequence, strengthened. When a man felt himself to be a Roman then he would be anxious to act as one.

There has, indeed, been some scholarly debate about just how strong this concept of Italian unity now was and to what extent the Italians now saw themselves as being one with Rome.[12] In other words, when Cicero claimed that *tota Italia* made him consul and brought him back from exile, could he really be said to command the sentiments of a united people? Again, when Octavius crushed Mark Antony he too boasted of the support of *tota Italia* which had taken a spontaneous oath in his favour. But was this true or had the oath been forced? Did Italian unity have to wait until Augustus to become a reality?[13] It has to be admitted that there are, in the first century, several phenomena observable which are clearly indicative of a lack of total unity and which in some cases, actually contribute to that state of affairs. It is impossible to believe the wars should not have left a great deal of bitterness and resentment against Rome in their wake among those who had chosen the losing side. Samnium is an obvious example.[14] For some, at least, the loss of their lands and the imposition of civic disabilities called for direct action and hence they lent their support to Lepidus, Catiline and Caesar.[15] Moreover, it has been argued that some of the former insurgent areas were slow to produce men of prominence in public life[16] and in the Caesarian period a general disinterest in politics is discernible among certain members of the Italian upper classes.[17] And even those who did participate did not always find a wholehearted acceptance. The contempt Romans felt for Italians did not vanish and we discover it alive and well and finding expression in the sneers which were directed at men of municipal origin.[18] Furthermore, as in the past, such contempt went hand in hand with an undiminished desire to keep Italians out of high office and so we learn that few of them reached the highest places.[19]

One cardinal factor helps us to put this evidence in perspective: all Italians now saw themselves as Romans, whether for good or ill. This is clear enough in the case of those who participated fully in the life of the new Italy which had emerged. After all, they had achieved that for which they longed: integration with the Roman state. If the truth of the above assertion appears, at first, less obvious in the instance of those whom we may call dissenters, a moment of reflection will, in fact, show that it was so. There is no evidence to suggest that any of these men cherished notions of independence. Rather, when they participated in political quarrels it was with a view to improving their own position within the existing framework. Once therefore, we have recognised that expressions of dissent, such as the alleged reluctance of some to swear for Augustus, were directed not against Rome itself but a particular regime then we can indeed speak of an Italy united in sentiment. Whatever disagreements there might be would not take from the fact that *tota Italia* was now Roman. The Roman city-state had vanished to be succeeded by Rome as *patria* of all.[20]

Notes

1. Sherwin-White (1973) pp. 151-5; Laffi (1973); Gabba (1978) p. 17, 21-2.
2. Gabba (1976) pp. 101-2. See further the concluding remarks of this section.
3. Gabba (1976) pp. 96-7, (1978) p. 18; Badian (1958) pp. 246-8, 250; Sherwin-White (1973) pp. 156-7. That the Italians were, indeed, willing to abandon independence and accept *civitas* is, I think, amply demonstrated by the fact that the only resistance to incorporation that we know of came from cities where a Greek tradition was still strong, cf. Gabba (1978) p. 18; Sherwin-White (1973) p. 138.
4. For these people see Keaveney *Crit. Stor.* (1982) pp. 519-20.
5. I believe that all Italians were now citizens. Since Sulla's recorded attempts to deprive some Italians of the citizenship were unsuccessful (Cic. *de Dom.* 79, *Pro Caec.* 97) we have, I think, to see in Sall. *Orat. Lep.* 12 an exaggeration of the true state of affairs which is probably seen in *Orat. Phil.* 14 and to reject the notion — see Laffi (1967) p. 187, n. 39 — that some of the Samnites were excluded from the citizenship, cf. Keaveney *Crit. Stor.* (1982) pp. 529-31, (1983) p. 182. Therefore, legally speaking, the position of the sons of the Italian proscribed was in no way different from that of the sons of the Roman proscribed. All were underprivileged members of the same state and there is no question of any group being picked out for especial treatment because they were foreigners. On the significance of this state of affairs see below.
6. Laffi (1967) pp. 185-7. Syme (1939) pp. 91-2, (1979) pp. 108-9 draws attention to the fact that some of Caesar's partisans were descended from Italian Social War leaders. It is possible, therefore, that some of these men numbered proscribed among their ancestors and that they were thus entering politics for the first time. But, it does not necessarily follow that all were in this position. Their status would surely have depended on positions taken in the Civil War, cf. Wiseman (1971) p. 8 and Gabba (1976) p. 236, n. 204.
7. Wiseman (1971) p. 59, 124-5, 136-141, 'The Census in the first century B.C.', *JRS* 59, 1969 pp. 59-75; Taylor (1960) p. 120.
8. Gabba (1976) pp. 59-67, 96-100; Laffi (1967) pp. 187-8; Syme (1979) pp. 110-13; Wiseman (1971) p. 59.
9. Wiseman (1971) pp. 6-10, 25-30, 63, 105.
10. Salmon (1967) pp. 395-6, (1982) p. 132, 135, 140-1; Gabba (1972).

There was a cultural price to be paid, see Gabba (1978) pp. 19-20.

11. The element of continuity between pre- and post-war Italy may be seen even in Samnium, cf. Gaggiotti pp. 140-1. On the other hand we have already seen (1.2) how the ruin of war here speeded up the process of Romanisation.

12. Compare, for example, Syme (1939) pp. 284-93, (1979) pp. 107-8 with Gabba (1976) pp. 96-103, (1978) pp. 22-3.

13. Wiseman (1971) p. 124; Syme (1939) pp. 284-93.

14. Salmon (1967) pp. 387-8.

15. Salmon (1967) pp. 387-8. As Gabba (1972) pp. 109-10 points out there must have been a political colouring to some of the violence which was so characteristic of Italy at the time.

16. Syme (1939) p. 91, (1979) pp. 111-12 and Salmon (1967) pp. 389-95. See, however, the important qualificatory remarks of Gabba (1976) p. 98.

17. Gabba (1976) p. 99.

18. Gabba (1976) p. 99.

19. Syme (1979) p. 112.

20. Sherwin-White (1973) p. 169; Gabba (1978) pp. 11-18.

Part Five
The Wolf and the Bull

5.1

The Wolf and the Bull: A Survey

The year 125 is a pivotal date. In that year we first hear of a scheme to give the citizenship to the Italians. Our investigation of the developing relationship between Italian and Roman in this period must, therefore, range backwards and forwards from this crucial central point. We first go backwards in order to determine why it was the Italians found the offer of 125 attractive or, to put it in simple terms, why they wanted the citizenship. We then move forward from 125 to see how what was first offered them was eventually granted.

Because Flaccus offered *provocatio* as an alternative to citizenship it has sometimes been claimed been that the main reason Italians wanted the citizenship was for the protection it might give. I do not think this is right. It seems to me that if both concessions were on offer then the possession of the citizenship must have meant something more than the right of *provocatio* to those who sought it. There is, therefore, no reason to disbelieve Appian when he says that those Italians who looked for it did so because it would make of them partners in empire rather than subjects. In other words, they wished to share in all the privileges, rights and duties of the Romans. They wished to become one with them, to become their equals in every respect.[1]

When subjects thus aspire to become equals it need hardly be said that we are witnessing a profound change in their outlook. There has come a great alteration in the way they see themselves and the world in which they live. It is precisely because of the momentous nature of this switch in perspective that I find it hard to believe it came about simply as a result of the events immediately preceding 125. Likewise, I doubt if Flaccus by his offer could have wrought this change. I consider it improbable he should have implanted in the minds of the Italians ideas they had never entertained before and have done his work so thoroughly that they put down such firm roots as never to be eradicated.[2] Come to that, if the Italians were totally disinterested in the citizenship, would Flaccus then have offered it to them? I would argue that the situation as revealed to us in 125 would only have come about as the result of a long and slowly maturing process and that we can, in part, trace that process.

To find the reasons for what may, not unfairly, be described as a great spiritual change in the Italians we must look at what had been happening to them in the years since 205. We have to look for those phenomena which helped to create the new mood. From the point of view of this investigation, the history of these years is a mist shrouded land through which certain significant seeming shapes loom. We have to turn a spotlight on each of them in turn to see if, in reality, they are of moment for our enquiries.[3]

Of prime importance is the dispersal of Italians, whether as soldiers or as businessmen, over the Mediterranean basin in the second century because they, in consequence, underwent what we may call 'the imperial experience'.[4] What this means is that as a result of their privileged position vis-à-vis the natives and their close contacts with the Romans, they came to a realisation of their affinity with the latter and of their own superiority to the other subject nations. When that realisation dawned it was natural that their disabilities should prove irksome and that they should long to be rid of them. They came to the conclusion that their present status was unsatisfactory in itself and hardly commensurate with the view they had now formed of themselves. Although most Italians will have been touched, not all will have reacted in the same way to the stimulus. The response of the common soldier will hardly have had the same degree of sophistication as that of his chief or the businessman. Again, not all will have had the will or the means to do something to change things. The businessmen seem to have had little effect on the course of events but it was far otherwise with the nobility of the Italian states. It was they who led the agitation for the citizenship and when they were refused it was they who declared war on Rome. And, in so doing, they could call upon their retainers who not only clung to their traditional loyalty to their masters but were also fired, in some degree, by the same ideals.

Those who brought back to Italy disturbing new ideas from

abroad found for them a ready audience. The process of Roman-isation, by which the Italians were assimilated with their rulers, was already making headway in certain areas. With it there seems to have come the idea that those thus affected were the equals of the Romans and that their present position was unacceptable. But, at the very moment when notions of equality were being born at home and abroad, the Italians saw even that position which they held being eroded. The nature of Roman rule was now such as to encroach upon their autonomy. The Italian nobles who were never ones to underestimate their own worth could ill-brook these incursions. Local patriotism was outraged at these slights to their native place in which they still took such a pride. Moreover, Rome's role as the leader of the Italian nations came to be questioned. It was she who had created a community of spirit and a sense of common identity among them and now these feelings gradually began to be turned against her.

So we may say that, both within and without Italy, Roman imperialism had inadvertently given the Italians notions about themselves which they determined to act upon.[5] Out of Rome's empire there came to the Italians the idea that they should be as one with those whom they had helped to create it.

Manifestations of an Italian desire for the citizenship occur long before 125 and may be seen in the migration from the countryside to Rome. For a long time this movement is devoid of any political significance since the people involved were of low degree and their aim was economic betterment. Nevertheless there is a very definite connection between these earlier assumptions of the citizenship and the events of 125. From our first glimpse of the phenomenon (in 187) it remains a constant factor in the history of the period; despite all efforts to stop it, migration continues throughout the century. But in 125 an important development has occurred. The same peoples, whether Latins or allies, are still looking for the franchise but we see now that the agitation does not reveal, as it once did, the aspirations of the common man but of his lord. What has happened is tolerably clear. For their own limited purposes the lower orders had long sought the citizenship. It was, therefore, easy for the aristocrats, once they had conceived their own peculiar ambitions, to capital-ise on these desires and turn them to their own uses. They were able to harness energies already existing and channel them in a direction beneficial to themselves.

It was Flaccus' peculiar achievement to introduce the Italian question into Roman politics. What he had, in effect, done was to teach the Italian nobility that the dreams they had conceived as a result of the 'imperial experience' might be made a reality. The year 125 therefore represents a coming together of the two strata of Italian society. High and low alike were united in their support of the ambitions of the aristocrats. Moreover, the characteristic features of the struggle for equality from now until the outbreak of the Social War are immediately discernible in the Gracchan age. In the first instance, it soon becomes clear that those who ruled Rome were not disposed to do anything about the problem unless it was forcibly brought to their attention. Nowhere do we learn of any initiative on their part. Moreover, when the Italians and their friends succeeded in attracting attention to themselves and their demands the reaction provoked was one of profound hostility and unrelenting resistance. The reasons for this stance are chiefly two. The Roman nobility was not, on the whole, opposed to the idea of admitting even large numbers to the citizenship always provided those so admitted posed no threat to their own position of power. The Italians with their clearly stated aim of achieving full equality with their masters posed just such a threat and hence they were to be resisted at all costs. Again, the acquisition of empire had given the Roman nobility very definite notions of their own superiority. The Italians might not be degenerates, like some of their other subjects, and might even be regarded as cousins to the Romans but there was no doubt that their natural place in the scheme of things was a lowly one.[6] It was altogether unacceptable that these poor relations should aspire to share power with those who rightfully occupied a position of superiority to them. A similar stubborn self-regard infected the plebs and manifested itself in the extreme touchiness they displayed whenever it was thought that something substantial was being offered to the Italians. But, as the commons did not have the same vested interest in clinging to power as the nobility, they could be seduced by fair promises. Hence, the changes in their attitude we find displayed in this period.

This state of affairs naturally drove the Italians to seek allies wherever they could and this meant, in effect, making common cause with the *populares*. Thus yoking their problem to other contentious issues and, in consequence, inflaming passions probably did them little real harm for there is no evidence that the Romans were prepared to consider their case, singly, dispassionately and on its merits. Hence they had little to lose and, we may add, a great deal to gain. It is only with hindsight that we can say they were unfortunate in their choice of champions.[7] Flaccus certainly put a lever into the hands of the Italians which they were not slow to use again when the opportunity presented itself, namely the land. Whatever other motives inspired people like Drusus they had to reckon with the fact that if they wished to lay hands on Italian land they would have to grant the citizenship in return.[8]

Particularly noteworthy are the divisions among the Italians at this period and their persistence despite certain changes of form. In the Gracchan age we discover three levels of political consciousness. The least sophisticated would be content with *provocatio* alone. Others, however, saw the citizenship as their goal. A third group seems to have come dangerously close to insurrection in the face of Roman obduracy although, in the event, only Fregellae allowed itself to be goaded into revolt. The proposed Roman legislation at this time clearly recognises the existence of these shades of opinion. A generation later, in the 90s, divisions are still apparent but they are of a different order. Now the desire for the citizenship is universal and the dissenters are the Etrurians and Umbrians who fully share that desire but are not prepared to barter their land in order to fulfil it. Their subsequent late entry into the war is wholly consistent with this attitude. Indeed, even after the war began, we hear of some who refused to join in and were treated as traitors by their own kind. Again, some of those who joined the confederacy showed certain signs of hesitancy. Before fighting became general they sent an embassy to Rome in a last effort to compose the quarrel and during the war itself engaged in parleys with the enemy.

Nowadays there is a tendency to study the Italian peoples individually and in their own right. For the purposes of our study, however, we must emphasise very heavily their close connection with Rome. This I believe to be correct since the Italians clearly felt themselves to be kin to the Romans and wished to be bound by even tighter links. Leaving to one side such matters as the patron-client relationship or Romanisation, we need only dwell on one cardinal point: in this period the Italians furnished the most unequivocal evidence that their desire was to become Romans. The attainment of the citizenship was for them the outstanding issue of the day and the lengths they went to in order to be enfranchised demonstrates the supreme importance they attached to it.

If we move forward from our pivotal point 125 in order to observe the development of the Italian question then the next significant date we encounter is 95 when the lex Licinia Mucia was passed. A generation has gone by and there had been a significant alteration in Italian attitudes. First of all, the Latins have withdrawn from the fray after having been among the most active participants in the agitation of the Gracchan age. Frightened by the intensity of feeling displayed by those to whom they felt especially close, the Romans had acted to quiet them. It was decreed that anybody who held a magistracy in a Latin state should automatically become a Roman citizen. This concession undoubtedly saved the Romans in the Social War for the Latins, well satisfied with it, held fast to their allegiance. More immediately though it cannot have done much to sweeten the tempers of the allies who must have looked with an envious eye on others' good fortune and asked themselves why they had not obtained a like boon. Further heavy calls on their manpower for service in the Jugurthine and Germanic Wars can hardly have done much to improve matters especially as nobody at Rome seemed willing to imitate Marius' example and give due recognition to the part Italians had played in the defence of the common homeland. Moreover, those processes which had given birth to the desire for citizenship in the first place had now had another thirty years or so to work on men's minds with the result that the ideas they spawned had acquired a firmer grip on those who had originally embraced them while at the same time laying hold on those who had hitherto been unaffected by them. As a result the demand for citizenship has now become universal and it is accompanied by a mood of determination which is new. No longer do we hear talk of lesser concessions such as *provocatio*, no longer do we find the allies, as in the time of Gracchus, asking for much but prepared to settle for less. The demand for citizenship had, at last, become universal and would be satisfied.

In this new mood of aggressive determination it was natural the allies should remember the lesson Flaccus had taught them: that theirs was a legitimate objective which might be obtained. Thus, when the Romans, as usual, showed no sign of making concessions, their sense of urgency and their self-confidence was such that they resolved to take the citizenship for themselves. So, at the census of 97, they simply came forward and declared themselves to be citizens. Obviously, this was a direct challenge to the Romans and much would hinge upon their response to it. It is for this reason that the lex Licinia Mucia of 95 is of supreme importance. In seeking to smother their pretensions it served only to enrage the allies beyond measure. Hence, they decided that if their champion Drusus could not undo the damage done by the *lex* and restore to them what they regarded as rightfully theirs then they would have no more to do with Rome.

The centrifugal forces which had always been present in Italy now come into prominence. If equality could not be achieved by integration then it would be achieved by separation. Even while Drusus laboured on their behalf the allies laid plans against the possibility of his failure. And when he was murdered they were prepared for just this eventuality. All over Italy men who had long been conspiring rose in revolt and established their own state, Italia, with its capital at Corfinium. A senate of five hundred represented the twelve rebel nations and a special council oversaw the war which was waged by two consuls and twelve praetors. Far different from the unitary state of Rome this confederation now made war on her. Although we may beg leave to doubt that the allies had worked out the full implications of what would happen should they achieve their aim, there can be no doubt what this aim was: independence.

From the purely military point of view the first full year of the Social War presents a number of interesting features. In the first place, there is the high degree of co-operation between the allied armies and the first rate co-ordination they showed in their campaigning.[9] The fruits of such efficiency can be seen in the fact that, for most of the year, the allies were able to mount a successful offensive. We should also add, perhaps, that although fewer in numbers, the superior quality of their troops to those of the Romans may, in some instances, have been a contributing factor to their success. Nevertheless, by the end of the year, there are clear indications that the tide of their victories had reached its high water mark and was now beginning to ebb. The failure to lift the siege of Asculum, their inability to advance beyond Acerrae and the swift collapse of the revolt in Etruria and Umbria before reinforcements could reach there are all unequivocal signs that the allied offensive was spent. Thus, in 89, their collapse was as sudden as their triumph had been. When the Romans had regained their nerve they threw their vast resources of manpower into the fray and the allies went down to a series of crushing defeats.

In the political sphere these years saw two important pieces of

203

legislation. The first of these was the lex Julia which granted the citizenship to those of Rome's Italian subjects who had not revolted.[10] Although this concession appears to have been wrung out of the Romans largely because it was necessary in order to stop further serious defections among the hitherto loyal, nevertheless their intransigence had been breached and it was, therefore, but a short step to embracing the principle of enfranchisement for all Italians. The year 89 then saw the passing of the lex Plautia Papiria under the terms of which all who surrendered by a certain date were to be admitted to the citizenship.

The Social War, therefore, constitutes another great landmark in the history of the Italian question. It was fought because the Italians, having failed to gain admission to the Roman state, determined that they should be independent of it. They failed to achieve this objective but their efforts to do so led the Romans directly to concede what they had been asking for in the first place. Although rebel resistance had by no means ended by the close of 89, the confederacy was in its death throes and so it is correct to say that by then the bulk of the Italians were citizens. Further grants of citizenship to remaining insurgents represent nothing more than an extension of the principles involved in the original enabling legislation just as declarations of independence by people like Telesinus are merely echoes from a time which is now past. Militarily defeated and with their hopes of independence now gone, the Italians gladly gave their allegiance to the state which had, at last, admitted them.

But the Social War did not put an end to the Italian question. Rather, it ushered in its final phase. With the defeat of the allies the problem now once more became entangled in the contemporary issues of Roman politics. The Social War, as we have just said, had not solved it but it had considerably altered its nature. Before the war the issue had been the winning of the citizenship. Now what was at stake was the full exercise of the rights attendant on that state for the Romans, in a bid to maintain their position of superiority, had circumscribed them. But there was also to come now a profound change in the way the Romans settled their own quarrels. For the first time the army became an instrument in politics, a circumstance which rapidly led from the urban brawls of the past to a full scale Civil War. And in this new situation the Italians were to be of particular importance and to acquire, yet again, a lever to compel others to their will.

At first it must have seemed as if little had changed. In the tribune Sulpicius the Italians found a disinterested champion who set about obtaining their re-distribution. By means of force and intimidation he was successful in this but unfortunately he had certain contractual obligations to Marius in the matter of the Mithridatic command. In fulfilling them he came into head-on collision with Sulla who with the aid of his army destroyed him utterly and so the Italian law perished in the general ruin of his schemes.

However, another soon came along who was ready to bestir himself on behalf of the Italians, namely, Cinna. Once more the familiar scenario was replayed; old and new citizens fought a pitched battle on the streets of Rome until Cinna was forced to flee. He had, however, thoroughly absorbed the lessons Sulla had taught and determined to return at the head of an army. He went, therefore, to the Italians, represented to them what he had suffered on their behalf and in consequence they willingly flocked to join his forces. Thus, it was with their aid that he and his associates made themselves masters of Rome and, however belatedly, this was acknowledged when the Cinnans redistributed the Italians among all the thirty-five tribes.

Now, if we remember that Cinna had yet to deal with Sulla then the crucial importance the Italians assume in the events of the years 86-82 becomes readily explicable. They represent a great pool of manpower whose support could be of considerable moment to either side. Their backing of Cinna and his allies was not unconditional. Rather, they would give their allegiance and their swords to whichever side seemed the most likely both to win and to respect, in the hour of victory, their newly gained rights.

Hence, in the period immediately preceding the Civil War and even after war had begun, the Italians found themselves being wooed with fair promises by both Cinnans and Sullans. Their fragmented response need not occasion surprise. With the demise of the confederacy they now had no organ through which they might speak with one voice.[11] Hence the peninsula was split as people decided for themselves whom they would support.

In the event those who chose Sulla chose wisely. Not only did he win but he remained faithful to his promises. Anomalies such as the disabilities imposed on the sons of the proscribed do not take from the fact that the bulk of the Italians were now confirmed in the possession of that which they had long sought: admission into the Roman state on the basis of full equality. Henceforth, Italians were to be Romans and they gladly accepted

it should be so. The Italian question, which has been the subject
of this book, was now dead.

Notes

1. Contra Sherwin-White (1973) pp. 134-5. We may remind ourselves, here, that those who sought merely *provocatio* now were, in the course
of time, to come to share in a universal desire for citizenship. See further
below.

2. This is aside altogether from the fact that there is evidence
(however we interpret it) that Italians had sought the citizenship before
125. We should also, perhaps, note that the effect of the deaths of Flaccus
and Gracchus was to strengthen the Italians in a resolve they already
had.

3. We do, of course, know of certain well articulated grievances but
they are only part of the story. It is only when they are set alongside other
elements that we can form a just appreciation of the great change in
Italian outlook.

4. We need, perhaps, to remind ourselves that the Romans were also
undergoing a similar experience with like results, at least as far as notions
of superiority went.

5. While it is obviously true to say, as does M. Crawford, *Coinage and
Money under the Roman Republic*, London, 1985 pp. 179-81, that, 'the Social
War is unthinkable without the wealth that flowed into Samnium and
other areas in the second century and the expressions of local pride that
this wealth made possible', such factors must, of course, be set firmly in
the context of the whole 'imperial experience'. We are not dealing solely
with matters of economics but with hearts and minds.

6. In fairness it should be pointed out that the actions of a man like
Scipio clearly show that this attitude was not necessarily a vicious one.

7. It is, for instance, true that when Drusus' Roman programme fell
it dragged his Italian proposals down with it. But, if we remember how
close he came to succeeding with his schemes for the Romans, then we
begin to appreciate how near the Italians were to getting what they
wanted.

8. Saturninus demonstrates the truth of this in the negative sense.

9. They can hardly be faulted for their failure to learn of the change
in the situation in Etruria. The bad weather conditions must have
rendered communication difficult.

10. It does not seem to me, however, that this legislation caused any
significant weakening in the Italian resolve to continue the war.

11. The need for such a forum can be readily appreciated when one
ponders the different attitudes displayed by Samnium and Calabria.

Appendix I
The Roman Commanders 90-87 BC

Any consideration of the Roman commanders in the Social War must begin with some prefatory remarks on two sources: Vell. Pat. 2.15. 3 and App. B.C. 1.40. Velleius says: *id bellum amplius trecenta milia juventutis Italicae abstulit. Clarissimi autem imperatores fuerunt Romani eo bello Cn. Pompeius ... C. Marius ... L. Sulla anno ante praetura functus, Q. Metellus.*

This would appear on the surface to be a list not of the most distinguished Roman commanders in 90 but in the whole war since while Marius did not serve beyond 90 there is no reason to suppose that Metellus took the field before 88.[1] However, we must reckon with the fact that one phrase, *anno ante praetura functus* seems to refer to 91 and this might lend support to the notion that Velleius is, after all, talking about the commanders of 90.[2]

The difficulty may be resolved if we accept that here, as in the rest of his account of the Social War, Velleius is careless and imprecise.[3] So, 2.15.1 describes how the war began — in 90 as Velleius believes. Then 15.2 lists the grievances of the Italians. The opening sentence of 15.3 gives their casualties in the whole war and the repetition of the expression *id bellum ... eo bello* shows clearly that commanders in the entire conflict are referred to in the next sentence. *Anno ante praetura functus* obviously does not pick up *id bellum* and it must surely refer back to Velleius' starting point of 90 in 15.1.

App. B.C. 1.40 presents less of a problem. It is a list of the Roman commanders at the beginning of 90.[4] Therefore, where names occur which Appian does not list here they are to be seen as generals in charge of those reinforcements he mentions as being sent out or as replacements for those killed in action.

Likewise, mention on this list but not in action — as in the case of Messalla[5] — is not an indication of error. This state of affairs is adequately accounted for by the fragmentary nature of our source material for the whole war. We may now proceed to list such Roman commanders as are known to us. In 90 the consul P. Rutilius Lupus had charge of the northern front. His colleague, L. Julius Caesar, had charge of the southern.[6] After Lupus' death, one of his legates, C. Marius, took command of his army. Then, for a time, he shared it with another legate Q. Servilius Caepio but, on the latter's death, he took sole charge once more. This pair probably operated as delegates of the urban praetor and it seems reasonable to assume the other legates did likewise. Eventually the proconsul Sextus Caesar took over command of the northern front and its *legati*. When he died C. Baebius took charge of his forces as *legatus propraetore*.[7] In addition it would appear that when the Etrurians and Umbrians rebelled a separate command was created. L. Porcius Cato, a propraetor, made war on them and among his legates was a certain A. Plotius.[8]

As we have seen, App. B.C. 1.40 furnishes us with a list of Lupus' *legati*. In some instances these same names occur on a list given by Cic. *Font.* 43. Unfortunately, however, Cicero does not differentiate between those who served only in 90 or 89 and those who served in both years. Nor does he specify under which commanders the legates served. In addition to Marius and Caepio Lupus' legates were: C. Perperna, Cn. Pompeius Strabo[9] and M. Valerius Messalla. From the same source we learn of the legates of Caesar who were: M. Claudius Marcellus, L. Cornelius Sulla, T. Didius[10] and P. Licinius Crassus.[11]

Thus far we have been dealing with men whose names and status are virtually certain. We now move on to others who present certain difficulties.

An otherwise unknown C. Caelius crushed a revolt in Transpadane Gaul in 90. He may have been a praetor or possibly he held a pro-magistracy.[12] If, however, the alternative reading *Coelius* is adopted then he could be C. Coelius Caldus cos. 94.[13] Rossbach's emendation, Caecilius, which would identify him with C. Caecilius Cornutus (q.v.) does not appear to be justified on textual or historical grounds.[14]

In B.C. 1.40 Appian says that Lentulus[15] was ἀδελφὸν αὐτοῦ Καίσαρος (the cos.). There are two distinct ways of interpreting this statement:

(a) It may be taken at its face value.[16] There is no corroborating evidence but then there is nothing to contradict it either. After all, Appian is given to inserting such explanatory notes after certain names[17] and it seems reasonable to suppose he took some care to get them right.

(b) The phrase, in fact, should refer to Q. Lutatius Catulus. We have independent evidence that he was, indeed, the half-brother of Caesar and, since he is mentioned by Cic. *Font.* 43, there is the possibility he was a legate in 90.[18] If that is so, then, one of three things may have happened:

(i) Catulus' name has fallen out of the text.

(ii) Appian may have got his names wrong as he has been known to do on previous occasions. The confusion over the two Caesars is an obvious example.[19] He will then have substituted Lentulus for Catulus.

(iii) Despite what was claimed in (a) above Appian does make blunders in writing explanatory notes on a name nor is he at his best when, as here, he is transcribing lists.[20] Bearing these matters in mind, it is not beyond the bounds of possibility that, in copying his list, Appian inadvertently omitted Catulus and then gave his explanatory gloss to Lentulus.

What conclusions are we to draw from all of this? It seems to me we cannot deny that Lentulus was in fact a legate to Caesar. Some indeed would expel him from Appian's text, [21] but the arguments advanced under b(ii) for this are not compelling. In the absence of supporting evidence proven error elsewhere does not establish the existence of error here. Whether or not Catulus should join Lentulus among the *legati* depends on our being able to show the gloss could not refer to the latter — something which cannot be done. Therefore we should mark the case of Catulus as 'not proven'.

P. Sulpicius, trib. pleb. 88, is known to have served as a legate in this war. Our source Cic. *Brut.* 304, hints, but does not definitely say, that he served in both 90 and 89. Mattingly, however, convincingly argued that he is the fourth *legatus* in *ILS* 8888. It was he therefore who fought at Asculum in 90 and vanquished the Vestini and the Marrucini in the following year.[22]

Another problem presents itself with regard to the man who won a battle over the Paeligni and is described (Liv. ep.73) as *sex. sul.* Dom. p. 25 thought that this was Sextus Julius Caesar but it is unlikely he had taken the field this early in the year.[23] It is most likely to refer to a Ser. Sulpicius Galba who may be identified with the man who fled Lucania in the previous year.[24] He may, perhaps, have been sent out after the death of Rutilius.

In 89, Pompey Strabo, now consul and with Q. Minucius Thermus as quaestor, commanded in the northern zone. The other consul L. Porcius Cato had charge of the south.[25]

In reconstructing the list of those who served under Pompey Strabo the famous inscription of his *consilium* (*ILS* 8888) is of vital importance.[26] As Cichorius points out the first five names must be those of his legates.[27] Of these five, three can be read without difficulty and they have been plausibly idenitified as L. Gellius Poplicola, Cn. Octavius Ruso and L. Junius Brutus Damasippus.[28] However, after the second name, that of Octavius, there occurs a gap of about twenty-four or twenty-five letters. The tribe of Octavius is missing and when the text resumes it is with the mutilated name CIUS. Thus the third legate has vanished entirely and the fourth is only recorded imperfectly. Now, we have seen that this last man is most likely to have been P. Sulpicius but have we any means of recovering the third which, as Cichorius believes, was one of about fifteen letters, including father's name and tribe?[29]

Here Cic. *Font.* 43 can come to our aid. By comparing it with other evidence it is possible to assign certain names on the list to their correct commanders in 89 and in the end just three names remain which cannot be so assigned.[30] The first of these is Catulus. We have seen that there is a faint possibility he may have served in 90 but that obviously does not preclude service in the next year as well.[31] The other two are L. Cornelius Cinna, and M. Caecilius Cornutus. Their presence on Cicero's list makes service in 90 at least possible but, most important from our point of view, is the fact that there is independent testimony which definitely establishes them as legates in 89. Together, we are told, they crushed the Marsi in several battles from which it would appear they had taken over operations in this area after the death of the consul Cato.[32] From this two possibilities present themselves, (a) both were legates of Cato,(b) one was a legate of Cato, the other of Pompey who had been seconded just as Sulla had been in the previous year.[33] Both notions are perfectly plausible and there would seem to be no way of choosing between the two. We must, therefore, conclude that the third legate of Pompey Strabo was either Catulus, Cinna or Cornutus but which one of the three it was exactly cannot be determined.

After the death of Cato it would seem that the supreme command on the southern front was taken over by Sulla. The evidence for his status may be set forth as follows:

(a) He is described as *legatus* in the early part of the campaigns (Liv. ep. 75; Diod. Sic. 37.2.8, cf. Cic. *Font.* 43) and that was still his rank on 29 April when he captured Stabiae (Pliny *NH* 3.70).

(b) Oros. 5.18.22-3 who describes him as a consul at the siege of Pompeii says Albinus (q.v.) was his *legatus*.[34] In describing an incident during the assault on Nola a little after this Val. Max. 1.6.4 also gives him the title of consul.[35]

(c) The manuscripts of Eutrop. 5.3.3 describe him as either *praetor* or *propraetore.*

As Salmon (1967) p. 364 emphasises it is clear from (a) that Sulla began the year as a legate to Cato. Salmon would appear to be sceptical of the notion that he achieved an elevation in status but the evidence of (b) and (c) would seem to justify our claiming he did.[36] It is true that Oros. and Val. Max. in (b) could be dismissed as a careless anticipation of his rank in the next year. But, with equal plausibility, it could be urged they are using *consul* as *proconsul.* The evidence of (c) lends support to this latter position. Whether he wrote *praetor* or *propraetore*, Eutropius, to judge from the context, was talking about 89. Again, irrespective of what reading we adopt, the word must refer to somebody who actually held an *imperium* since, by the usage of Eutropius, it cannot refer to a *legatus* of praetorian rank.[37] And, since Sulla must have had his office conferred on him by the senate, *propraetore* is a more likely reading than *praetor* because Eutropius usually differentiates between magistracies and pro-magistracies.[38] Therefore, from (b) and (c) we receive, at very least, a strong hint that Sulla was given *imperium* at some time in the course of 89. What we know of the military situation at the time leads us to conclude that there is, indeed, nothing untoward in this. As with the death of Lupus on the northern front in the previous year so the loss of Cato now must have created a gap which had to be filled. The fathers may have feared to confer the widest powers on Marius but they would have had no such hesitation in the case of Sulla. Hence it is legitimate to infer from the combined evidence of (b) and (c) that the *privatus* Sulla was given an *imperium pro consule.* [39]

Sulla will then have taken over Cato's legates. Three of these are definitely known. They are T. Didius, A. Gabinius and A. Postumius Albinus.[40] It also seems probable that a man called Carbo took over the war against the Lucanians on the death of Gabinius.[41]

A certain Cosconius is called στρατηγός by App. B.C. 1.52

and Diod. Sic. 37.2.8. A glance at Diodorus' use of the term in the passage in question shows it is impossible to determine what he meant by it. Appian is just a little more informative. He tells us (B.C. 1.53) that Metellus Pius who was praetor in 89 and probably proconsul in 88[42] succeeded Cosconius in the στρατηγίαν. What that last word means is not altogether clear[43] but the context does strongly imply that both men were more or less equal in status. If a man is succeeded by someone in an important theatre of war who has an *imperium proconsule* then it is not straining credulity to suggest that he holds a similar *imperium* too. If we accept the general view that Cosconius is to be identified with a man who was praetor about 79[44] then we may suggest his position is most likely to have resembled that of Sulla. He was a *privatus* on whom the *imperium proconsule* had been bestowed.[45]

A man who is most probably a legate of Cosconius is mentioned by Liv. ep. 75. Following the majority of manuscripts Rossbach prints his name as Lucanus. It has, however, been suggested that the name be corrected to Lucanius. Thus, while not idenitical with the M. Lucanius of *ILS* 8888, this man might be a relative of his.[46] One other possibility should, however, be borne in mind as we attempt to establish the identity of this legate. One manuscript reads *Luceius* and this has been corrected to Lucceius by Gronovianus. If this were accepted, then we could have here L. Lucceius who was also a legate in 92.[47]

Metellus retained the command he obtained in 88 up until the time he fled from Rome in 87. In fact he does not appear to have been officially stripped of his *imperium* until the winter of 83/82 when he and other followers of Sulla were declared *hostes*.[48] In 88 we hear of a legate of his called Mam. Aemilius Lepidus and, in 87, of another, a certain Plautius.[49] With the exception of a brief period when he was deprived of his command by Sulla, Pompey Strabo with pro-consular *imperium* continued to command in the north in 88 and he still retained his position at his death in 87.[50] Although Sulla was designated to fight Mithridates he spent part of his consular year besieging Nola and was aided by his quaestor L. Lucullus. Upon his departure in 87 charge of the siege was left to Ap. Claudius Pulcher as *legatus pro-praetore* and he remained at his post until his army was subverted by Cinna.[51]

Notes

1. See 3.3 and Keaveney and Madden pp. 47-51.
2. Keaveney *LEC* (1980) pp. 148-50.
3. For a further example see Appendix II.
4. Cf. Haug p. 226.
5. Lentulus presents his own problems — see below.
6. *MRR* 2.25.
7. Keaveney *RhM* (1983) pp. 274-8. Baebius probably arrived on this front with Sextus.
8. *MRR* 2.28, 29. It may be noted here that Q. Lutatius Cerio (*MRR* 2.27) was probably not a quaestor at this time, cf. Crawford no. 305.1. We may also mention here Otacilius a legate who served with the fleet, cf. 3.2.
9. Oros. 5.18.10 cannot be taken as an indication of his status.
10. Cos. 97 — Gabba (1967) p. 131.
11. See 3.2.
12. Liv. ep.73, cf. *MRR* 2.25, 27.
13. *MRR* 2.12.
14. *RE* 'Caecilius' no. 12, 'Coelius' no. 6.
15. Probably P. Cornelius Lentulus, one of Marius' later victims, cf. Gabba (1967) p. 131.
16. As is done in *RE* 'Cornelius' no. 203.
17. See, for example, B.C. 1.80.
18. See Gabba (1967) p. 131.
19. See also B.C. 1.116 with Gabba (1967) p. 319 and Marcks p. 47. n.l.
20. Cf. B.C. 1.37 with Gabba (1967) p. 125 and B.C. 1.59 with Keaveney *Eirene* (1983) pp. 71-2.
21. Cf. e.g. Cichorius p. 140, n.l and Marcks p. 47, n.l.
22. See Mattingly pp. 264-5. The dating of the events in App. B.C. 1.47 would seem to indicate that Sulpicius was not Pompey's legate to start with, cf. 3.2.
23. See 3.2.
24. See Rossbach and Criniti pp. 96-7.
25. *MRR* 2.32; Cichorius p. 143.
26. On its dating to 89 see Cichorius pp. 130-2 and Criniti pp. 47-61. As a legate in 90 Pompey Strabo could hardly grant the citizenship.
27. Pp. 136-7.
28. Cichorius pp. 139-42; Criniti pp. 99-101.
29. Cichorius pp. 137-8.
30. See the discussion of the legates of Cato below.
31. In my view Cichorius p. 140 too readily assumes Catulus was actually a legate in 90. Moreover, bearing in mind the nature of our source, he is wrong to neglect the possibility of service in 89.
32. Liv. ep.76 with Keaveney and Madden pp. 50-1. Some (e.g. Haug p. 240) emend the *Conmutus* of Sisenna fr. 20P to *Cornutus* but this is not the only possible correction, cf. Peter's apparatus. The pair probably continued to serve into 88. See further 3.3.
33. It would seem that neither *MRR* 2.36 nor Cichorius pp. 140-1 has thought of (b).

34. *MRR* 2.38, n.7 wrongly says *legatus* is the only title to appear in our sources — compare *MRR* 2.36.

35. Cf. *de Div.* 1.72, 2.65; Keaveney (1983) p. 60 is erroneous.

36. It is not altogether clear what Salmon thinks Sulla's position at the end of the year was. Taking my cue from his discussion I once assumed — (1983) p. 55, n. 41 — he remained a *legatus* but now I am not so sure.

37. Cf. 3.10.4, 5.9.2, 6.20.4.

38. Cf. 4.6.4, 13, 6.1-4, 7.16.2.

39. See Jashemski pp. 20ff.

40. *MRR* 2. 36-37. Didius may have died before Sulla took command. He is mentioned by Cic. *Font.* 43. Note that *MRR suppl.* p. 50 does not classify Albinus as a pro-magistrate in 89 as Salmon (1967) p. 364, n. 2 claims it does. Salmon seems to have confused him with L. Postumius, the only Postumius listed as a pro-magistrate on that page.

41. Flor. 2.6.13. See 3.3. He may possibly be C. Papirius Carbo (*MRR* 2.37).

42. *MRR* 2.42.

43. In view of the uncertainty Gabba's, 'il suo successore nel comando' is preferable to the Loeb, 'his successor in the praetorship'.

44. *MRR* 2.39, n. 21, 86, 88, n. 4.

45. It is not quite certain whose legate he was before this, but I am inclined to favour the notion he was Cato's, cf. 3.3.

46. Cichorius pp. 171-2.

47. *ILLR* 210.

48. *MRR* 2. 42, 47-8. Cf. Keaveney (1983) pp. 130-1, 135.

49. *MRR* 2. 43, 51.

50. *MRR* 2. 42, 48.

51. Keaveney (1983) pp. 56-77. *MRR* 2.44 gives L. Minucius Basilus and C. Mummius the rank of legates under Sulla in 88 but this is unlikely, cf. Keaveney *Klio* (1984) pp. 123-4.

Appendix II
The Italian Commanders 90-87 BC

Here, as in the case of the Roman commanders, it is necessary for us first to say something about two of our sources. Vell. Pat. 2.16.1 gives a list of *Italicorum ... celeberrimi duces* in this war. Although there is some slight evidence to support the notion that Telesinus might have served earlier in an inferior capacity, he could not be said to be a prominent leader until 82. The most likely explanation for his presence on the list therefore is that Velleius saw the Social and Civil Wars as one.[1] Flor. 2.6.6-7 gives a list of Italian leaders as well. As printed in the texts of Malcovati (1938 and 1972) and Jal (1967) the commanders and the nations they led appear as follows:

Poppaedius Marsos et Paelignos, Latinos Afranius Umbros Plotius, Egnatius Etruscos; Samnium Lucaniamque Telesinus.

It is usual to approach Florus with caution but in the present instance even more circumspection than is habitual is called for. The passage has been heavily emended and some of those emendations are dubious. The supplement Paelignos is acceptable enough since it is not straining credulity to suggest that if Florus thought Telesinus was the leader of the Samnites and the Lucanians[2] then he might well believe Poppaedius to have led both the Marsi and the Paelignians. Likewise, although the name is not mentioned elsewhere, Afranius should probably not be rejected since the manuscripts have *Afrienos*, *Affranius* and *Affranios*. Plotius, which is the correction of Tollius for the *totos* and *totus* of the manuscripts, is a different matter. Tollius drew the name from Liv. ep. 74. However, the Plotius there is not the commander of the Umbrians but a Roman legate who helped subdue them.[3] By the same token, the reading Egnatius Etruscos for *senatus et consules* proposed by Lipsius is unacceptable. This was made on the basis of App. B.C. 1.40 but the Egnatius there is almost certainly a Samnite.[4]

The allies had two supreme commanders who are styled consuls and each had under him six praetors who commanded the national contingents.[5] The multiplicity of names in our sources confirms what we would anyway have guessed at; the praetors had subordinate officers whom, for the sake of convenience, we shall call legates. On the northern front the supreme command was held by the Marsian leader Q. Poppaedius Silo. The other consul who had charge of the south was a Samnite C. Papius Mutilus.[6] We may now go on to list, insofar as they are known to us, the praetors and legates of the various nations:

Apuli, Campani, Frentani, Hirpini: no commanders are known.

Lucani: Their praetor was Marcus Lamponius.[7] One of his legates was a certain Clepitius or Cleptius.[8]

Marrucini: Herius Asinius is attested as their praetor (Liv. ep. 73).[9] If it is not simply a mistake, his inclusion among the Marsi by Eutropius may be due to the close connections between the two nations.[10] Asinius' successor may have been a man called Obsidius although the possibility that the latter was a Marsian legate of Poppaedius Silo cannot be ruled out.[11]

Marsi: Since P. Vettius Scato is called *dux Marsorum* by Cic. *Phil.* 12.27 we may legitimately infer that he was their praetor. As Cicero was a contemporary who actually saw Scato his evidence is obviously to be preferred to that of Macrob. 1.11.24 who makes a Paelignian of him.[12] This error could have arisen because the two nations were closely associated in the Sabellic League.[13] Like Haug p. 241, Gabba (1967) p. 133 accepts the evidence of Macrobius and he further makes Scato a native of Corfinium. There is no ancient evidence for this notion which appears to derive from Dom. p. 14 the source of whose error may be divined.[14] He appears to have combined the evidence of *de ben.* 3.23.5 with that of *de ben.* 3.24 which actually does mention Corfinium. However, there is no connection between the two passages and the second actually refers to the second Civil and not the Social War.[15]

A certain Fraucus is mentioned as commanding a Marsian force near Asculum in the winter of 90/89. Having due regard to the military situation at that time it seems safe to conclude that he was one of Scato's legates.[16]

Paeligni: Salmon (1967) p. 353 suggests that P. Praesenteius may have been their praetor. His role in the war, however, does not exclude his being a Marsian legate.[17]

Picentes: C. Vidacilius played a prominent part in the war, he was a native of Asculum and is styled *dux* in one of our sources — all of which make it virtually certain he was the Picentine praetor.[18] A man called P. Ventidius who was the father of the 'muleteer' served as one of his legates.[19] Likewise, T. Herennius, whose Picentine origins seem fairly certain, may also be numbered among Vidacilius' legates.[20] A slightly more exotic Picentine legate was Agamemnon. He was a Cilician pirate who had been lodged in Asculum for safe keeping. When the rebellion started he was set free and in gratitude gave his services to his benefactors.[21]

Samnites: Their praetor was Marius Egnatius.[22] A commander called Duilius operated against Sulla at Aesernia. From this it is reasonable to infer he was a Samnite legate. He has been identified with the man whose name has been read on a coin as Lucilius.[23] Trebatius appears to be the name of yet another legate of this nation.[24]

Since the family of the Cluentii is attested in Campania this might appear to support the theory of Salmon (1967) p. 366 that the L. Cluentius who fought in that area was the leader of the rebel Campanians.[25] A closer examination of the context suggests, however, that this is not necessarily so. Pompeii, an important centre of the insurrection, is being put under siege by Sulla. Cluentius is not being depicted as the leader of the Campanian resistance but as the general of an army which came from elsewhere. Thus, I would accept the view of Haug p. 242 that he belonged to one of the neighbouring nations. Three considerations make me reject her further contention that he belonged to the Hirpini. The Cluentii are also attested at Larinum as well as in Campania, Cluentius fled back to Nola, a town in Samnite hands and his men are called Samnites.[26] From this evidence I would deduce that he was a Samnite legate.

Venusini: If the evidence of Florus (2.6.6) is to be trusted their praetor was called Afranius.

Vestini: Dom. p. 18 says their praetor was C. Pontidius but gives no cogent reason for this choice. While Pontidius certainly had the rank of praetor we know so little about him that it is impossible to say which nation he led.[27] In my view, Salmon (1967) p. 353 is probably right to suggest that the Vestinian praetor was T. Lafrenius. Münzer apud Gabba (1967) p. 133, indeed, thought he was the Picentine praetor but, as we know, this position was held by Vettius Scato. Dom. pp. 17-18 made of him the Marsian praetor but his arguments are not compelling. Accepting yet another emendation of Flor. 2.6.6 (*Latinos Lafrenius* instead of *Latinos Afranius*), he then goes on to say, 'Da Titus Lafrenius die Latiner angriff, so war er Prätor der Marser'. Now, since Lafrenius was not the Picentine praetor, but was active there late in 90 we may assume that he belonged to one of the neighbouring nations and had come to the aid of his allies.[28] On the widest possible definition the phrase 'neighbouring nations' may be applied to the Marsi, Paeligni, Frentani, Marrucini and Vestini. We know the names of the praetors of the Marsi, Marrucini and Paeligni so this means Lafrenius could have belonged to one of the other two. Of these, the Vestini are the most likely since, being closest, they would be the ones we would naturally expect to come to help.[29]

Notes

1. See Keaveney *Crit. Stor.* (1982) pp. 501-2.
2. On the Lucanian leadership see below. This mention of Telesinus would seem to indicate that Florus, like Velleius, believed the Social and Civil Wars were one conflict.
3. See Appendix I and 3.2.
4. See below. This must cast doubt on the hesitant theory of Ruoff-Väänänen pp. 76-7.
5. See 3.1.
6. Diod. Sic. 37.2.5-7. See Salmon (1967) pp. 351-2; Gabba (1967) pp. 132-3. Their names appear on some coins (Sydenham nos. 634-41) while that of Mutilus has been found on a temple he had built at Schiavi d'Abruzzo (Gaggiotti p. 139).
7. Sources: Gabba (1967) p. 133.
8. Diod. Sic. 37.2.11 with Walton *ad loc.* and Magaldi p. 171, n. 3. Cf. also Diod. Sic. 37.23.
9. Cf. Eutrop. 5.3.2; App. B.C. 1.40; Vell. Pat. 2.16.1.
10. On which see Salmon (1967) p. 340.
11. Oros. 5.18.25. See 3.3.
12. Valuable confirmation for Cicero comes from Sen. *de ben.* 3.23.5 who calls Scato *praetor Marsorum*. Although Peter does not list this passage among the fragments of that author's work, I would agree with Haug p. 256 that Seneca must have drawn this from another contemporary, Quadrigarius (cf. *de ben.* 3.23.1).
13. Cf. Salmon (1967) p.340.
14. Haug p. 241, n. 2 is perhaps too pessimistic when she says it came 'aus der Luft'.
15. Scato is most likely the Cato of App. B.C. 1.40 and Vell. Pat.

2.16.1. See Gabba (1967) p. 133 and Drumann-Groebe vol. 2 p. 558.
  16. Oros. 5.18.18. See 3.3.
  17. App. B.C. 1.41. See 3.2.
  18. App. B.C. 1.48; Oros. 5.18.21.
  19. App. B.C. 1.47. Cf. Syme (1939) p. 71, 92.
  20. Serv. ad *Aen.* 9.587; Eutrop. 5.3.2, cf. Syme (1939) p. 92. Haug p. 242 fails to take the evidence of Eutropius into account and does not consider the war theatre in which Herennius operated. See 3.2.
  21. Diod. Sic. 37.16; Oros. 5.18.10. The circumstances of his release make it more likely he served the Picentes (Diod.) rather than the Marsi (Oros.). *RE* 'Agamemnon' no. 2 is fantasy. The reputation of the Cretans in antiquity (H.A. Ormerod, *Piracy in the Ancient World*, Liverpool, 1978 repr. *passim*) makes it likely that the one who struck a bargain with L. Julius Caesar (Diod. Sic. 37.18) was also a pirate who had been released by the allies.
  22. Gabba (1967) p. 132. Dom. p. 18, followed by Haug p. 242, makes him a praetor of the Frentani. This conclusion is, however, arrived at on the basis of a reconstruction of the allied command which I find unconvincing and which I have implicitly tried to refute in this appendix.
  23. Front. *Strat.* 1.5.17; Sydenham no. 642, cf. Salmon (1967) p. 359, n. 5.
  24. App. B.C. 1.52 with Gabba (1967) p. 155. He is called a praetor by *RE* 'Trebatius' no. 1. but this seems unlikely.
  25. App. B.C. 1.50; Eutrop. 5.3.2. Cf. Gabba (1967) p. 150.
  26. Oros. 5.18.23 with Gabba (1967) pp. 150-1.
  27. He is mentioned in Vell. Pat. 2.16.1 and App. B.C. 1.40. Since all the others on Appian's list were clearly praetors, then we must assume that Pontidius was too. By a process of elimination Haug p. 224 arrives at the same conclusion as Dom. However, as her attribution of other commands is not always persuasive, this cannot be accepted (cf. n. 22).
  28. See 3.2.
  29. Haug p. 241 does not seem to give due weight to this fact when she argues, from Lafrenius' presence in Picenum, for his being a Marsian.

Appendix III
The Social War: Table of Events 90-89 BC

In this table events are listed in chronological sequence. Where events on either front occurred simultaneously they are enclosed within a bracket. Contemporaneous events on both fronts are grouped together in the numbered sections.

90 BC

	Northern Front	Southern Front
(1)	Defeat of Pompey Strabo by the Picentes Perperna defeated by Praesentius	L. Julius Caesar defeated by Scato Venafrum falls to Marius Egnatius Defeat of Crassus by Lamponius Vidacilius invades Apulia Papius takes Nola and advances into Campania
(2)	Defeat and death of Rutilius Marius receives command Ser. Sul. Galba defeats Paeligni Minor victory of Caepio who receives command Defeat and death of Caepio	Vidacilius completes conquest of Apulia Lucanians take Grumentum Papius, after subduing Campanian towns, advances on Acerrae and is there defeated.
(3)	Marius' campaign against the Marsi Marius and Sulla defeat the Marsi Rebellion of Saluvii Sex. Caesar marches on Picenum	Defeat of L. Julius Caesar in Samnium Caesar returns to Acerrae

Pompey Strabo engages
enemy in Picenum   }

(4)   Siege of Asculum begins   Caesar remains at Acerrae
Sulla temporarily relieves
Aesernia

(5)   Brief rebellion of Etruria and
Umbria

89 BC

(1)   Defeat of the Marsi at   Sulla's campaign in
Asculum   Campania up to siege of
Defeat of force sent to aid   Nola
Etruria   Cosconius' campaign in
Cato's campaign against the   Samnium
Marsi

(2)   Campaigns against Marsi,   Sulla's campaigns against
Vestini, Marrucini   Samnites/Hirpini
Siege of Asculum continues   Campaigns in Lucania
and culminates in its fall   Campaigns of Cosconius in
                                 Apulia

Bibliography

Badian, E. (1958) *Foreign Clientelae (264-70 BC)*, Oxford
—— (1968) *Roman Imperialism in the late Republic*, Oxford
—— (1972) *Publicans and Sinners*, Oxford
—— (1955) 'L Papirius Fregellanus', *CR*5, pp. 22-3
—— (1969) 'Quaestiones Variae', *Historia* 18, pp. 447-91
—— (1970/71) 'Roman Politics and the Italians 131-91 BC', *D. Arch* 4/5, pp. 373-421
Beloch, K.J. (1926) *Römische Geschichte*, Berlin
Bennett, H. (1923) *Cinna and his Times*, Menasha
Bernardi, A (1944/45) 'La Guerra Sociale e le lotte dei partiti in Roma'. *NRS* 28/29, pp. 60-99
Bernareggi, E. (1966) 'Problemi della monetazione dei Confederati Italici durante la Guerra Sociale', *RIN* 5ª S. 14, pp. 61-90
Bodei Giglioni, G. (1977) 'Pecunia Fanatica: l'incidenza enonomica dei Templi Laziali', *RSI* 89, pp. 33-76
'Bourgeoisies' (1983) *Les 'Bourgeoisies' Municipales Italiennes aux 11ᵉ et 1ᵉʳ Siècles, av. J.C.*, Paris/Naples
Brizzi, G. (1982) *I sistemi informativi dei Romani*, Wiesbaden
Broughton, T.R.S. (1965) 'Comment' pp. 150-62 in *Deuxième Conference* (q.v.)
Brunt, P.A. (1971) *Italian Manpower: 225 BC-AD14*, Oxford
—— (1965) 'The *equites* in the Late Republic', pp. 117-49 in *Deuxième Conference* (q.v.)
—— (1965) 'Italian aims at the time of the Social War', *JRS* 55, pp. 90-109
Bruun, P. *et al.* (eds) (1975) *Studies in the Romanisation of Etruria*, Rome
Bulst, C.M. (1964) 'Cinnanum Tempus', *Historia* 13, pp. 307-37
Campanile, E. and Letta, C. (1979) *Studi sulle magistrature indigine e municipali in area Italica*, Pisa
Carcopino, J. (1929) in G. Bloch and J. Carcopino, *Histoire Romaine*, Paris, vol. 2
—— (1929) 'Les Lois Agraires des Gracques et la Guerre Sociale', *BAGB* 22, pp. 3-23
Carney, T.F. (1970) *A biography of C. Marius*, Chicago, 2nd ed.
Cassola, F. (1970/71) 'Romani ed Italici in Oriente', *D. Arch* 4/5, pp. 305-22
Castrèn, P. (1975) *Ordo Populusque Pompeianus*, Rome
Catalano, P. (1961/62) 'Appunti sopra il più antico concetto giuridico di Italia' *AAT* 96, pp. 198-228
Cichorius, C. (1922) *Römische Studien*, Leipzig
Coarelli, F. (1983) 'I Santuari del Lazio e della Campania', pp. 217-40 in *'Bourgeoisies'* (q.v.)
Crawford, M. (1964) 'The Coinage of the Age of Sulla', *NC*4, pp. 141-58
—— (1983) 'Le Monete Romane nelle Regioni d' Italia', pp. 47-50 in *'Bourgeoisies'* (q.v.)

Bibliography

Criniti, N. (1970) *L'Epigrafe di Asculum di Gn. Pompeio Strabone*, Milan
Cuff, P.J. (1967) 'Prolegomena to a critical edition of Appian B.C. 1.'
Historia 16, pp. 177-88
Deroux, C. (ed). (1983) *Studies in Latin Literature and Roman History III*,
Brussels
Deuxième Conference, (1965) *Deuxième Conference Int. d'Histoires Economique (1962)*, Paris vol. 1.
Devoto, G. (1956) 'La Romanisation de l'Italie Mediane', *CHM*3, pp. 443-62
Domaszewski, A. von (1924)*Bellum Marsicum*, Vienna/Leipzig
Earl, D.C. (1963) *Tiberius Gracchus: A study in politics*, Brussels
—— (1967) *The Moral and Political Tradition of Rome*, London
Frank, T. (1933) *An economic survey of ancient Rome*, Baltimore, vol. 1.
Frederiksen, M. (1970/71) 'The contribution of archaeology to the
agrarian problem in the Gracchan period', *D. Arch* 5, pp. 330-67
Gabba, E. (1956) *Appiano e la storia delle Guerre Civili*, Florence
—— (1967) *Appiani Bellorum Civilium Liber Primus*, Florence, 2nd edn
—— (1976) *Republican Rome, the army and the allies*, trans. by P.J. Cuff,
Oxford
—— (1951) 'Ricerche su alcuni punti di storia mariana', *Athenaeum* 29,
pp. 12-24
—— (1972) 'Urbanizzazione e rinnovamenti urbanistici nell' Italia
centro-meridionale de 1 sec. a.C., *SCO* 21, pp. 73-112
—— (1978) 'Il problema dell' 'unita' dell' Italia Romana', pp. 11-27 in
*La Cultura Italica: atti del convegno della società italiana di Glottologia, Pisa,
Dicembre 1977*, Pisa
—— (1983) 'Strutture sociali e politica Romana in Italia nel 11 sec.
A.C.', pp. 41-5 in '*Bourgeoisies*' (q.v.)
Gaggiotti, M. (1983) 'Tre casi regionali italici: il Sannio Pentro', pp. 137-43 in '*Bourgeoisies*' (q.v.)
Galsterer, H. (1976) *Herrschaft und Verwaltung im Republikanischen Italien*,
Munich
Goehler, J. (1939) *Rom und Italien*, Breslau
Greenidge A.H.J. (1901) *Roman Public Life*, London
—— (1904) *A History of Rome*, London, vol. 1.
Gros, P. (1978) *Architecture et Société à Rome et en Italie Centro-méridionale aux
deux derniers siècles de la République*, Brussels
Grueber, H.A. (1910) *Coins of the Roman Republic in the British Museum*,
London, vol. 2
Gruen, E. (1968) *Roman Politics and the Criminal Courts*, Cambridge, Mass.
—— (1965) 'Lex Varia', *JRS* 55, pp. 54-73
Hackl, U. (1982) *Senat und Magistratur in Rom*, Kallmünz
Hardy, E.G. (1912) *Roman Laws and Charters*, Oxford
Harris W.V. (1971) *Rome in Etruria and Umbria*, Oxford
—— (1979) *War and Imperialism in Republican Rome*, Oxford
—— (1977) 'Economic conditions in northern Etruria in the second
century BC.' pp. 56-63 in Martelli and Cristofani (q.v.)
Hatzfeld, J. (1919) *Les Trafiquants Italiens dans l'Orient Hellenique*, Paris
Haug, I. (1947) 'Der Römische Bundesgenossenkrieg 91-88 v. Ch. bei
Titus Livius', *WJA* 2, pp. 201-58

Heurgon, J. (1963) 'L'Ombrie a l'époque des Gracques et de Sylla', pp. 113-31 in *Atti 1 Congresso Studi Umbri*, Florence

Humbert, M. (1978) *Municipium et Civitas sine suffragio*, Rome

Ilari, V. (1974) *Gli Italici nelle Strutture Militari Romane*, Milan

Jashemski, W.F. (1950) *The origins and history of the proconsular and propraetorian imperium to 27 BC*, Chicago

Jolowicz, H.F. (1961) *Historical Introduction to the study of Roman Law*, Cambridge

Kaimio, J. (1975) 'The ousting of Etruscan by Latin in Etruria' pp. 85-246 in P. Bruun (q.v.)

Keaveney, A. (1983) *Sulla—the last Republican*, London

—— (1983) 'Sulla and the Gods, pp. 44-79 in Deroux (q.v.)

—— (1978) 'Pompeius Strabo's second Consulship', *CQ*28, pp. 240-1

—— (1979)'Sulla, Sulpicius and Caesar Strabo', *Latomus* 38, pp. 451-60

—— (1980) 'Deux dates contestées de la carrière de Sylla', *LEC*48, pp. 149-59

—— (1982) 'Young Pompey', *AC*51, pp. 111-32

—— (1982) 'Sulla and Italy', *Crit. Stor.* 19, pp. 499-544

—— (1983) 'What happened in 88?', *Eirene* 20, pp. 53-86

—— (1983) 'Caesars in the Social War', *RhM*126, pp. 273-81

—— (1984) 'Civis Romanus Sum', *Crit. Stor.* 21, pp. 345-72

Keaveney, A. and Madden, J.A. (1983) 'Metellus Pius: the evidence of Livy, Epitome 76', *Eranos* 81, pp. 47-51

Klingner, F. (1956) *Römische Geisteswelt*, Munich, 3rd edn

Knapp, R.C. (no date) *Aspects of the Roman experience in Iberia 206-100 BC.*, Valladolid

Laffi, U. (1975) In U. Laffi and M. Pasquinucci, *Asculum*, Pisa, vol.1.

—— (1973) 'Sull' organizzazione amministrativa dell' Italia dopo la Guerra Sociale' pp. 37-53 in *Akten des VI Internationalen Kongresses für Griechische und Lateinische Epigraphik*, Munich

—— (1983) 'I senati locali nell' italia repubblicana', pp. 59-74 in '*Bourgeoisies*' (q.v.)

—— (1967) 'Il Mito di Silla', *Athenaeum* 45, pp. 177-213 and pp. 255-77.

Letta, C. (1972) *I Marsi e il Fucino nell' antichità*', Milan

Letta, C. and d'Amato, S. (1975) *Epigrafia della regione dei Marsi*, Milan

Levick B.M. (1982) 'Sulla's March on Rome in 88 BC', *Historia* 31, pp. 503-8

Lewis, R.G. (1968) 'Appian B.C. 1. 49, 214 δεκατεύοντες: Rome's new tribes 90-87 BC', *Athenaeum* 46, pp. 273-91

Lintott, A.W. (1972) 'Imperial Expansion and moral decline in the Roman Republic', *Historia* 21, pp. 626-38

Luraschi, G. (1978) 'Sulle 'Leges de civitate''', *SDHI* 44, pp. 321-70

McDonald, A.H. (1939) 'The History of Rome and Italy in the Second Century BC', *Cam. Hist. Journ.* 6, pp. 124-46

—— (1944) 'Rome and the Italian confederation (200-186 BC)', *JRS* 34, pp. 11-33

Magaldi, E. (1947) *Lucania Romana*, Rome

Malcovati, E. (1955) 'L. Papirius Fregellanus', *Athenaeum* 33, pp. 137-40

Bibliography

Marcks, E. (1884) *Die Überlieferung des Bundesgenossenkriegs 91-89 BC*, Marburg

Martelli, M. and Cristofani, M. (eds.) (1977) *Caratteri dell' ellenismo nelle urne etrusche*, Florence

Mattingly, H.B. (1975) 'The consilium of Cn. Pompeius Strabo in 89 BC' *Athenaeum* 53, pp. 262-66

Meyer, H.D. (1958) 'Die Organisation der Italiker in Bundesgenossenkrieg', *Historia* 7, pp. 74-9

Mommsen, Th. (1876) *The History of Rome*, trans. by W.P. Dickson, London, vol. 3.

Nagle, D.B. (1970) 'The failure of the Roman political process in 133 BC', *Athenaeum* 48, pp. 372-94

—— (1973) 'An allied view of the Social War', *AJA* 77, pp. 367-78

Niccolini, G. (1946) 'Le leggi de civitate Romana durante la Guerra Sociale', *RAL* 8ᴬ S.1, pp. 110-24

Nicolet, C. (1966) *L'ordre équestre à l'époque républicaine (312-43 av. J.C.)*, Paris, vol. 1.

Onorato, G.O. (1949/50) 'La partecipazione di Cicerone alla Guerra Sociale in Campania', *RAAN* 24/25, pp. 415-26

—— (1951) 'Pompeii municipium e colonia Romana', *RAAN* 26, pp. 115-56

Pareti, L.(1953) *Storia di Roma e del mondo romano*, Turin, vol. 3

Paul, G.M. (1984) *A historical commentary on Sallust's Bellum Jugurthinum*, Liverpool

Reid, J.S. (1878) *Cicero Pro Balbo*, Cambridge

Richardson, J.S. (1980) 'The ownership of Roman Land: Tiberius Gracchus and the Italians', *JRS* 70, pp. 1-11

Ruoff-Väänänen, E. (1975) 'The Etruscans and the civitas romana problems during the years 91-84 BC', pp. 71-82 in Bruun (q.v.)

Salmon, E.T. (1967) *Samnium and the Samnites*, Cambridge

—— (1969) *Roman colonisation under the Republic*, London

—— (1982) *The making of Roman Italy*, London

—— (1962) 'The cause of the Social War', *Phoenix* 16, pp. 107-19

de Sanctis, G. (1976) *La Guerra Sociale*, ed. by L. Polverini, Florence

Seager, R. (1967) 'Lex Varia de Maiestate', *Historia* 16, pp. 37-43

Shatzman, I. (1972) 'The Roman General's authority over booty', *Historia* 21, pp. 177-205

Sherk, R.K. (1969) *Roman documents from the Greek East*, Baltimore

Sherwin-White, A.N. (1973) *The Roman Citizenship*, Oxford, 2nd edn

—— (1972) 'The date of the Lex Repetundarum and its consequences', *JRS* 62, pp. 83-99

Shochat, Y. (1970) 'The lex agraria of 133 BC and the Italian allies', *Athenaeum* 48, pp. 25-45

Smith, R.E. (1955) *The failure of the Roman republic*, Cambridge

—— (1954) 'Latins and the Roman citizenship in Roman colonies: Livy 34. 42.5-6', *JRS* 44, pp. 18-20

Stockton, D. (1979) *The Gracchi*, Oxford

Strachan-Davidson, J.L. (1902) *Appian Civil Wars: Book 1*, Oxford

Syme, R. (1939) *The Roman Revolution*, Oxford

—— (1979) *Roman Papers*, ed. by E. Badian, Oxford, vol. 1

Bibliography

Taylor, L.R. (1960) *The Voting Districts of the Roman Republic*, Rome
Thomsen, R. (1942) 'Das Jahr 91 v. Chr. und seine Voraussetzungen', *C & M* 5, pp. 13-47
Tibiletti, G. (1950) 'Ricerche di storia agraria Romana', *Athenaeum* 28, pp. 183-266
—— (1953) 'La politica delle colonie e città Latine nella Guerra Sociale', *RIL* 86, pp. 45-63
Torelli, M. (1983) 'Una nuova epigrafe di Bantia e la cronologia dello statuto municipale Bantino', *Athenaeum* 61, pp. 252-7
Toynbee, A.J. (1965) *Hannibal's Legacy*, Oxford, vol. 2
Tra Grecia (1980) *Tra Grecia e Roma*, Rome
Treggiari, S. (1969) *Roman Freedmen during the late Republic*, Oxford
Voirol, A. (1954) 'Die Münzen des Bellum Sociale und ihre Symbolik', *GNS* 4, pp. 64-7
Wegner, M. (1969) *Untersuchungen zu den lateinischen Begriffen socius und societas*, Göttingen
Whatmough, J. (1937) *The Foundations of Roman Italy*, London
Willems, P. (1968) *Le Senat de la république romaine*, Aalen, repr. vol. 2
Wilson, A.J.N. (1966) *Emigration from Italy in the Republican age of Rome*, Manchester
Wiseman, T.P. (1971) *New men in the Roman Senate 139 BC-AD 14*, Oxford
—— (1983) 'Domi nobiles and the Roman cultural elite', pp. 299-307 in *'Bourgeoisies'* (q.v.)

Index